REVELATION
and the End of All Things

REVELATION

and the End of All Things

CRAIG R. KOESTER

WILLIAM B. EERDMANS PUBLISHING COMPANY
GRAND RAPIDS, MICHIGAN / CAMBRIDGE, U.K.

© 2001 Wm. B. Eerdmans Publishing Co.
All rights reserved

Wm. B. Eerdmans Publishing Co.
2140 Oak Industrial Drive N.E., Grand Rapids, Michigan 49505 /
P.O. Box 163, Cambridge CB3 9PU U.K.

Printed in the United States of America

13 12   14 13

Library of Congress Cataloging-in-Publication Data

Koester, Craig R., 1953-
Revelation and the end of all things / Craig R. Koester.
p.   cm.
Includes bibliographical references and index.
ISBN 978-0-8028-4660-0 (pbk.: alk. paper)
1. Bible, N.T. Revelation — Commentaries.
I. Title.

BS2825.53 K64 2001
228'.07 — dc21

00-069199

www.eerdmans.com

For Matthew and Emily

CONTENTS

Contents

Contents

PREFACE

Embarking on a study of Revelation is one of the most engaging ventures in biblical studies. Interest in Revelation is perennially high even among those who do not otherwise give much attention to questions of biblical interpretation. Curiosity is fed by the popular use of Revelation in print, film, and other media. This book, *Revelation and the End of All Things,* grows out of years of teaching courses on Revelation to seminary students, pastors, and congregational groups. Many of the questions that people ask in these settings are sparked by sensationalistic interpretations of Revelation, but these questions also point to major issues concerning our understanding of God and the future, death and life, judgment, hope. Rather than ignoring popular interpretations of Revelation, the first chapter of *Revelation and the End of All Things* considers how these approaches work and why they are problematic. The rest of the book takes a careful look at each section of Revelation, keeping the situations of first-century and twenty-first-century readers in mind. The goal is to present the message of Revelation in a manner that is accessible, engaging, and meaningful to modern readers, while taking account of the best in recent scholarship.

Many people helped to make this book possible. Photographs of the woodcuts by Albrecht Dürer were made from original prints in the Lutheran Brotherhood Collection of Religious Art. I would like to thank Richard Hillstrom for making the prints available. I also want to express my gratitude to Luther Seminary and Lutheran Brotherhood for supporting a sabbatical leave in which to complete the manuscript. Thanks are due to Nancy Koester and Todd Nichol for reading portions of the manuscript and to Alice Loddigs for technical assistance at many points. Finally, I want to acknowledge my appreciation to Allen Myers, Jennifer Hoffman, and the rest of the Eerdmans staff for all they have done to bring this project to completion.

BIBLIOGRAPHY OF WORKS CITED

Aune, David E. "The Influence of Roman Imperial Court Ceremonial on the Apocalypse of John." *Biblical Research* 28 (1983): 5-26.

————. *Prophecy in Early Christianity and the Ancient Mediterranean World.* Grand Rapids: Eerdmans, 1983.

————. *Revelation.* 3 vols. Word Biblical Commentary 52. Dallas: Word, 1997-98.

Bauckham, Richard. *The Climax of Prophecy: Studies on the Book of Revelation.* Edinburgh: T. &. T. Clark, 1993.

————. *The Theology of the Book of Revelation.* Cambridge: Cambridge University Press, 1993.

Beale, G. K. *The Book of Revelation: A Commentary on the Greek Text.* Grand Rapids: Eerdmans; Carlisle: Paternoster, 1999.

Boring, M. Eugene. *Revelation.* Interpretation. Louisville: John Knox, 1989.

Boyer, Paul. *When Time Shall Be No More: Prophecy Belief in Modern American Culture.* Cambridge, MA: Harvard University Press, 1992.

Caird, G. B. *A Commentary on the Revelation of Saint John the Divine.* New York: Harper & Row, 1966.

Clouse, Robert G., Robert Hosack, and Richard V. Pierard. *The New Millennium Manual: A Once and Future Guide.* Grand Rapids: Baker, 1999.

Collins, Adela Yarbro. *The Apocalypse.* New Testament Message 22. Wilmington, DE: Michael Glazier, 1979.

————. *Crisis and Catharsis: The Power of the Apocalypse.* Philadelphia: Westminster, 1984.

Collins, John J. *The Apocalyptic Imagination: An Introduction to Jewish Apocalyptic Literature.* 2nd ed. Grand Rapids: Eerdmans, 1998.

Grenz, Stanley J. *The Millennial Maze: Sorting Out Evangelical Options.* Downers Grove, IL: InterVarsity, 1992.

Hemer, Colin J. *The Letters to the Seven Churches in Their Local Setting.* Grand Rapids: Eerdmans, 2001.

Jeffrey, Grant. *The Millennium Meltdown: The Year 2000 Computer Crisis.* Wheaton, IL: Tyndale House, 1998.

Koester, Nancy. "The Future in Our Past: Post-Millennialism in American Protestantism," *Word & World* 15 (1995): 137-44.

LaHaye, Tim, and Jerry M. Jenkins. *Left Behind: A Novel of the Earth's Last Days.* Wheaton, IL: Tyndale House, 1995.

————. *Tribulation Force: The Continuing Drama of Those Left Behind.* Wheaton, IL: Tyndale House, 1996.

————. *Are We Living in the End Times?* Wheaton, IL: Tyndale House, 1999.

Lindsey, Hal. *The Late Great Planet Earth.* Grand Rapids: Zondervan, 1970.

Schüssler Fiorenza, Elizabeth. *Revelation: Vision of a Just World.* Minneapolis: Fortress, 1991.

Tabor, James D. "The Waco Tragedy: An Autobiographical Account of One Attempt to Avert Disaster." In *From the Ashes: Making Sense of Waco,* edited by James R. Lewis, 13-21. Lanham, MD: Rowan & Littlefield, 1994.

Wainwright, Arthur W. *Mysterious Apocalypse: Interpreting the Book of Revelation.* Nashville: Abingdon, 1993.

Chapter 1

INTERPRETING THE MYSTERY

The power of a book can be seen in what it does to people, and few books have affected people more dramatically than Revelation. In positive terms, Revelation has inspired countless sermons and theological treatises, artistic works, and musical compositions ranging from the triumphant "Hallelujah Chorus" to the gentle strains of "Jerusalem My Happy Home." On the negative side, it has fed social upheaval and sectarian religious movements that have often foundered on misguided attempts to discern the date of Christ's return. Some are attracted to sensationalistic interpretations that find Revelation's prophecies reaching fulfillment in the rise of the modern state of Israel, the outbreak of the Persian Gulf War, volcanic eruptions, and oil spills. Others, repelled by these speculations, suggest that Revelation might best be kept on the shelf, sealed and unread. Yet attempts to ignore or dismiss Revelation are generally not successful; its secrets are too alluring.

A sketch of some of the ways in which Christians have interpreted the book over the centuries can provide a valuable preface to reading Revelation. Sometimes intriguing, sometimes disturbing, the story of Revelation's checkered history of influence on previous generations provides contemporary readers with an opportunity to think about the kinds of questions that our predecessors have asked, the assumptions that shaped their reading, and the effects of their interpretations on their communities. As we consider the perspectives of others, we are challenged to consider the questions and assumptions that we ourselves bring to the text, as well as the effects that our interpretations might have on our own communities. Looking at the past is a prelude to the task of seeking faithful and compelling ways to read Revelation in the present.

Future Prediction or Timeless Truth?

Good questions are often very simple questions. One of the most important of these questions is whether the visions in Revelation refer to future events or to timeless realities. Since the early centuries of the church, Christians have had different viewpoints on this issue. Since at least the second century, some have understood the book to be primarily a message about the future of the world, with its visions offering glimpses into events that would transpire in days to come. For nearly as many years, others have insisted that Revelation contains a timeless message, with its visions showing how God relates to people of every generation. Still others have proposed an alternative to these two options, preferring to read Revelation as visions concerning events that are now in the past. Since readers today find themselves asking these same basic questions, a look at what our predecessors have said might help us think about what we might expect to find when we open the book of Revelation.

Revelation and the Future

A passage that has long been a test case for interpretations of Revelation is John's reference to the saints reigning with Christ for a thousand years at the end of time, just prior to the last judgment: "And I saw thrones, and they sat upon them, and judgment was given unto them: and I saw the souls of them that were beheaded for the witness of Jesus, and for the word of God, and which had not worshipped the beast, neither his image, neither had received his mark upon their foreheads, or in their hands; and they lived and reigned with Christ a thousand years" (Rev. 20:4). The vision of the millennial kingdom is intriguing, in part, because it leaves so much to the imagination that readers inevitably disclose their own ideas when they explain what they think the passage means.

Justin Martyr (ca. 100-165) was one of the early Christian writers who thought that John's vision of the thousand-year kingdom pointed to a future reign of the saints on earth. An articulate and philosophically-minded convert to Christianity, Justin came to Rome from the eastern part of the empire. In one of his writings, he tried to show how the promises that God made through the prophets of the Old Testament are fulfilled through Christ. His argument is that Christians do not reject the older Jewish tradition, but recognize how God accomplishes his purposes in Christ and the church.

Justin assumed that the prophetic visions concerning the transformation of the earth into a peaceful paradise would be realized in the millennial kingdom mentioned in Revelation. He quoted Isa. 65:17-25, which spoke of a time when life expectancy would be increased and people would "build houses and inhabit them," they would "plant vineyards and eat their fruit," able to enjoy the work of their hands without fear of loss. In that day the "wolf and the lamb shall feed together, the lion shall eat straw like the ox" (Isa. 65:20-25). Only after these promises concerning an earthly paradise were fulfilled would the last judgment take place and the faithful enter into life everlasting (*Dialogue with Trypho* 80-81). Many later interpreters followed Justin's lead, even though the passage from Isaiah actually refers to the new heaven and new earth, something that John identifies with the New Jerusalem in Rev. 21:1-5, not with the millennial kingdom of Rev. 20:4-6.

Irenaeus (ca. 130-200) was another Christian writer who read Revelation futuristically. Born in the eastern part of the Roman Empire, Irenaeus spent much of his career in Lyons in southern France, where he became the bishop of a Christian community that had suffered persecution. Like a number of other writers, Irenaeus thought that world history would last for six thousand years, followed by a seventh span of a thousand years that would be a period of rest for the world. His reasoning was that God created the world in six days and rested on the seventh day (Gen. 1:1–2:4). If one day could symbolize a thousand years (Ps. 90:4), then history would last for six thousand years, and the millennial reign of the saints (Rev. 20:4-6) would be the final period of blessedness for the world (*Against Heresies* 5.28.3).

Irenaeus's insistence that there would be a future millennial kingdom on earth was connected to his belief in the justice of God. Since Christians lost their lives within the created order for the sake of their faith, it would be within the created order that God would give them life again. Out of divine abundance and mercy, God would restore the creation to a condition of perfection, making it subject to the righteous before the last judgment (*Against Heresies* 5.32.1). The millennial kingdom was also a way to affirm the goodness of creation. In contrast to Gnostic teachers, who thought that the material world was inherently evil and irredeemable, Irenaeus envisioned a future for the creation, a time when it would be lavishly transformed into a place of blessing: "the days will come in which vines will grow, each having ten thousand branches, and in each branch ten thousand twigs, and in each twig ten thousand shoots, and in each shoot ten thousand clusters, and on every cluster ten thousand grapes . . . and when any one of the saints shall lay hold of a cluster, another cluster will cry out, 'I am a better cluster, take me; bless the Lord through me'" (*Against Heresies* 5.33.3).

A more extreme form of futuristic hope was sparked by the preaching of Montanus (late second century), who launched a new religious movement in Phrygia, in what is now northern Turkey. Montanus claimed to be the mouthpiece of the Holy Spirit, who Jesus had said would lead people into all the truth (John 14:26; 16:13). Christianity had long revered those who had prophetic gifts (Acts 21:9; 1 Cor. 14:1), but Montanus broke with tradition by claiming to bring what he called the "New Prophecy." Proclaiming that the end of the world was near, Montanus called people to follow a strenuous path of self-denial, fasting, and celibacy. He was joined by two women prophets named Priscilla and Maximilla, one of whom declared that the New Jerusalem (Rev. 21:1–22:5) would soon descend to earth at the Phrygian town of Pepuza, which became a focal point for the group (Epiphanius, *Panarion* 49.1.2-3).

Montanism came under attack by leaders of the wider Christian church. An elder named Gaius was sharply critical of the movement and of Revelation, since the book had helped to inspire the Montanist belief that the end times had arrived. In order to discredit Revelation, Gaius argued that the book had not been written by the apostle John, as many believed, but had been penned by Cerinthus, a notorious heretic, who falsely attributed it to John the apostle in order to obtain a wide readership. Gaius insisted that people were attracted to the thought of a future millennial kingdom on earth because they thought that in it they could indulge their lust for pleasure (Eusebius, *Ecclesiastical History* 3.28.1-2). Despite such criticisms, however, the book of Revelation continued to be read and valued by Christians in the western part of the Roman Empire.

The moderate type of futuristic interpretation that we saw in Justin and Irenaeus was further developed by Victorinus (died 304), bishop of Pettau in what is today Slovenia. Martyred in the great persecution conducted by the Roman emperor Diocletian, Victorinus wrote the oldest extant commentary on Revelation. Assuming that Revelation portended disasters that would occur in the course of human history, he pointed out that "Babylon," the persecutor of the saints, symbolized Rome, and that Revelation's portrayal of the beast included traits of Nero, the emperor who slaughtered Christians in the first century. This insight continues to be accepted by scholars today. Victorinus also assumed that the millennial kingdom in Revelation 20 would be an earthly kingdom in which the nations would be placed under the rule of the saints, as earlier interpreters had thought.

Victorinus's most important contribution, however, was his observation that Revelation does not depict the final events of history in a clear chronological sequence. John's visions are sometimes repetitive, so that one cannot assume that the book makes step-by-step predictions about the future. Instead, the book repeats or recapitulates the same message in different ways, much as the Old Testament said that the two dreams of pharaoh symbolized the same periods of bounty and famine in the time of Joseph (Gen. 41:26). Victorinus recognized that the seven trumpets in Revelation 8–9 and the seven bowls of plagues in Revelation 16 depict the same series of threats. John may speak of the heavenly lights being darkened twice (Rev. 8:12; 16:10) and the sea turning to blood twice (Rev. 8:9; 16:3), but that does not mean that these events will happen twice. This observation about the repetitive quality of the visions has also gained a wide following in recent interpretation of Revelation, and we will explore the idea further below.

Jerome (ca. 342-420), the brilliant and prickly biblical scholar who produced the Latin translation of the Bible that the western church used for centuries, preserved and revised Victorinus's commentary. A vigorous promoter of monasticism and ascetic practice, Jerome rejected the idea that the saints would inherit an earthly kingdom of material bounty that would endure for a thousand years. Although he valued many of Victorinus's insights, Jerome developed a different understanding of the millennial reign of the faithful. In a postscript to Victorinus's commentary, Jerome argued that Revelation must be understood spiritually. John's vision of the millennial kingdom does not refer to earthly rule or to a thousand calendar years, but to obedience and chastity, for Satan is bound whenever people resist evil thoughts. Although many Christians in the Latin-speaking world had read Revelation in a futuristic way, Jerome's edited version of Victorinus's commentary moved many to read Revelation in a more timeless fashion, as a vision of the spiritual battle that Christians in all times and places were to wage against sin.

Revelation as Timeless Truth

The idea that Revelation could be read in a timeless way did not begin with Jerome. Several generations before his time, a similar approach emerged among Christians at Alexandria and Caesarea, leading centers of learning in the eastern part of the Roman Empire. Dionysius, bishop of Alexandria (died ca. 264), reacted strongly against the idea that Christ would establish a thousand-year kingdom on earth, a kingdom that some apparently thought would be "devoted to bodily indulgence." Since self-indulgence ran counter to Christian teaching, Dionysius insisted that some deeper meaning must underlie John's vision of the millennial kingdom (Eusebius, *Ecclesiastical History* 7.24.1; 7.25.3-4).

Some of Revelation's "deeper meaning" was suggested by Dionysius's teacher, Origen (ca. 185-254), who was a leading biblical interpreter in the third century. Origen showed little interest in the time or the place of the battle of Armageddon (Rev. 19:11-21), since he understood that Revelation's vision of the great conflict dealt with the triumph of God over sin and vice. He pointed out that the text identifies the warrior Christ with "the word of God" (19:13), so that "heaven is opened" (19:11) when the divine word gives people the light of truth and victory is won when the knowledge of truth destroys all that is wicked and sinful in the soul. Later advocates of this approach thought that the seven heads of the beast were the seven deadly sins and its ten horns were violations of the Ten Commandments.[1]

---

1. See Origen, *Commentary on John* 2.4 (Ante-Nicene Fathers, 10:325-27); Wainwright, *Mysterious Apocalypse: Interpreting the Book of Revelation* (Nashville: Abingdon, 1993), 203.

Interpretation of Revelation took a major turn in the late fourth century when a North African writer named Tyconius (died ca. 400) proposed that the thousand-year reign of Christ and the saints had already begun with Christ's first coming. He argued that the millennial kingdom of Rev. 20:1-6 was not a future hope, but a present reality, supporting his claim by bringing together two New Testament texts. First, he noted that the millennium was to begin when Satan was "bound" (Rev. 20:2). Second, he pointed out that Jesus had already "bound" Satan by his exorcisms, since Jesus said that he was casting out demons in order to "bind" Satan, whom he called a "strong man" (Matt. 12:29). By putting these two texts together Tyconius concluded that the thousand-year kingdom began with the first coming of Christ.

Many found that this interpretation helped to make sense of Christian experience. On the one hand, the conversion of the emperor Constantine and the spread of Christianity throughout the Roman Empire gave some evidence that false gods were on the retreat and that the rule of the saints had begun. On the other hand, Tyconius was keenly aware that the kingdom of God had not yet fully arrived. He belonged to a group known as the Donatists, who refused to recognize the legitimacy of church leaders who had handed over the Scriptures to be burned during the persecution under the emperor Diocletian. Because of their uncompromising stance, the Donatists experienced conflict with the wider church. Yet Tyconius helped to show that such conflict was to be expected during the millennium, since Satan was only "bound" (Rev. 20:1-3) and would not be annihilated until the end of time (Rev. 20:7-10). Until then, the righteous and the unrighteous would exist side by side.

Tyconius's view of the millennium gained wide currency when it was adopted by Augustine (354-430), a North African theologian whose work has had tremendous impact on western Christianity. Augustine dealt with this material in his own great work *The City of God* (20.6-7). Although Augustine opposed the Donatists, he found that Tyconius's interpretation provided a way to read Revelation that could be applied to the interior life of Christians in all times and places. People entered the millennial kingdom through the "first resurrection" (Rev. 20:4-6), which referred to the dying and rising that took place through baptism (cf. Rom. 6:4). The second resurrection (Rev. 20:11-

13) would be the bodily resurrection at the end of time (cf. 1 Cor. 15:35-58). When Revelation said that Satan has already been confined to "the abyss," Augustine explained that this referred to the abyss of human hearts, where wickedness would reside until God destroyed it.

Augustine opposed speculations as to when the end would come and proposed that the thousand-year kingdom was not an exact period of time but a way of speaking about time as a totality (*City of God* 18.53; 20.7). History would reach its culmination in the second coming of Christ, but until then, the principal movement reflected in Scripture concerns the movement of the soul from the earthly to the heavenly city. Augustine's use of Tyconius's interpretation of Revelation, together with Jerome's edited version of Victorinus's commentary, made a timeless and spiritualized reading of Revelation the dominant viewpoint for centuries to come.

History, Politics, and Reform

Some modern readers may feel at home with the kind of spiritual reading of Revelation that was outlined above, but many ask different questions of the book, inquiring how its visions can be related to current events in global and church politics. We will consider some of the more recent attempts to do this below, but since the question is not new, it can be helpful to see how people tried to make these connections generations ago. A quick look at the eleventh and twelfth centuries is instructive, because that was a time of ferment, in which reform movements arose within the church, conflicts between the emperor and the pope intensified, and new monastic orders appeared. Questions about the meaning of history led to a different approach to reading Revelation, in which people read it not only for its message concerning the interior spiritual life, but for what it said about historical events of the past, the present, and especially the future.

Mystics, Popes, and Kings

One of the leading figures of this age was Joachim of Fiore (ca. 1135-1202), who was a mystic and the abbot of a monastery in southern Italy.

Interpreting Scripture in light of visions that he received, Joachim taught that history could be divided into three interlocking periods, corresponding to the three persons of the Trinity. The period of the Father began at creation and extended until the first coming of Christ. The period of the Son began to dawn at the time of King Josiah's reforms in the seventh century B.C., but it arrived in its fullness with the coming of Christ. The period of the Spirit overlaps with that of the Son, beginning under the monastic reforms of Saint Benedict in the sixth century A.D., and fully arriving at some point in the future.

The seven heads of the beast in Revelation provided a pattern for Joachim's view of the persecutions that would take place during the period of the Son. Since Rev. 17:10 indicates that the seven heads correspond to seven kings, Joachim proposed that they represented successive foes of Christianity: Herod and Nero in the first century; Constantius the heretical emperor in the fourth century; Muhammad and other figures in subsequent centuries, including the sixth king, Saladin, the Muslim leader who defeated the Crusaders in Jerusalem in 1187. The seventh head would be the Antichrist, whose future coming would be part of the tribulation that would usher in the age of the Spirit. During this coming crisis, Joachim predicted that two new monastic orders would arise to bear witness to the truth in the spirit of Moses and Elijah (Rev. 11:1-13). The goal of this final time of affliction was the purification of the church.

Many of Joachim's interpretations remained cryptic, but his work gave the impression that the age was rapidly coming to a close. His followers had the sense that the people of his own time had important roles to play in the final acts of the drama of world history. Joachim had predicted that two new monastic orders would arise as harbingers of the new age, and few could resist seeing the fulfillment of this prophecy in the emergence of the Franciscan and Dominican orders. Some of the Franciscans, noting how Joachim had connected figures from church history with characters in the Bible, extended his practice by filling out the apocalyptic scenario in greater detail. Among the heroes of the end times was Saint Francis, whom many identified as the angel who appeared after the opening of the sixth seal (Rev. 7:2), making Francis the harbinger of the final age.

Attempts to identify the villains in the apocalyptic drama were also commonplace. Joachim had identified the sixth head of the beast with his contemporary, the Muslim leader Saladin (1137-1193). Since this suggested that the end was near, some of those influenced by Joachim identified the beast's seventh head with the Holy Roman Emperor, Frederick II (1194-1250). Conflicts between the pope and emperor had led Pope Gregory IX (ca. 1170-1241) to denounce Frederick as the beast that ascends from the sea (Rev. 13:1-2), but Frederick made a similar charge against Gregory, calling the pope the great dragon who leads the world astray, namely the Antichrist. Later, some of Frederick's followers extended the charge to Pope Innocent IV (ca. 1200-1254), claiming that the numerical values of his name and title *Innocencius papa* added up to 666, the number of the beast (Rev. 13:18). Frederick died in 1250, initially creating confusion among those who thought he was the Antichrist. Some, however, began claiming that he was not really dead, but since he was the Antichrist, he would come to life again, as Rev. 13:3 said would happen to the beast.

Some of Joachim's most enthusiastic followers calculated that the present age would end by the year 1260. They noted that Joachim had pointed out that the first chapter of Matthew's gospel said that forty-two generations had preceded the coming of the Son. If forty-two generations were to come after the arrival of the Son, and if each generation lasted for thirty years, one could expect the era of the Spirit to arrive fully by A.D. 1260 (cf. Rev. 11:3). Although the end did not arrive on schedule, conflict escalated between church leaders and the radical Franciscans, who insisted that Christ had called true Christians to practice poverty. They understood their own order to be the vanguard of the new age, charging that Pope Boniface VIII (1234-1303) was the beast that was to rise from the sea and that the numerical values of the name of his successor, Benedict XI (1240-1304), when written in Greek, added up to 666, the number of the beast (Rev. 13:18).[2]

Luther's Love/Hate Affair with Revelation

Martin Luther (1483-1546), the German monk turned reformer and Bible translator, inherited the diverse spiritual, historical, and polemi-

2. The values of the Greek letters for *Benediktos* are b = 2, e = 5, n = 50, e = 5, d = 4, i = 10, k = 20, t = 300, o = 70, s = 200.

cal traditions of earlier generations. During his career, he dealt with Revelation in several different ways, all of which appear in various forms today.

First, Luther dismissed Revelation as a book that was of little value for Christian faith and life. His rejection stemmed in part from his recognition of the book's power to draw people into dangerous speculations about the future. In December of 1521, for example, three radical preachers from the town of Zwickau arrived in Wittenberg, where Luther taught. They claimed unmediated divine inspiration, renounced infant baptism, and proclaimed the imminent end of the world. In 1522, following the turbulence created by the radicals, Luther published a preface to his German translation of Revelation that roundly declared it "to be neither apostolic nor prophetic," and that Luther could "in no way detect that the Holy Spirit produced it." Not only did Revelation's visionary language confuse readers, but Luther declared that "Christ is neither taught nor known in it." Therefore, he advised people to stick to the biblical books that present Christ clearly.[3]

Second, Luther later engaged in decoding Revelation in light of the political events of his own time. In 1530, he published a second preface to Revelation that treated Revelation as a map of history between Christ's first and second comings. Some interpreters in the later Middle Ages noted that Revelation began with messages for churches in the first century (Revelation 1–3) and it ended with a vision of the New Jerusalem (Revelation 21–22). They inferred that the intervening chapters must cover the centuries in between. Luther adopted this approach, calculating, for example, that the angels in Revelation 8–9 represented the heretics of antiquity, such as Marcion, Montanus, and Novatian. His own continuing conflict with Rome, and the joint attempts of the pope and emperor to dominate affairs in Germany, convinced him that the beasts from sea and land in Revelation 13 and 17 were the papal empire. Earlier interpreters sometimes identified individual popes or emperors with the beast, but Luther went further, identifying the beast and harlot with the papacy itself. Moreover, the relent-

---

3. "Preface to the Revelation of St. John [I]," in *Luther's Works*, vol. 35, trans. Charles M. Jacobs and E. Theodore Bachman (Philadelphia: Fortress, 1960), 398-99.

less advance of Turkish armies into Europe suggested that they might be Gog and Magog, who were expected to threaten the faithful in the end times (20:8).

Finally, however, Luther's most significant comments ask about the *function* of Revelation's imagery. In his often neglected conclusion to the second preface, Luther shifts from decoding Revelation to asking about how the book addresses readers with a message of warning and comfort. As a warning, Revelation shows that the church will be marked by so many tribulations and heresies that it will be unrecognizable. The survey of history that Luther provided earlier in the preface showed that such afflictions were not unique to one period, but characterized the church's life on earth. Therefore, Revelation warns readers not to be deceived into despair by this impression. As a promise, Revelation assures readers that if "the word of the gospel remains pure among us, and we love and cherish it, we shall not doubt that Christ is with us, even when things are at their worst." For "through and beyond all plagues, beasts, and evil angels, Christ is nonetheless with his saints and wins the final victory."[4] These final comments provide a helpful alternative to reading Revelation without either dismissing its message or reducing it to a code.

Evangelism and Social Reform in America

Interpretations of Revelation that appeared during the sixteenth-century Reformation and in subsequent generations varied greatly. John Calvin (1509-1564) maintained a discreet silence about Revelation, writing commentaries on every book in the New Testament except Revelation. Others in the Reformed tradition were more venturesome, looking for clues to the future in Revelation's visions. Two tendencies emerged among those who read Revelation as a message concerning the future, rather than as a record of past history. One tendency was to anticipate that the kingdom of God would arrive through tribulation and cataclysmic change. Those who work with this cataclysmic view are sometimes called "premillennialists," since they expect conditions on earth to worsen, until Christ returns before ("pre-") the kingdom is es-

4. *Luther's Works,* 35:409-11.

tablished on earth. Some modern forms of this view will be considered in the next two sections. A second tendency was to anticipate that the kingdom of God would come more progressively through evangelism and social reform.

Those who worked with this latter view are sometimes called "postmillennialists," because they expected Christ to return after ("post-") the kingdom had been inaugurated.[5] According to Revelation 19:11-21, the battle that precedes the millennial age is won by Christ, the rider on the white horse, who brings the sword of God's word. Postmillennialists understand that Christ wields the sword of the word through the evangelistic activities of his followers. Therefore, they conclude that the vision in Revelation 19 does not have to do with the battle of Armageddon or Christ's second coming, but with the missionary outreach of the church. The "first resurrection," which takes place at the beginning of the millennium (20:5-6) is not a physical resurrection, but a spiritual one — an awakening to new life in faith. Only after the millennial period will Christ return to raise the dead bodily (20:11-15). In the meantime, the kingdom comes gradually and progressively, like a mustard seed growing or yeast leavening a loaf of bread (Matt. 13:31-33).

Postmillennialism was widespread in colonial America. Many New Englanders understood the book of Revelation as a cosmic story of redemption in which the world passes through affliction as God redeems it, just as individuals suffer under judgment before experiencing grace. Jonathan Edwards (1703-1758), the premier American theologian of the eighteenth century, believed Christians serve as instruments by which God carries out his plan of redemption, which is to increase over the entire world until Christ's kingdom becomes universal. Edwards expected the millennium to be inaugurated through outpourings of the Spirit, which Edwards saw in the revivals of his own time, and through bowls of wrath being poured out upon the enemies of God. For example, Edwards thought that the fifth bowl (Rev. 16:10) was the Protestant Reformation, which made the papal "Beast" agonize. Writing in the mid-1700s, Edwards reckoned that it would take about two hun-

---

5. See Nancy Koester, "The Future in Our Past: Post-Millennialism in American Protestantism," *Word & World* 15 (1995): 137-44; Grenz, *Millennial Maze: Sorting Out Evangelical Options* (Downers Grove, IL: InterVarsity, 1992), 65-89.

dred fifty years to convert the nations to Christ, so that he expected the millennium to begin about the year 2000.

Postmillennialism found one of its most powerful advocates in the fiery evangelist Charles Finney (1792-1875), who devoted his energies to converting the American masses and to reforming society through the abolition of slavery and promotion of temperance. Finney envisioned the millennium as an age of benevolent action, and insisted that people could hasten the millennium's coming by actively showing goodwill toward others, while those who remained obstinately selfish delayed its arrival. By the late nineteenth century, the ideals associated with postmillennialism were absorbed into the Social Gospel movement, which sought social reform without the older emphasis on evangelism and personal conversion, and without thinking specifically in terms of the "millennium" envisioned by Revelation 20.

Apocalyptic Fever, Disappointment, and Tragedy

Members of sectarian groups have long been attracted to Revelation as a source of clues concerning the time of Christ's coming. The groups described below exemplify a pattern in which a charismatic individual develops a distinctive interpretation of biblical texts and gathers a group of followers who anticipate that time will end in the near future. Memories of groups taking to the mountaintops in the futile expectation that the end has arrived, the door-to-door evangelism of the Jehovah's Witnesses and their emphasis on 144,000 being especially chosen by God, as well as news reports about the violent end of the Branch Davidian group at Waco, Texas, have awakened both curiosity and hesitancy about the meaning of Revelation and its relationship to religious groups that fall outside the mainstream.

William Miller and the Seventh-Day Adventists

One of the most important end-times movements in America began through the preaching of William Miller (1782-1849), a veteran of the War of 1812, who converted from deism to Christianity in 1816. He settled in New York State, and after intensively studying Daniel and Revelation, reasoned that according to Dan. 8:14 there were to be 2300 days from the decree to restore Jerusalem "until the sanctuary be cleansed." If the decree to restore Jerusalem was given in 457 B.C., and if one could calculate that each "day" symbolized a year, as it did in Ezek. 4:6, then the consummation would come 2300 years later, in 1843-1844. Miller became a Baptist lay preacher, spreading his message through public speaking and a number of publications.

As the time approached, thousands were attracted to the movement, and tensions between the adventists and older established churches increased. Eventually, Miller refined his calculations, announcing that Christ's return would come between March 21, 1843, and March 21, 1844. When the dates that Miller set came and went without Christ's visible return, the group faced an initial disappointment. The movement's leaders acknowledged that they had misunderstood the time foretold by the biblical prophecies. By recalculating, they concluded that the correct date would be October 22, 1844. When this date also passed, the movement faced its second major crisis, the Great Disappointment. In response, many simply left the movement.

Others argued that Miller had indeed been correct about the *time* of Christ's return, but not about the *manner* of Christ's return. They concluded that the biblical prophecies did not point to Christ's visible return to earth, but his invisible return to cleanse the heavenly sanctuary, as depicted in Heb. 8:1-2. Those who espoused this view claimed that this is precisely what happened in 1844, so that the faithful can still anticipate Christ's visible return to earth at a future (unspecified) time. A woman named Ellen White (1827-1915), who experienced trances, gathered a number of Miller's followers who adhered to this spiritualized view into the group that became the Seventh-Day Adventists.

Charles Taze Russell and the Jehovah's Witnesses

In the decades that followed the Great Disappointment, new dates for the coming of Christ continued to be proposed. One group identified 1874 as the key date, but again the year came and went without cataclysmic change. A man named Charles Taze Russell (1852-1916), however, began popularizing the view that Christ returned spiritually in 1874, inaugurating a millennial dawn period that would climax with the arrival of the kingdom of God on earth in 1914. Russell spread his views by organizing Bible studies and producing literature through the Watch Tower Tract Society. Sensing the imminent coming of the end, he proclaimed that "Millions now living will never die." The outbreak of World War I in 1914 generated excitement among Russell's followers, but Russell himself died in 1916 and never saw the war's outcome. In the decades that followed, his followers organized themselves as the Jehovah's Witnesses, continuing to hold that 1914 had been a pivotal year in God's plan.

Calculations that point to 1914 are based in part on Luke 21:24, which warns that "Jerusalem will be trodden down by the Gentiles until the times of the Gentiles are fulfilled." Jehovah's Witnesses teach that the times of the Gentiles began in 607 B.C., the year that is (mistakenly) thought to be the time that Israel went into exile. According to Dan. 4:25, the Gentile king Nebuchadnezzar was debased for seven years until he came to recognize God as ruler. This seven-year period is taken to foreshadow the duration of "the times of the Gentiles." Seven years include 2520 days, according to a lunar calendar in which each year has 360 days. If one day represents one year (cf. Ezek. 4:6), then the times of the Gentiles should last for 2520 years, beginning in 607 B.C. and ending in 1914.

Revelation has had a central place in the thinking of Jehovah's Witnesses. Perhaps their most famous teaching is the idea that a group of 144,000 saints will have a special place in heaven as priests and kings of God. The idea comes from Rev. 7:4-8 and 14:1-5. Some Jehovah's Witnesses have taught that the group of 144,000 was identified by 1914, while others have thought that the gathering process continued beyond that time. In either case, the Jehovah's Witnesses continue to sponsor an aggressive missionary movement because Rev. 7:9-14 says that a great multitude of other people will share in the benefits of God's kingdom on earth, though without the special status of the 144,000.

Tragedy at Waco: Branch Davidians

The Branch Davidians were an obscure adventist group until they seized national attention when federal agents attacked their compound near Waco, Texas, in 1993. The founder of the Davidians was Victor Houteff (died 1955), a Seventh-Day Adventist, who by 1929 was convinced that the seven seals described in Revelation 6 contained the secret to God's plan for the final days of the world, and he felt called to gather a group of 144,000 people prior to the arrival of God's kingdom (Rev. 7:1-8; 14:1-5). Establishing the Mount Carmel Center near Waco in 1935 as a temporary gathering point for the group, Houteff eventually intended to go to Palestine where his followers would found a Davidic kingdom. After Houteff died in 1955, his widow prophesied on the basis of texts like Rev. 11:1-3 that in a mere 1260 days, on April 22, 1959, God would intervene in Palestine to prepare for the establishment of the kingdom. About nine hundred Davidians from the U.S. and Canada sold their homes and businesses and gathered at Mount Carmel in anticipation of an imminent move to the Holy Land. When the prophecy failed, the group fractured, and the faction known as the Branch Davidians assumed control of the Mount Carmel Center.

In 1981, a charismatic figure named Vernon Howell (died 1993) joined the group, eventually becoming its leader. He called himself David Koresh. Koresh is the Hebrew form of the name "Cyrus," the Persian king who defeated the Babylonians and allowed the Jews to return to Jerusalem after 539 B.C. Since Isaiah 45:1 calls Cyrus or "Koresh" God's "anointed one" (*christos* in Greek), David Koresh argued that many New Testament references to the "christ" referred to a latter-day warrior rather than to Jesus. For example, he insisted that the Lamb who would break the seals on the scroll that contained God's plan for the ages (Rev. 5:2) was not Jesus, but Koresh himself. He also claimed to be the conqueror on the white horse that appeared when the first seal was broken (Rev. 6:1-2). Like Cyrus before him, Koresh envisioned himself as the adversary of "Babylon," the term he used for federal agents and other outsiders.

Koresh further developed his identity by appealing to the "key of David" (Rev. 3:7), which he took to mean the Psalms. Like the book of Revelation, Psalm 45 speaks of a conquering king who fights for truth.

The psalm's references to the king marrying princesses and begetting children were used to support Koresh's claim that he was to beget children through the former wives of his followers. This was his version of "the marriage supper of the Lamb" (Rev. 19:9). Allegations of polygamy and child abuse prompted federal agents to raid the compound on Feb. 28, 1993. The Davidians resisted, several of their members were killed, and federal agents began a siege. Koresh attempted to understand the siege by correlating his experience with Revelation's account of the fifth seal. Key words are in boldface:

> 9And when he had opened the fifth seal, I saw under the altar the souls of **them that were slain** for the word of God and for the testimony which they held: 10And they cried with a loud voice, saying, **How long**, O Lord, holy and true, dost thou not judge and avenge our blood on them that dwell on the earth? 11And white robes were given unto every one of them; and it was said unto them, that they should **rest yet for a little season**, until their fellowservants also and their brethren, that **they should be killed** as they were, should be fulfilled. (Rev. 6:9-11, KJV)

Since the text refers to "them that were slain," Koresh connected this with the first federal attack, in which some Davidians were killed. When asked "how long" he would resist, Koresh refused to surrender because Rev. 6:11 told him to remain in the compound "for a little season." The prospect of death did not deter the group because they expected others to "be killed," as the passage from Revelation predicted. From their perspective, the scene was unfolding as God had scripted it, with the agents of Babylon opposing the faithful. Progress toward a solution was made when negotiators used Revelation to convince Koresh that since his motives were so poorly understood, he must "prophesy again before many peoples, and nations, and tongues, and kings" (Rev. 10:11). Koresh agreed, saying that he would surrender after writing an exposition of the seven seals. Federal agents interpreted this as a delaying tactic and attacked on April 19. Most members of the group died when a fire broke out in the compound (Tabor, "The Waco Tragedy").

Rapture, Tribulation, and Armageddon

The groups mentioned above have sometimes captured public attention for brief periods, but their beliefs are not widely known outside their own circles. The situation is quite different for another form of end-times belief that circulates broadly on the currents of modern evangelicalism. Its key features are summed up on the cover of *Tribulation Force* by Tim LaHaye and Jerry Jenkins: "In one cataclysmic moment, millions around the globe disappear. Those left behind face war, famine, plagues, and natural disasters so devastating that only one in four people will survive. Odds are even worse for enemies of the Antichrist and his new world order," during "the seven most chaotic years that the planet will ever see."

These words represent a system of thought that was developed in the early 1800s by a British writer named John Nelson Darby (1800-1882). Darby was associated with a small group known as the Plymouth Brethren, but his views reached a broad audience through the study notes that Cyrus Scofield included in *The Scofield Reference Bible*, which was first published in 1909. More recently, Hal Lindsey's *Late Great Planet Earth* and the *Left Behind* series by Tim LaHaye and Jerry Jenkins, which have sold millions of copies, have helped to make "rapture," "tribulation," and "Armageddon" into household words for many Americans.

Those who hold this view are called "dispensationalists" because they usually divide world history into a series of periods or "dispensations" that will culminate with the thousand-year kingdom of Christ on earth. They are also "premillennialists," because they argue that world conditions will worsen until Christ returns before ("pre-") the millennial kingdom begins. They insist that prophecy is actually history that has been written in advance, so that the prophetic passages in the Bible constitute a script that will be played out to the letter in the end times. They also assume that no single book of the Bible contains the entire script, and that verses from various parts of the Bible must be joined together like the pieces of a jigsaw puzzle so that people can see the whole picture.

Basic to this approach is a clear distinction between Israel and the church. Dispensationalists have traditionally insisted that Old Testament prophecies concerning Israel will be literally fulfilled in the national history of the Jewish people rather than spiritually in the life of the church. God promised the descendants of Abraham a kingdom that would stretch "from the river of Egypt to the great river, the Euphrates" (Gen. 15:18), but when the Jews rejected Jesus in the first century, God postponed fulfilling his promises concerning the land. A church comprised largely of Gentiles came into existence. At some point, dispensationalists believe, the church will be mysteriously whisked up to heaven. After this event, God's final steps toward giving an earthly political kingdom to Israel will be carried out.

The Script of the End Times

A key text for this scenario is Dan. 9:20-27, which describes a period of seventy weeks of years that will pass before the end comes (a "week" of years equals seven years). According to Darby's reckoning, all but one of these seven-year periods elapsed prior to the time of Christ. After the Jews rejected Christ, God stopped the clock of prophecy with just one seven-year period remaining, much as a referee might stop a basketball game with seven seconds left on the clock. For the past two thousand years, people have gone about their activities, as the players and spectators do during a time-out in a basketball game, waiting for the clock to start so that the game can be played out. Thus, all of time from the first century to the present lies in the gap between Dan. 9:26 and 9:27.

> 24Seventy weeks are determined upon thy people and upon thy holy city, to finish the transgression and to make an end of sins, and to make reconciliation for iniquity, and to bring in everlasting righteousness; and to seal up the vision and prophecy, and to anoint the most Holy. 25Know, therefore, and understand, *that* from the going forth of the commandment to restore and build Jerusalem unto the Messiah, the Prince, *shall be* seven weeks, and threescore and two weeks; the street shall be built again, and the wall, even in troublous times. 26And after threescore and

two weeks shall Messiah be cut off, but not for himself; and the people of the prince that shall come shall destroy the city and the sanctuary, and the end of it *shall be* with a flood, and unto the end of the war desolations are determined.

2000 or
more years
of church
history

^{27}And he shall confirm the covenant with many for one week; and in the midst of the week he shall cause the sacrifice and the oblation to cease, and for the overspreading of abominations he shall make *it* desolate, even until the consummation, and that determined shall be poured upon the desolate.

Premillennial dispensationalists have intently watched developments in the Middle East for signs that God might start the clock moving again. Tremendous excitement was generated by waves of Jewish immigration into Palestine following persecutions in Europe in the nineteenth and twentieth centuries. The formation of the modern state of Israel in 1948 and the Israeli capture of east Jerusalem in 1967 led many to believe that God was divinely protecting the Jewish nation, and that conditions were emerging in which the temple could be rebuilt on its ancient site, where the Dome of the Rock now stands. Along with global politics, dispensationalists have seen signs of the nearness of the end in computer technology, which could allow the Antichrist to attain mastery of the planet, as well as in nuclear weaponry, which for the first time could bring about the kind of worldwide devastation foretold by Revelation. Although dispensationalists usually avoid predicting the dates of final events, Hal Lindsey for a time spoke as if the end would come in 1988, a forty-year generation after the founding of the modern state of Israel. Later, fears that the Y2K computer problem would bring widespread chaos led Grant Jeffrey to warn that if computer networks collapsed on January 1, 2000, nations might yield their authority to a global economic czar, who would be delegated to stem the tide of chaos. Using the crisis as a pretext, this figure could institute emergency laws that would consolidate his power, establishing the

21

Antichrist's world government.[6] The year 2000, however, arrived without incident.

The signal that God's clock is about to begin ticking again is expected to be the rapture of faithful Christians. The term "rapture" refers to believers being caught up to meet the Lord in the air, as Paul said in 1 Thess. 4:16-17. Since the first century Christians have usually understood that Paul was referring to Christ's second coming at the end of time; but during the last couple of centuries some have taken Paul to mean that the faithful will be snatched from the earth to spare them from the tribulation that is to occur before Christ's second coming. Popular presentations of this idea speak of believers vanishing bodily, leaving their clothes, eyeglasses, contact lenses, hairpieces, and jewelry behind, to the astonishment of the unbelievers and half-hearted Christians who will face the horrors of the tribulation. Proponents point out that the word "church" appears often in Rev. 1:1–3:22, then it vanishes until 22:16. Since the word vanishes, they conclude that the church itself will vanish during the tribulation. The central chapters of Revelation do refer to "saints" on earth being afflicted during the tribulation, but those who hold to a pre-tribulation rapture position respond that these "saints" will be the people who come to faith *during* the tribulation, not those who had sincere faith before it.

A world leader known as the Antichrist (1 John 2:18), "the man of lawlessness" (2 Thess. 2:3-4), and the beast (Rev. 13:1-8) is expected to form a single world government during the tribulation. He will form a group of ten nations to help exert his influence over the world. After World War II, many expected the European Common Market to become this ten-nation coalition. Although more than ten nations have now joined, dispensationalists continue to speculate that the Antichrist might ally himself with ten especially powerful nations within the European Union, or perhaps with a group of ten countries in the United Nations. One of the beast's supporters is expected to use computers to control the global economy, forcing all people to use the

---

6. Grant Jeffrey, *The Millennium Meltdown: The Year 2000 Computer Crisis* (Wheaton, IL: Tyndale House, 1998), 155-59. For those who have forgotten, the Y2K problem was that the dates on computers commonly listed only the last two digits of the year, and when the millennium changed, computers that did not know what time it was could malfunction.

"number" of the beast in order to conduct their transactions. Some assume that this "number," which Rev. 13:18 identifies as 666, will be something like a social security number or credit card number. Others have claimed that the international product codes are based on a secret numerical foundation of sixes.

Since true believers will have been raptured to heaven before the tribulation, the beast will be able to promote a new global religion to support his policies on earth. The agent of this new religion is pictured as a harlot (Rev. 17:1-18), who will both seduce and compel people into giving up their distinctive beliefs in order to embrace a single world religion. The World Council of Churches is sometimes seen as the precursor of the harlot. Nevertheless, God will not leave people without an opportunity to learn the truth, for he will appoint two witnesses to preach in Jerusalem. They will give evidence of the truth of their message by performing signs like those of Moses and Elijah before being martyred and raised to life again (11:1-13). A group of 144,000 Jews will convert to Christianity (7:1-8; 14:1-5), and they in turn will bring innumerable people of other nations to faith (7:9-17).

The tribulation is expected to last for seven years, the final "week" of years mentioned in Dan. 9:27. During its first half, Israel will make a diplomatic agreement or "covenant" with the Antichrist, thinking that this will give them the peace and security needed to rebuild the temple in Jerusalem and restore the system of sacrifice. After three and a half years, however, this will prove to be a "covenant with death" (Isa. 28:15) that will bring a "time of trouble for Jacob" (Jer. 30:7), for the Antichrist will double-cross the Jews by defiling the temple and making true sacrifice cease (Matt. 24:15; Dan. 9:27).

"Armageddon" is the name given to the cataclysmic conflicts that are expected to occur at the end of the tribulation. The word "Armageddon" (Rev. 16:16) probably means "mountain of Megiddo," and those who take it as a literal geographic description assume that it points to the place named "Megiddo" in northern Israel. Popular pictures of the battle involve linking multiple puzzle pieces together. A common scenario is that Russia, which is identified as the nation of Gog (Ezekiel 38–39) and the king of the north (Daniel 11), attacks Israel in order to gain control of the Middle East. The conflict escalates into global war when the Russians are joined by the king of the south — assumed to be an Arab confederacy — and by the kings from the east — who are taken to be a Chinese army of two hundred million soldiers (Rev. 9:13-19; 16:12). The battle culminates when Christ returns and defeats his enemies in Jordan (Isa. 63:1-6), at Megiddo (Rev. 16:12-16), in the valley of Jehoshaphat (Joel 3:1-2, 9-17), and at Jerusalem (Zech. 12:1-9), leaving carnage on the battlefield (Ezek. 39:18).

The millennial kingdom begins after Armageddon is over and Satan has been bound for a thousand years (Rev. 20:1-6). This kingdom is pictured as the time when many of the Old Testament prophecies come to their fulfillment. People will live long and peaceful lives, building homes to live in and eating the fruit of their vineyards (Isa. 65:20-21). The natural order will be transformed so that the "wolf and the lamb shall feed together" and "the lion shall eat straw like the ox" (Isa. 65:25). The nations will "beat their swords into plowshares and their spears into pruning hooks," giving up the practice of war (Isa. 2:4; Mic. 4:3). After the thousand years have ended, Satan will be released and utterly defeated, the last judgment will occur, and eternity will begin.

Many have found this system appealing. Its dark view of coming events corresponds to perceptions that the world is sliding into increasing violence and moral decay, that modern military technology has created a situation that will result in nuclear holocaust, and that conditions of poverty and environmental degradation are irreversible. In the face of these threats, however, the dispensationalist system not only assures its adherents *that* God's purposes will be carried out, but that they can anticipate *how* his purposes will be carried out, step by step, by following the script that has been pieced together from various verses of Scripture. The teaching about the rapture also holds out the hope that those who come to faith now will escape before the horrors of the end times are unleashed.

Problems with the Script

Despite its appeal, dispensational premillennialism is fraught with difficulties. First, the system has a mechanistic view of prophecy fulfillment that is foreign to Revelation. Darby's system maintains that God continued fulfilling prophecies through Dan. 9:26, then stopped the clock for over two thousand years without fulfilling 9:27; yet when read in context these two verses seem clearly to speak of the same period.

Darby's calculations depend not only on the wording but even on the punctuation found in the King James and New International versions of Dan. 9:25; his reckoning collapses under the punctuation used in the New American Bible, Today's English Version, the New Revised Standard, and other versions.[7] In contrast, Revelation frequently paraphrases the Old Testament, but *never quotes it verbatim.* John weaves Old Testament prophecies into his book in a way that shows *that* God will fulfill his promises but without clearly disclosing *how* he will do so.

Second, neither Daniel nor Revelation refers to the rapture. Dispensationalists sometimes try to find the rapture in God's summons to John of Patmos: "Come up hither" (Rev. 4:1), yet when read in context, God's command calls John into a temporary visionary ascent; it does not refer to the ingathering of all the faithful in heaven. The idea that true believers vanish when the word "church" vanishes from the scenes of tribulation in Revelation 4–19 is forced. The central chapters of Revelation refer to the saints, who follow the Lamb, undergoing affliction (Rev. 13:7, 10; 14:12; 17:6), and there is no reason to think that the faithful who suffer include only those Christians converted after the beginning of the tribulation.

Third, the sharp distinction between Israel and the church is not warranted. New Testament writers assume that the story of Israel continues within the Christian community. Paul pictures the people of God as an olive tree: non-Jews are grafted into the tree on the basis of their faith in Christ, so that there remains just one tree (Rom. 11:13-24). In Christ, the wall dividing Jew from Gentile is broken down, so that the two peoples are no longer separated on the basis of ethnicity or the Law (Eph. 2:11-22). The term "Israel" is extended to include all who share in the blessings promised to Abraham (Gal. 6:16).

---

7. Dan. 9:25 refers to seven weeks of years (= 49 years) and sixty-two weeks of years (= 434 years), a total of 483 years. The King James and New International versions say that all 483 years elapse between the command to rebuild the wall of Jerusalem and the coming of the anointed one, Jesus. The New Revised Standard and most other recent translations say that an anointed one is to appear after a mere forty-nine years, that is, shortly after the exile. Thus this anointed figure would be Joshua or Zerubbabel (Ezra 3:2; Zech. 4:14) or perhaps Cyrus (Isa. 45:1). The remaining period of 434 years is roughly the period from the rebuilding of Jerusalem to the Seleucid persecution in the second century B.C., the time most scholars think Daniel was written.

Finally, the system confuses the literal and the symbolic. Dispensationalists regularly insist that the biblical prophecies must be taken literally, as history written in advance; but their own readings often strain the notion of what is literal. For example, it is difficult to think that a literal reading of Daniel would put a gap of over two thousand years between Dan. 9:26 and 9:27, as noted above. Dispensationalists usually assume that the reference to the "temple" in Rev. 11:1-2 must be taken literally, as a temple building that will be constructed in Jerusalem at some point in the future; yet they also assume that the olive trees and lampstands in 11:4 symbolize human beings. They maintain that the number of the beast in Rev. 13:18 literally has to do with computerized control of the economy, yet they do not assume that the beast will literally have seven heads and ten horns, even though 13:1 describes him this way. (Usually the Antichrist is pictured as an appealing, though cunning, human being.) Ezekiel is taken to predict that the Russians, identified as "Gog," will attack Israel; but where Ezek. 39:3 says that God will destroy the enemy bows and arrows, dispensationalists assume that the text really refers to the destruction of Russian aircraft and missiles. The interpretation of Revelation that will be given below devotes special attention to the symbolic dimensions of Revelation's message.

Historical Study of Revelation

Recent scholarly study interprets Revelation very differently from the futuristic approaches described above. A good way to show the difference is to look at the way that the book introduces itself. Futuristic interpreters tend to read Revelation as if it begins, "John, to the Christians in North America, who live in the twenty-first century," assuming that Revelation is primarily a book for those living at the end of time. Most scholars today, however, note that Revelation begins, "John, to the seven churches that are in Asia" (Rev. 1:4). To take this statement literally means that Revelation is primarily a book for its own time, and that it was written to communicate with Christian congregations in first-century Asia Minor (modern-day Turkey). If futuristic interpreters assume that Revelation's message will become clearer as the final days approach, many scholars take the opposite view. Assuming that Revelation's message would have been clearest to those who lived in John's own time, they search for clues to understanding the book not by combing recent headlines or news broadcasts, but by studying the language and literature of the ancient world.

Revelation and Apocalyptic Literature

One of the most basic questions that scholars ask is "What kind of literature is Revelation?" The assumptions that people make about a text affect the way that they read it. People do not read a science fiction novel in the same way that they read a history textbook, or approach a newspaper's comic strips in the same way that they read the front page. Accordingly, those who assume that Revelation is essentially a history of the end of the world that has been written in advance will read the book one way, while those who assume that the book is not a script for the end times, but another form of literature, will read it quite differently.

Revelation is commonly grouped with other writings known as "apocalypses," a term that comes from the Greek word *apokalypsis,* which means "revelation." The word, which appears in Rev. 1:1, is now used for a category of ancient writings that have features like those of Revelation. By comparing Revelation with similar writings, scholars try to discern how the book would have communicated with its intended audience. Within the Bible, the book most like Revelation is Daniel, which begins with stories about Daniel and his companions in Babylonian and Persian courts, and which ends with visions of beasts, battles, the coming of the son of man on the clouds of heaven, and the resurrection of the dead. Other apocalypses include 2 Esdras 3–14 — often called 4 Ezra — which is included among the apocryphal or deuterocanonical books in many Bibles, as well as 1 and 2 Enoch, 2 and 3 Baruch, the Apocalypse of Abraham, and other writings.

Apocalypses are a form of literature with a narrative framework, in which a revelation of transcendent reality is given by an angel or otherworldly being to a human recipient. Usually the revelation unveils a supernatural world and points to salvation at the end of time. The apocalypses describe revelations coming in various ways, including visions and journeys into another world, and conversations with an angel, who helps the seer interpret what he sees. The seer may also be given a heavenly book. Apocalypses assume that the world of ordinary life is mysterious, so that revelation comes from a supernatural source. They tell readers about a hidden world of angels and demons, whose activities affect human life, and about a final, future judgment of the wicked.

Some of these elements do appear in texts that are not, in themselves, apocalypses. For example, Isaiah 24–27 speaks of judgment followed by a final end to death; the gospels speak of tribulations at the end of the age (Matt. 24:1-51; Mark 13:1-37); Paul's letters tell of future resurrection and the defeat of death (1 Cor. 15:1-58; 1 Thess. 4:13-18); and the Dead Sea Scrolls tell of a final conflict between the forces of good and evil. An "apocalypse" differs from these writings in that it brings these elements together in a narrative framework (J. J. Collins, *Apocalyptic Imagination,* 2-9).

Broadly speaking, there are two types of apocalypses. Some are mainly accounts of heavenly journeys that tell how a seer ascends through celestial regions in the company of an angelic guide to see things that are inaccessible to other human beings. The "Book of Watchers," for example, tells how Enoch is shown the foundations of the universe, the prison where the stars of heaven are kept, and the places where the spirits of the dead are held in anticipation of the coming day of judgment (1 Enoch 17–36). Other apocalypses focus on the movement of history, often dividing time into periods that lead up to catastrophic upheavals, which are followed by a time of salvation that may include the restoration of the land of Israel and the transformation of the world. Second Baruch 53–74 tells of alternating dark and bright waters that represent periods of history from the time of Adam to the tribulations of the end time, when illness and fear will vanish, and the world will be filled with joy. The seer in 4 Ezra understands the present age to be dominated by sin and sadness, but he learns that salvation will arrive in the age to come, when the messiah will reign for four hundred years before the resurrection and last judgment.

Knowing something about apocalyptic literature helps readers of Revelation check the kind of expectations that they bring to the book. First, readers today sometimes are intrigued with Revelation because it seems to be a uniquely mysterious writing in comparison to other biblical books. Readers in John's own time, however, would have recognized that Revelation was written in an established literary form that had features in common with other texts. Like the apocalypses that recount heavenly journeys, Revelation tells how John was taken up into the heavenly world to receive visions that are interpreted for him by angelic beings (e.g., Rev. 4:1; 5:5; 7:13-14). Like the apocalypses that focus on the movement of history, Revelation uses symbolic language to depict the powers of this age engaging in conflict with the power of God. Nations may be pictured as animals. Daniel, for example, has a vision in which four successive empires are depicted as a lion, a bear, a leopard, and a horned beast (Dan. 7:1-8). In another apocalypse, Ezra sees a vision of an eagle with twelve wings and three heads, which is said to be the fourth kingdom mentioned by Daniel (2 Esdras 11:1-12:3; 12:11). Revelation, in turn, combines the traits of Daniel's four beasts into a single seven-headed beast that was slaughtered and came to life (Rev. 13:1-4).

Second, Revelation's world of thought is not entirely unique, but is similar in some ways to the thought worlds of other apocalypses. These writings typically understand the present age to be dominated by the powers of sin, evil, and death; but they anticipate that in the future the wicked will be defeated or judged by God, and the world will be transformed into a state of blessedness and joy. Similarly, Revelation envisions the satanic powers of the beast and its allies making war against the saints until God's adversaries are defeated by Christ. Afterward, the dead are raised and judged, a new heaven and earth appear, and the saints reign in glory forever. Specific scenarios vary, and no two apocalypses envision the movement of history in exactly the same way. The underlying message is often similar, however, and the basic message of salvation is as important as the details in the scenarios that describe its coming.

Third, people generally wrote apocalypses to assure readers that God would be faithful, despite conditions of evil in the present age, and to encourage readers to remain loyal to God, rather than giving in to powers that oppose God. Apocalyptic writers were concerned about the future realization of God's purposes, but exhortation and assurance seem to have been more important than simple prediction of future events. We will find that this is also true of Revelation. In chapter 2 below, we will see that John's own statements about his reasons for writing and his references to prophecy indicate that Revelation was more concerned with his readers' faithful service to God than with the specific sequence of events that would transpire in the end times.

Revelation also differs from apocalypses that divide time into periods that occur in a linear sequence. As noted above, 2 Baruch 53–74 outlines periods of history from Adam to the end times, and a similar outline appears in the "Apocalypse of Weeks" in 1 Enoch 93:1-10 and 91:11-17. Daniel offers a variation on this approach by repeated visions of a series of kingdoms. In Daniel 7, the lion, bear, leopard, and horned beast represent the empires of the Babylonians, Medes, Persians, and Greeks. In Daniel 8, a two-horned ram symbolizes the empires of the Medes and Persians while a goat represents the Greeks (8:20-22). Despite the repetition, each vision moves sequentially through the rise and fall of world powers.

Revelation, however, does not offer a review of history but instead, as we will see, leads readers through overlapping cycles of visions that do not fall into a clear chronological sequence. The result is that Revelation does not disclose future events in a linear fashion, but gives alternating messages of warning and encouragement that are designed to promote faithful endurance. Revelation also differs from other apocalypses in that authors of apocalypses regularly adopted the name of an ancient figure like Enoch, Baruch, or Ezra, giving the impression that the text had been composed many generations before the author's own time. Revelation, however, is written in John's own name for Christians of his own time, who apparently knew him and considered him a "brother" in the faith (1:9).

Revelation and Roman Imperialism

Historical study has often focused on the way that Revelation urges Christians of the first century to resist Roman imperial authority. Issues of persecution (2:9-11) and eating food that had been sacrificed to idols (2:14, 20) probably stem from pressures to participate in the imperial cult, which had shrines in a number of cities in Asia Minor. John remembers that the blood of the saints was shed by the power of Rome, the city set on seven hills (6:9-11; 17:6, 9; 18:24). He himself had probably been sent to the island of Patmos because of Roman uneasiness about his Christian commitments (1:9-11). Although some Christians found it prudent to accommodate Roman domination, even when this meant compromising their faith, John writes to urge a more tenacious commitment to God, Christ, and the Christian community, even when this generated opposition from those in authority.

Revelation emphasizes that God, not Caesar, is Lord of the world. The splendor of God's heavenly throne room shows that the pageantry of the Roman court is but a mockery of the true sovereignty of God (4:1-11). When the Lamb opens the seals on God's scroll, a mounted bowman appears, resembling the Parthian warriors that threatened the borders of the Roman Empire, and another horseman takes away the "peace" that Rome claimed to provide (6:1-4). The beast that persecutes the saints seems to be another Nero, while the beast's chief ally promotes idolatrous worship like that of the imperial cult (13:1-18). The harlot that rides upon the beast is the city set on seven hills — clearly Rome — and it is called "Babylon," since Babylon destroyed the first temple and the Romans destroyed the second temple (17:1-18). Yet Revelation warns that the Roman "Babylon" will fall, and Christians are called to separate themselves from it in the confidence that God's purposes will triumph (18:4).

These historical insights are valuable because they show how Revelation's earliest readers would have interpreted some of its symbolism, and how the book issued a call to commitment that would have had direct consequences for Christians living in a non-Christian world. The problem with historical study, however, is that modern readers often find it difficult to see how such an ancient text might relate to the modern world. The interpretation of Revelation that is offered in chapters 2-7 below modifies the usual historical approach in two ways. One is that it emphasizes that Revelation addressed a number of different issues, not just one issue, and that there are valuable analogies between first-century life and modern life. The other is that it considers how Revelation's imagery evokes associations that fit multiple periods of time, not only one period of time. The idea is not that Revelation's images are "timeless," but that they disclose things that apply to many generations.

Silence or Song?

Surveys of approaches to Revelation usually do not comment on how the so-called mainline churches view the book, presumably because there seems to be so little to say. Christians in these churches often treat Revelation with the kind of uneasy silence that is usually reserved for the more eccentric members of one's extended family. Pride of place in mainline preaching and teaching usually goes to Matthew, Mark, Luke, and John, while the Revelation-inspired end-times antics among some Christian groups make those in the mainline wince. While not willing to deny all connection with the book, many in the mainline treat Revelation like the distant cousin who does not quite fit in with the rest of the family. They prefer not to talk much about it or invite it to family gatherings more often than necessary.

One measure of mainline churches' use of Revelation is *The Revised Common Lectionary,* which lists the Scripture passages that are read in many Protestant and Roman Catholic congregations each week. Although Revelation is twenty-two chapters long, the lectionary selects only six short passages to be read. These include the opening and concluding greetings from God and Christ as the Alpha and Omega, together with four scenes of the saints in glory. These texts are read during the Sundays after Easter once every three years, and occasionally, one of these same texts is also read on All Saints Day or Christ the King Sunday in November. The lectionary conveniently avoids passages mentioning the beast and the harlot, and passes by the seven seals and other plagues without inviting comment. Some rather stern warnings do interrupt the greetings at the end of Revelation, but these are omitted from the assigned reading so that worshipers do not hear them.[8] The result is a rather pleasant selection of texts that minimizes the likelihood that anyone will be embarrassed or confused by Revelation's more bizarre or disturbing images.

The problem is that many people know that there is much more to Revelation than these few scenes, and most of the questions that people ask come from passages that are not included in the lectionary. When questions do arise, a common response is to dismiss the more speculative and sensationalistic ideas that people encounter in popular culture, and perhaps to show how Revelation can be read as a critique of Roman imperial power. The result, however, is that many people have difficulty seeing Revelation's value for readers today.

8. The assigned texts for the Sundays after Easter in series C are Rev. 1:4-8; 5:11-14; 7:9-17; 21:1-6; 21:10, 22–22:5; 22:12-14, 16-17, 20-21.

A different and intriguing perspective on Revelation emerges, however, when we consider how often Christians of all sorts encounter passages from the book in their hymns and liturgies. Mainline Christians might not read Revelation, but they sing it all the time. Revelation has inspired songs and hymns that range from traditional compositions to contemporary praise choruses; and words from Revelation are woven into many liturgies. Worshipers often become acquainted with images from Revelation more through music than through reading the text. A brief musical tour of Revelation can show how each of its six vision cycles culminates with songs and images that continue to be used in Christian worship.

The book of Revelation is framed by declarations that God and Christ are the Alpha and Omega, the first and the last, the beginning and the end (1:8, 17; 21:6; 22:13). This announcement corresponds to Revelation's structure, because the book begins and ends with visions that bring readers into the presence of God and the risen Christ. A hymn that conveys this is "Of the Father's Love Begotten." The text was composed in the fourth century A.D., and today it is usually sung to a melody of thirteenth-century chant:

The first cycle of visions begins when John encounters the risen Christ, who directs him to send messages to seven congregations in Asia Minor. After being told about each of the seven churches in turn, John is taken into God's heavenly throne room, where he sees the throne of God beside a glassy sea. The throne is surrounded by twenty-four elders wearing golden crowns, and by four living creatures, whose faces resemble those of a lion, an ox, an eagle, and a human being. When the creatures raise the song of praise, "Holy, holy, holy, Lord God Almighty," the elders cast down their crowns before the throne (4:8-10). The traditional hymn "Holy, holy, holy" by Reginald Heber (1723-1826) is one of many that paraphrase this text:

> Holy, holy, holy, Lord God Almighty!
> Early in the morning our song shall rise to thee.
> Holy, holy, holy, merciful and mighty,
> God in three persons, blessed Trinity.
>
> Holy, holy, holy! All the saints adore thee,
> Casting down their golden crowns around the glassy sea.
> Cherubim and seraphim falling down before thee,
> Which wert and art and ever more shalt be.

The heavenly chorus of praise continues after John sees a Lamb, who had been slaughtered and yet was alive, take the scroll from the hand of God in order to open its seven seals. The four living creatures and twenty-four elders fall down before the Lamb in praise (5:8-10). They are joined by myriads of angels who declare that the Lamb is worthy to receive "power and wealth and wisdom and might and honor and glory and blessing" (5:11-14). One of the hymns inspired by this scene of praise to Christ the Lamb is "All Hail the Power of Jesus' Name," by Edward Perronet (1726-1792). The second verse draws on the image of the martyrs under the altar, which appears in 6:9-11.

> All hail the pow'r of Jesus' name!
> Let angels prostrate fall;
> Bring forth the royal diadem,
> And crown him Lord of all.
> *(repeat)*
>
> Crown him ye martyrs of your God,
> Who from his altar call;
> Extol the stem of Jesse's rod
> And crown him Lord of all.
> *(repeat)*

The Lamb opens the seven seals, unleashing the four horsemen that bring conquest, violence, economic hardship, and death. In their wake, John sees a vision of martyrs and another vision in which all the inhabitants of the earth are threatened with destruction. An angel, however, interrupts the threat to show John a vision of a great multitude in heaven. They are dressed in white and hold palm branches in their hands. The words of their song (7:10-12) were paraphrased by Charles Wesley (1707-1788), among others, who wove them into the third and fourth verses of his hymn, "Ye Servants of God":

> Salvation to God, who sits on the throne!
> Let all cry aloud, and honor the Son.
> The praises of Jesus the angels proclaim,
> Fall down on their faces, and worship the Lamb.

> Then let us adore and give him his right,
> All glory and power, all wisdom and might
> All honor and blessing, with angels above,
> And thanks never ceasing, and infinite love.

The choruses of heavenly praise give way to more visions of threat, in which a number of angels blow trumpets to call down plagues upon the earth and sea. As the horror of the plagues intensifies, an angel again interrupts the movement toward final judgment by giving John a scroll to eat. He does so, and sees a vision of the oppressed community of faith, represented by the temple and the holy city under siege. God's witnesses testify, are martyred, and raised; but afterward people do give glory to God. The angelic announcement that summons the twenty-four elders to worship (Rev. 11:15) was memorably put to music by Georg Friedrich Handel (1674-1748), in his Hallelujah Chorus:

The next cycle of visions shows Satan being cast out of heaven to persecute the faithful on earth, extending his influence through a great seven-headed beast, who is the adversary of the Lamb. Visions of judgment follow, culminating in the ingathering of the faithful and the trampling of the vintage of the winepress of the wrath of God (14:19-20). This vision of judgment, which occurs just before the end of the cycle, was one of the passages that inspired Julia Ward Howe (1819-1910) to compose the "Battle Hymn of the Republic." Writing in late 1861, during the early phases of the American Civil War, she wove images from Revelation together with images of the conflict in which she found herself. Like the book of Revelation, her hymn served as an uncompromising call to commitment:

> Mine eyes have seen the glory of the coming of the Lord.
> He is trampling out the vintage where the grapes of wrath
>   are stored.
> He hath loosed the fateful lightning of his terrible swift sword.
> His truth is marching on.
>
> Glory, glory hallelujah! Glory, glory, hallelujah!
> Glory, glory, hallelujah! His truth is marching on.

After returning briefly to the heavenly throne room at the close of the cycle, a new series of visions depicts bowls of plagues falling upon the earth. John sees Babylon the harlot, riding on a seven-headed beast. The beast destroys the harlot, and after her fall, the kings and the merchants of the earth mourn her passing; but voices of celebration are heard again from heaven, singing "hallelujah" with joy because Babylon's violent reign has come to an end (19:6). Again, the words appear in Handel's "Hallelujah Chorus":

The fall of Babylon is quickly followed by the defeat of the beast and its allies. Satan is bound for a thousand years and the saints are brought to life to reign with Christ. Although Satan is briefly released to deceive the nations once more, he is quickly and finally defeated. All the dead are raised, the last judgment occurs, and John finally sees the new heavens and the new earth, where the New Jerusalem descends from heaven as the bride of the Lamb. Scenes from the New Jerusalem have inspired many hymns, ranging from Philipp Nicolai's (1556-1608) majestic "Wake, Awake, for Night Is Flying" to the gentle strains of "Jerusalem, My Happy Home" and Robert Lowry's (1826-1899) "Shall We Gather at the River." The sense of triumph is captured well by the final verse of William How's (1823-1897) "For All the Saints":

From earth's wide bounds, from ocean's farthest coast,
Through gates of pearl streams in the countless host,
Singing to Father, Son, and Holy Ghost: Alleluia! Alleluia!

Recognizing how images from Revelation are used in Christian music and worship can be illuminating for contemporary readers of the book. By translating the book into song, musicians have helped to give Revelation an integral place in a living faith tradition. One of the greatest barriers that people face when opening Revelation is the fear of being confused or misled by its images. People may overcome some of this uneasiness when they realize that Revelation's most abiding contribution has not been to stir people into a frenzy over the date of Christ's return, but to give communities of faith some of the language that they have used for generations when giving praise to God and the Lamb. Those who enjoy singing hymns based on Revelation 4–5 do not keep the book at arm's length, but add their voices to the heavenly chorus. Rather than speculating about what it might mean to "worship God" (19:10; 22:9), they actually join in the act of worship. Moreover, the hymns lift up passages that stress hope, joy, and faithfulness. Readers cannot ignore Revelation's many warnings about divine judgment, but the worship scenes help readers interpret the warnings in light of the promises, and to understand that God's purposes are directed toward the joy of salvation.

Venturing Forward

So how can we best read Revelation, given the astonishing (and confusing) range of viewpoints sketched above? Looking at previous attempts to make sense of the book should rightly make us cautious about claiming to have found yet another key to unlocking the mysteries contained in Revelation, but a number of points are worth keeping in mind as we embark on a journey through the visions that John of Patmos included in his book.

One basic insight is that we do well to take Revelation as a whole, as a book with its own integrity. Some of the approaches mentioned above assume that verses of the Bible are like pieces of a jigsaw puzzle, and that our task is to put pieces from various books together to create a complete picture. To take Revelation as a whole means following its message from the introduction in Revelation 1 to the final blessing at the end of Revelation 22, instead of jumping from Daniel 9 to 1 Thessalonians 4 and then to Revelation 6, etc. Read in this way, John's message remains compelling, yet it will seem different from many of the sensationalistic interpretations outlined earlier.

Reading Revelation as a whole shows that the book moves in a non-linear way. This insight goes back to the third century, when Victorinus wrote the earliest existing commentary on Revelation, and many recent interpreters have found this approach quite helpful. An outline of the book looks like a spiral, with each loop consisting of a series of visions: seven messages to the churches (Rev. 1–3), seven seals (Rev. 4–7), seven trumpets (Rev. 8–11), unnumbered visions (Rev. 12–15), seven plagues (Rev. 15–19), and more unnumbered visions (Rev. 19-22). Visions celebrating the triumph of God occur at the end of each cycle (4:1-11; 7:1-17; 11:15-19; 15:1-4; 19:1-10; 21:1–22:5). This pattern, which provides an outline for the remaining chapters of this book, looks something like this (A. Y. Collins, *Apocalypse,* ix-xiv):

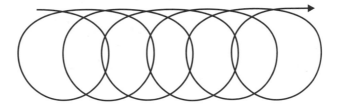

Those who read Revelation as a whole encounter visions that alternatively threaten and assure them. With increasing intensity the visions at the bottom of the spiral threaten the readers' sense of security by confronting them with horsemen that represent conquest, violence, hardship, and death; by portents in heaven, earth, and sea; and by seemingly insuperable adversaries who oppose those who worship God and Christ. Nevertheless, each time the clamor of conflict becomes unbearable, listeners are transported into the presence of God, the Lamb, and the heavenly chorus. These visions appear at the top of the spiral. Threatening visions and assuring visions function differently, but they serve the same end, which is that listeners might continue to trust in God and remain faithful to God.

Revelation is designed to unmask false sources of security while beckoning readers to join the heavenly host in singing praises to God and the Lamb. The musical compositions listed above direct our attention to Revelation's festive scenes of worship, reminding us that these scenes show us the goal of God's saving work. The many songs and hymns that are based on worship scenes from Revelation continue to be sung in Christian communities around the world, enabling many — including those who have never read the book — to *experience* its message with compelling immediacy. Readers will encounter many threatening images in Revelation, but those who keep the musical scenes in mind will not lose sight of the book's goal. Moving through kaleidoscopic cycles of visions can be confusing, but readers who keep the strains of the "Hallelujah Chorus" in the backs of their minds will remember where the story is going.

Finally, we will take Revelation contextually, as a book written by "John, to the seven churches that are in Asia" (1:4). Accordingly, instead of first asking how Revelation relates to the headlines in today's newspaper, we will ask how it relates to the situation of the Christians of John's own time. This approach is not designed to keep Revelation safely confined to the first century, so that modern readers can be protected from its message. Rather, it recognizes that Revelation is not a coded collection of secrets that will finally become intelligible at the end of time, for from the beginning it has been an open book that was designed to communicate with Christians living on earth. Looking at ways in which the book addressed the situation of its first readers invites modern readers to explore ways in which it continues to address our situations today.

The next chapter will help in this process, because the messages to the seven churches that appear at the beginning of Revelation show that not all of its readers were alike. Revelation addresses not only those Christians who feel the threat of persecution, but Christians who are being lulled into complacency because of their prosperity, and those who are inclined to back away from the claims of faith in order to assimilate into the surrounding culture. A look at the spectrum of readers first addressed by the book is a stimulating way to begin considering how the ancient message continues to speak.

Chapter 2

CHRIST AND THE CHURCHES

Revelation 1–3

Revelation is a drama in two acts. The first half of the book (Revelation 1–11) takes readers from the valleys and hills of Asia Minor to the heights of heaven, where choruses of praise resound in the halls of God's heavenly throne room. The thundering hoofbeats of the four horsemen and visions of the collapse of the universe, with stars falling from heaven and ghoulish armies rising from the underworld, promise to thrill those with a taste for high adventure and special effects. Two heroic witnesses battle the forces of evil by bearing fiery testimony to the truth before being slain in the streets; yet as the curtain falls at the end of chapter 11, they are vindicated, and the forces of God regroup before the agents of the evil empire can strike back.

Before the curtain rises, so that the action can begin, the theater darkens and a single spotlight focuses attention upon John, the writer of Revelation, who walks out on to the stage alone in order to address the audience. His opening lines indicate that readers will encounter a "revelation" and a "prophecy," but John presents his message in the form of a letter to seven congregations. After telling about the circumstances that prompted him to write, John takes his audience through the first cycle of visions, one in which each of the seven congregations is discussed in turn (Revelation 1–3). Those in search of seven-headed monsters may find the messages to the seven churches to be rather tame, yet these chapters are among the most important in the book because they create the context in which the later visions can be understood. They make clear that John's visions do not float freely in heaven but address issues confronting Christian congregations on earth. By taking the opening chapters seriously, readers can better ask how the visions in the later part of the book address the situations of people engaged in a struggle of faith.

A Revelation — A Prophecy — A Letter (1:1-8)

A Revelation

The last book of the Bible introduces itself as a "revelation" or *apokalypsis* in Greek (Rev. 1:1), which suggests that it discloses things that would not otherwise be known. Although "revelation" could simply mean the "uncovering" of what is hidden, New Testament writers used the word in a more dynamic sense for a manifestation of God's power (Rom. 2:5), for the second coming of Christ (1 Cor. 1:7; 1 Pet. 1:7), and for messages inspired by the Spirit (1 Cor. 14:6). When Paul insisted that the gospel he proclaimed came through "a revelation of Jesus Christ" (Gal. 1:12), he referred to an encounter with the risen and glorified Christ. Similarly, when the writer of Revelation calls his book "the revelation of Jesus Christ," he refers to a message that he understood to come from the glorified Christ, who received it from God and communicated it through an angel (Rev. 1:1-2).

Modern readers do not have unmediated access to the revelation that John received, but encounter it only through the text that he wrote. We must ask, therefore, what it means to encounter this revelation in written form, as a piece of literature. Readers of mystery stories expect the final chapter to offer them a "revelation" that will unlock the secrets of the text. Clues scattered throughout such stories frequently take readers down false trails, building suspense by intimating that a solution may be close at hand, only to show that the obvious answers are the wrong ones. In the end, however, a Sherlock Holmes inevitably resolves the mystery by revealing the identity of the thief and showing how puzzling pieces of evidence fit into a coherent whole. Those who read the last book of the Bible expecting to find the same kind of "revelation" are frequently baffled, since its visions often conceal more than they reveal and confuse more than they clarify. The bewildering array of viewpoints that were summarized in the previous chapter attests to the problem.

Much of the challenge arises because the revelation was "signified" to John (1:1). Although many translations simply read that it was "made known," the Greek word *sēmainein,* like the English word "signify," is related to a word meaning "sign" (*sēmeion* in Greek). There is an old theory that Revelation's signs and symbols functioned as a kind of code that revealed its message to some readers while concealing it from others. The story is that John wrote in symbolic language while he was in prison on the island of Patmos and needed to slip his message past the Roman censors. The assumption is that the bizarre visions in the book would have confused non-Christians, but that other Christians could have decoded the message. A modern analogy might be the way that people in wartime communicate in code, so that their enemies will find their messages to be unintelligible, while their allies, who possess the key to the code, will be able to understand them. This explanation is colorful, to be sure, but it is implausible. For example, when John says that the seven heads of the beast represent seven hills (Rev. 17:9), only the most obtuse censor would fail to see that the beast represented Rome, the city built on seven hills.

Some texts we read do have symbols that work like a code, in which an image must have one and only one meaning for effective communication to take place. The symbols on a map, for example, are regularly explained in the key that the mapmaker provides in the corner of the page, indicating that one symbol stands for a school building and another for a post office.

Religious symbols like those in Revelation, however, communicate in a more complex way, often conveying several meanings at once. They engage readers in an ongoing process of reflection, rather than giving information that eliminates the need for future thought. The image of the Lamb who was slain (Rev. 5:6) is one of the principal images in Revelation. The symbol is not difficult to decode, so that readers can easily recognize that the Lamb is Jesus, who was crucified. By depicting Christ as a Lamb, the book does not conceal his identity but discloses or "signifies" something about Christ. The image works by evoking a range of associations — sacrifice and atonement, Passover and liberation, purity and innocence — that enhance the readers' understanding of Christ's significance.

Symbols also help to move readers by affecting the emotions and will. Portrayal of the Lamb as a slain victim can help to awaken the readers' sympathy toward the one whom the Lamb represents, even before they consciously analyze the sacrificial implications of the imagery. Conversely, the ugly portrayal of a violent beast with seven heads, ten horns, and blasphemies pouring from its mouth can awaken an intuitive sense of aversion that precedes any attempt to interpret the beast's significance. People may not understand exactly what the beast is, but they quickly recognize that they want nothing to do with it. The images through which Revelation "signifies" its meaning are an element of persuasion. The book is not so much designed to dispense information as it is designed to strengthen the readers' commitments. When the images move readers to renounce evil and to affirm their loyalty to God and Christ, they are effective in their communication even if readers cannot explain the meaning of each detail.

A Prophecy

Revelation also identifies itself as a "prophecy" (1:3). Its character as a book of prophecy is reinforced indirectly by the similarities between its introduction (1:1-3) and the introductions that appear on some of the prophetic books in the Old Testament (Jer. 1:1-2; Ezek. 1:1-3; Amos 1:1). The term "prophecy" means very different things to readers. Some, who take a narrow view of prophecy, essentially limit it to inspired predictions of future events (e.g., Acts 11:27-28). Others — seeking to avoid treating Revelation as step-by-step guide to events at the end of time — expand the notion of prophecy to include bold preaching of almost any sort. The view of prophecy that emerges from Revelation itself has some affinities with both views, but does not fit neatly into either category.

The book of Revelation assumes that prophets are specially inspired messengers of God, the risen Christ, and the Spirit. In other words, "prophecy" is a distinctive form of divine communication, not a general term for Christian preaching. John says that he received his visions through the power of God's Spirit (Rev. 1:10; 4:2; 17:3; 21:10) and that the Spirit communicated through his words (2:7, 11, 17, 29). John conveys words from God (1:8; 21:5-8) and the glorified Christ (2:1–3:22) in the first person singular. Some, but not all of the faithful in the seven churches were considered prophets (22:9). This view of prophecy has affinities with Israel's tradition, in which prophets were understood to have spoken because they were filled with the Spirit (e.g., Micah 3:8; Ezek. 2:2) or because the word of the Lord "came" to them (Jer. 1:4). The same was true among early Christians, who spoke of God's Spirit being present and active in the life of each person in the community of faith (Acts 2:38; 1 Cor. 12:7), yet continued to refer to prophecy as a special manifestation of the Spirit's work (Acts 13:1; 15:32; 1 Cor. 12:10, 29).

The content of John's message pertains, in part, to the future, since his visions extend as far as the appearance of a new heaven and new earth (21:1); but John's prophecy is not limited to the future. If, as seems clear, the entire book of Revelation is to be considered "prophecy" (Rev. 1:3; 22:7, 10, 18, 19), then John understood prophecy to be more than predictions of coming events. For example, the messages to the seven churches in Revelation 2–3 include condemnations of sin, calls for repentance, and words of encouragement. The threats to the churches are not simple predictions of future disasters, but are given in conditional form, so that the threat will only be carried out if repentance does not occur (2:5, 16; 3:3); and the promises are not so much predictions as expressions of God's commitment to bless those who "conquer" (2:7, 10-11, 17, 26-28; 3:5, 12, 20-21). Similar warnings and promises appear elsewhere in the book, as do prophetic pronouncements of salvation and blessing (14:13; 19:9; 22:7). This view of prophecy is not unique to Revelation. The prophetic books of the Old Testament encompass a comparable range of material, including conditional oracles of salvation and judgment, messages of censure and encouragement, as well as references to future events (Aune, *Prophecy,* 274-88).

The criterion for authentic prophecy is finally whether the prophet's message promotes faithfulness to God or whether it leads people away from God. This is evident in the way that Revelation distinguishes true from false prophecy. False prophets include the woman nicknamed "Jezebel," who is denounced because she encouraged people to eat what had been sacrificed to idols and to practice immorality (2:20). Revelation does not suggest that she was a false prophet because she spoke wrongly concerning the future, but because her teaching drew people away from God. Later visions depict a false prophet as a beast that seems to have the ability to perform miracles. Again, the false prophet is condemned for encouraging people to worship a false god, not for erroneous predictions (13:11-18; 16:13-14; 19:20). True prophets include the two "witnesses" that "prophesy" during a time of oppression (11:3). These prophets can consume their adversaries with fire and prevent the rain from falling, as the prophet Elijah did; and they can turn water into blood and bring other plagues, as did the prophet Moses. The fact that they were dressed in sackcloth, however, implies that their primary function was to call people to repentance. Nothing is said about their ability to predict the future. To say that "the spirit of prophecy is the testimony of Jesus" (19:10) underscores that the integrity of a prophetic message has to do with its witness to Christ.

Identifying the confession of faith in God or Christ as the touchstone for true prophecy is part of the wider biblical tradition. A famous passage in Deuteronomy recognizes that false prophets sometimes do perform miracles and predict things that actually come to pass, but the text warns that successful prediction does not necessarily mean that the prophet is legitimate. If the prophet whose word comes true encourages people to follow other gods, the people must not heed the prophet, for the prophet's message is ultimately false (Deut. 13:1-5). Early Christians faced similar problems of discernment. The author of 1 John urges Christians to "test the spirits to see whether they are from God; for many false prophets have gone out into the world" (1 John 4:1). When counseling readers on how to test the prophets, the author says nothing about the power to predict the future, but emphasizes that true prophecy is consistent with the community's confession of Christ (1 John 4:2-3; cf. 1 Cor. 12:1-3).

The preface to Revelation says that John wants people to respond to his prophecy by "keeping" it (Rev. 1:3), which has to do with the listeners' fundamental commitments. If John primarily intended to dispense information about the future, we might have expected 1:3 to speak of the blessing that comes on those that "understand" his book. The word "keeping," however, is associated with repentance and a manner of life that is consistent with Christ (2:26; 3:3). It entails obedience to God's commands (12:17; 14:12) and a refusal to deny one's relationship with Christ (3:8). To "keep" the message of Revelation's prophecy means to "worship God" (22:9).

A Letter

John conveys his prophecy in the form of a letter. People in the ancient world wrote letters that included certain standard elements, just as letters do today. Modern letters usually have the sender's address at the top of the page, followed by the date. They begin with a formula like "Dear ———" and conclude with an expression like "Sincerely yours," followed by the sender's name. Ancient letters had their own conventional introductions and conclusions. The opening regularly identified the sender, identified the intended recipients, and extended a greeting. These conventional components regularly appear at the beginning of Paul's letters, as they do in Rev. 1:4-5. At its conclusion, Revelation reads, "The grace of the Lord Jesus be with all the saints" (Rev. 22:21). This resembles the conclusions on the Pauline letters (e.g., Gal. 6:18; Phil. 4:23; 1 Thess. 5:28).

Letters served as vehicles for preaching among early Christians. Paul expected his letters to be read aloud in congregations (1 Thess. 5:27; Col. 4:16) and Revelation also was to be read aloud. The introduction says, "Blessed is the one who reads aloud . . . and blessed are those who hear" (Rev. 1:3). Recognizing that Revelation is a letter that was designed to be read aloud to a group helps modern readers envision the way in which communication would take place.

Sender

The writer of letter identifies himself as "John" (1:4), a name that also appears in 1:1, 9 and 22:8. There is a general consensus that the author was writing in his own name rather than under a penname or pseudonym. The author does not give any information that enables us to identify him further. Some early Christians assumed that the writer was John the son of Zebedee, who was one of Jesus' twelve disciples. This seems unlikely. "John" was a rather common name, and the author of

Revelation does not claim to have seen Jesus during his earthly ministry and makes no reference to Jesus' teaching, miracles, or other actions. The only encounter with Christ that he mentions is the one that occurs through a vision. Later, John refers to the twelve apostles (21:14), but does not suggest that he himself was among them. Since Revelation does not link itself with John the apostle, we do well to identify him as an early Christian named John, without assuming that he was one of the twelve disciples.

Recipients

The letter is sent to "the seven churches that are in Asia" (1:4). It is an open letter that is designed to communicate with Christian groups in Ephesus, Smyrna, Pergamum, Thyatira, Sardis, Philadelphia, and Laodicea. The importance of these churches is underscored in Revelation 2–3, which specifically address conditions in these congregations. It is not clear why these seven congregations were the intended recipients, since the Roman province of Asia included most of what is now western Turkey, and there were Christians at Colossae (Col. 1:2) and Hieropolis (Col. 4:13), Troas (Acts 20:5), and other towns at the time that Revelation was written. The fact that Revelation so often uses the number seven to imply completeness suggests that these seven congregations represent the whole church. Revelation is an open prophetic letter that is sent to seven particular congregations, yet it contains a message that applies to the church as a whole.

Greetings

Like Paul's letters, Revelation begins with the salutation, "Grace to you and peace" (Rev. 1:4b). Instead of a form of the word *chairein* ("greetings"), which was common in Greco-Roman letters, Paul and John used *charis,* which means "grace." This is coupled with the word "peace," which recalls the Hebrew greeting *shalom.* Paul sometimes elaborated the greetings theologically by identifying characteristics of God or Christ: "Grace to you and peace from God our Father and the Lord Jesus Christ, who gave himself for our sins to set us free from the present evil age, according to the will of our God and Father, to whom be glory forever and ever. Amen" (Gal. 1:3-5). John does the same when he ex-

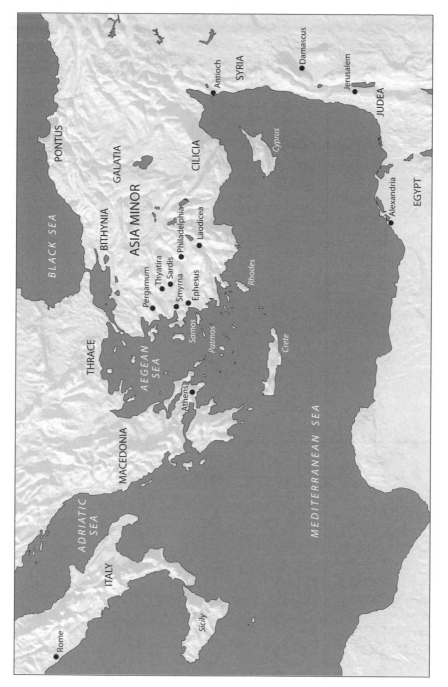

tends greetings from God, from the seven spirits that are before God's throne, and from Christ the faithful witness (Rev. 1:4-5).

The theology expressed in John's greeting begins the proclamation of his message. John calls God "the One who is and who was and who is to come" (1:4). Readers familiar with the Old Testament would almost certainly hear in this greeting an echo of the way that Moses spoke in the name of God, who said, "I Am the One who is" (Exod. 3:14 LXX). Readers might also hear a provocative recasting of claims made about other gods in their culture. For example, some said, "Zeus was, Zeus is, Zeus shall be" (Pausanias, *Description of Greece,* 10.12.10), but John insists that these traits belong to one true God. He begins with God's present existence ("the One who is"), following the precedent of Moses; and instead of speaking of God's future existence, he speaks of God's future "coming," since God will come through the advent of Jesus Christ. Identifying God in this way also prepares for later polemics against the beast, whose traits are a demonic imitation of divine power, for the beast "was and is not and is about to ascend from the bottomless pit" (Rev. 17:8).

Christ is introduced as "the faithful witness, the firstborn of the dead, the ruler of the kings of the earth" (1:5), underscoring his death, resurrection, and lordship. Although the Greek word for "witness" *(martys)* was not a technical term for a "martyr" when John wrote Revelation, Christ's faithfulness did result in death. Therefore, Christ has the credibility to summon others to be faithful in their witness, even at the cost of their lives (2:13; 11:3; 17:6), since he has already done this himself. Christ's resurrection, in turn, provides assurance that death is not the end for the faithful, because Christ is the first of many who will die and rise. Finally, Christ died at the hands of the rulers of the earth, but through his resurrection Christ will rule over them. Their temporal power is subordinate to his eternal power. Therefore, John can call upon readers to give their ultimate allegiance to Christ, rather than to submit to lesser authorities who oppose the will of God.

The implications of Christ's death and reign are considered from two different perspectives in the final part of the introduction. First, the praises in 1:5b-6 show how the faithful respond to Christ. John uses the first person plural, which emphasizes that the whole community gives glory to the one "who loves *us* and freed *us* from our sins by his blood and made *us* to be a kingdom, priests to his God and Father." Communal praise will be central in the visions of heavenly worship later in Revelation (5:9-14; 7:9-17; 11:15-18; 15:3-4; 19:1-8). Reasons for praise are that Christ's death manifests divine love, and divine love is the presupposition for Revelation's warnings and the calls for repentance (3:19), as well as for its promises of salvation (3:9) and exhortations to love others (2:4, 19). Christ's death frees people from sin for life in God's kingdom, but this freedom does not mean that believers are liberated from commitments to others in order to focus on their own desires. Rather, freedom means being brought into a new relationship with God in which they have the dignity of serving as God's priests.

Second, the warning in 1:7 continues to consider the themes of Christ's death and lordship, but this time as a threat. The words of the warning are freely drawn from Old Testament passages. John frequently paraphrases and alludes to Old Testament passages when recounting his visions, but he never gives exact quotations of the Old Testament according to any known version (Beale, *Book of Revlation,* 77):

Rev. 1:7	**Old Testament**
Look!	I saw one like a son of man
He is coming with the clouds.	coming with the clouds. (Dan. 7:13)
Every eye will see him,	They will look on him
even those who pierced him.	whom they have pierced. (Zech. 12:10)
On his account all the tribes	The land shall mourn,
of the earth will wail.	each family by itself. (Zech. 12:12)

Here the death of Christ is not the source of liberation from sin, but a reminder of the way that opposition to Christ led to his being "pierced" by crucifixion. Similarly, his lordship is not an occasion for celebration on the part of those who belong to God's kingdom, but that which brings an occasion for judgment and wailing. The contrast between the community's praise (Rev. 1:5b-6) and the tribes' grieving (1:7) eliminates the possibility of neutrality. People will respond to Christ; the question is whether they will join in the praises of the faithful or suffer the anguish of the rest of society.

In 1:8 the voice of God speaks directly: "I am the Alpha and the Omega, says the Lord God, who is and who was and who is to come, the Almighty." God's voice is only given in direct terms twice in Revelation, here and in 21:5-8. In both places the message is the same, namely, that God is the Alpha and Omega. The intrusion of the voice of God at the beginning and end of Revelation gives these words particular emphasis. If God is the beginning and God is the end, then God is the focus of the book. The point is significant. The book does not say that the four horsemen are the beginning and that the great judgment is the end, but that God is the beginning and God is the end. We will find that the structure of the book reinforces this point, as the visions move from God and Christ to God and Christ.

In the Presence of the Living One (1:9-20)

When the curtain rises on Act I, the audience hears the narrator introduce himself as "I, John, your brother" (1:9). John does not introduce himself in terms of his authority — as a prophet or other figure — but in terms of his relationship with the readers: he is their brother. John says that he received visions while he was on Patmos "because of the word of God and the testimony of Jesus" (1:9). Patmos is a small island that is separated from the mainland by thirty-seven miles of water. A mere ten miles long and six miles wide, the island has a deeply indented coastline consisting of hills and ridges that rise from the Aegean Sea. John does not explain why he was on Patmos, but he may have been banished there because of his Christian preaching. The references to the "affliction" and "endurance" that people experience because their identity is "in Jesus" (1:9), and comments about suffering "because of the word of God and the testimony of Jesus" (6:9) make it likely that John was on Patmos under duress. Islands in the group to which Patmos belonged were places where political prisoners were banished (Pliny, *Natural History* 4.69-70; Tacitus, *Annals* 4.30) and it seems likely that Patmos was also used for this purpose. Banishment was a common form of punishment that was used for various offenses, including magic and astrology, and the Romans probably sent John to Patmos because his prophesying seemed to pose a threat to the social order.

John says that his message comes from a visionary experience that he had while he was "in the Spirit" (Rev. 1:10). The earliest readers of Revelation would probably have accepted that a genuine spiritual experience underlies the book. The Old Testament refers to visions received by prophets (e.g., Isa. 6:1-13; Jer. 1:11-19; Ezek. 37:1-14) and the New Testament recounts visions that were experienced by Peter (Acts 10:10) and Paul (Acts 16:9), who told of being caught up into the third heaven (2 Cor. 12:2-3). The phrase "in the Spirit" could simply mean that John was "in a trance," but as Revelation progresses, spiritual activity will be connected to the Spirit of God. Thus, the Spirit conveys the words of the risen Christ to the churches (Rev. 2:7, 11, 17, 29; 3:6, 13, 22), the seven spirits of God are associated with Christ the Lamb (5:6), and the "spirit of prophecy" conveys the "testimony of Jesus" (19:10).

John is told, "Write what you see in a book" (1:11), but what he wrote was more than a simple record of what he saw and heard. Note that when John turned toward the voice that spoke to him, he saw a divine figure whose appearance was difficult to describe in human language. John said: "His head and hair were white *as* white wool . . . his eyes were *like* a flame of fire, his feet were *like* burnished bronze . . . his voice was *like* the sound of many waters . . . and his face was *like* the sun" (1:14-16). The repeated use of the words "as" and "like" indicates that John was describing something that did not fit within the confines of ordinary speech. He used analogies from ordinary human experience in order to give readers a sense of something that belongs to the divine realm.

The Old Testament provided some of the language through which John conveyed his vision. To readers familiar with the Scriptures, speaking of one "like a son of man" in Rev. 1:13 recalls how Daniel saw "one like a son of man coming with the clouds of heaven" to receive dominion over the peoples of the world (Dan. 7:13; cf. Rev. 1:7). Daniel told of seeing a heavenly being, who was clothed in linen with a belt of gold around his waist. His "face was like lightning, his eyes like flaming torches, his arms and legs like the gleam of burnished bronze, and the sound of his words like the roar of a multitude" (Dan. 10:5-6). By repeating and adapting much of this imagery, John implies that his vision of the glorified Christ has continuity with what was made known to previous generations.

The glorified Christ declares: "I am the first and the last" (Rev. 1:17). His words echo the way that God declared: "I am the Alpha and the Omega," using the first and last letters of the Greek alphabet (1:8). Not only here, but again at the end of the book, Christ (22:13) identifies himself in terms of deity, calling himself the Alpha and Omega, the beginning and the end along with God (21:6). Christ's words are startling because in the Old Testament God was the one who said, "I am the first and I am the last; besides me there is no god" (Isa. 44:6; cf. 48:12). Like the Old Testament prophets, Revelation opposes worship of any being other than God, warning readers against worshiping angels (Rev. 19:10; 22:8-9) and false gods (13:4). Therefore, it seems clear that John does not consider Christ to be an alternative object of worship alongside God. The Lamb is not seated on his own throne, but appears on God's throne along with God (7:17; 22:1, 3). John assumes that Christ shares in the power, the rule, the glory, and the being of the one true God.

Revelation does not simply convey information, but confronts readers with the presence of a living being. Calling God and Christ the Alpha and Omega, the beginning and the end, corresponds to the book's literary structure. The first vision in Revelation is not one of an event, but of a person: the crucified and risen Christ, the one who could say, "I was dead, and see, I am alive forever and ever" (1:18). The last vision in Revelation brings readers not only to the New Jerusalem, but to the throne of God and the Lamb (22:3); so that the expected response to the book's message is "Amen. Come, Lord Jesus" (22:20).

The initial revelation, a startling one perhaps, is not of a future event, but of a present reality. The exalted Christ is already present among the churches that are represented by the golden lampstands. The woodcut by Albrecht Dürer puts this into visual form. The vision discloses the presence of the exalted Christ in a manner that is not available to the senses. Its message is that the churches are not alone, but have Christ in their midst, both as savior and judge. This disclosure of the presence of Christ may be reassuring or unsettling depending upon the position of the reader. For those that are insecure, the disclosure of Christ's presence is assuring. For those who would prefer to keep their distance from Christ, this intrusion can be unsettling.

Not All Readers Are Alike (2:1–3:22)

Modern readers hear the message of Revelation differently depending on the situations in which they encounter the book. Wealthier Christians in North America are often disturbed by Revelation's uncompromising denunciations of evil and calls for justice, while poorer Christians in Latin America value the book precisely because they hear it

Christ among the Lampstands or Churches (Rev. 1:12-20)
by Albrecht Dürer

calling for resistance to oppressive powers (Schüssler-Fiorenza, *Revelation,* 10-12). The first readers addressed by the book were similarly diverse: (1) On one end are the Christians that are threatened by overt hostility from others in society. (2) In the middle we find congregations engaged in internal conflicts over leadership and the extent to which Christians should accommodate themselves to non-Christian culture. (3) On the other end are Christians that are comfortable and complacent in prosperous communities. Despite the differences, all the congregations were alike in that they were subject to currents that threatened to undermine their commitments, whether blatantly through persecution, or more subtly through the erosion of the basis of their faith.

Each congregation is addressed individually, but not privately, since all the messages are available for all the congregations to read. The messages to all the churches follow the same basic pattern:

— Address from Christ
— Words of rebuke and encouragement
— Summons to listen and promise to the conqueror

The opening address from Christ includes a command for John to write to the "angel" of each congregation (2:1, 8, 12, 18; 3:1, 7, 14). Although some have suggested that the "angel" might actually be the local leader who was to read the message to the church, this seems unlikely because elsewhere in Revelation the "angels" are heavenly beings. This unique mode of addressing the angels seems to assume that each congregation has a heavenly representative. Nevertheless, the messages themselves speak directly to the members of the congregations.

The address to each congregation mentions traits from the vision of the glorified Christ in 1:12-20. This device repeatedly presses readers to consider their situation in relationship to Christ. At stake is an issue of perspective. For example, one might evaluate a congregation by assessing the social or economic status of its members in relation to others in society. From this perspective, the Christians at Smyrna are poor (2:9) while those at Laodicea are rich (3:17). In relationship to Christ, however, the situation is reversed: those at Smyrna are truly rich while those at Laodicea are wretched and poor (2:9; 3:17). Because the messages are repeatedly tied to the inaugural vision, they insist that the readers see their situation in relation to Christ.

The promises at the end of each section depict the faithful as "conquerors." This military metaphor assumes that the faithful in each congregation are engaged in a struggle to remain faithful. The notion of conquest can be seen in two different ways. On the one hand, Revelation speaks of a horseman and a beast that "conquer" by making war, killing, and oppressing people (6:2; 11:7; 13:7). On the other hand, Christ the Lamb and his followers "conquer" the forces of evil by faithful suffering (5:5; 12:11). The first is a victory of violence, the second a victory of faith. It is the conquest of faithful endurance to which the readers are called. The conquest metaphor seeks to alter the readers' perceptions of their situations. The persecuted "conquer" their opponents by remaining faithful to the point of death, while the first step in conquest for complacent churches is to wake up to the way in which their levels of comfort are eroding their commitments.

The Problem of Assimilation

Three of the seven churches — Ephesus, Pergamum, and Thyatira — were dealing with internal conflicts over acceptable and unacceptable forms of Christian faith and practice. On one level the disputes have to do with issues of leadership: opposition to false apostles at Ephesus, an errant teacher at Pergamum, and a false prophet at Thyatira. On another level, the objectionable teachings that are associated with these figures and with the group known as the Nicolatians had to do with the extent to which Christians could accommodate pagan practices. John opposed those who encouraged Christians to eat meat offered to idols and practice immorality, urging Christians to maintain a distinctive identity.

Ephesus (2:1-7)

The risen Christ, who walks among the golden lampstands that represent the churches (1:13, 20; 2:1), first addresses the congregation at Ephesus, which was one of the chief urban centers of Asia Minor. Located along the coast, where the Cayster River poured into the Aegean Sea, the city was a major hub for commerce and governance. Columns, marble pavement, and monumental buildings graced its major streets and public squares. Athletic festivals were held in its stadium, and events in its theater could be seen by up to twenty-four thousand people. The massive temple of Artemis, a fertility goddess, was considered one of the architectural wonders of the ancient world, attracting a steady traffic of worshipers. The city was also known for its temple to the goddess Roma and the divinized Julius Caesar; and by the end of the first century it added a temple to the emperor Domitian. Along with the dominant pagan population there was a Jewish community and a congregation of Christians whose origins extended back to at least the time of Paul in the mid-first century (Acts 18:24–19:41).

The principal challenge which faced the congregation at Ephesus grew out of the need to oppose false teaching. Distinguishing acceptable from unacceptable forms of Christian practice was a difficult task for early Christians. The term "apostle," which means "one who is sent out," was used for various itinerant evangelists, who preached and taught in towns around the Roman world, often relying on the hospitality of local Christian communities. The "apostles" were not limited to Peter, James, John, and other early followers of Jesus, but included missionaries like Paul, Barnabas, and others (Acts 14:14). The teachings of self-identified "apostles" sometimes conflicted and some who claimed to be apostles were actually charlatans (2 Cor. 11:4-5; Didache 11:3-6). The congregation at Ephesus is commended for having "tested those who claim to be apostles but are not," and for exposing their false teaching (Rev. 2:2). They also maintained strong opposition to the teachings of the Nicolatians, who apparently encouraged Christians to accommodate themselves to practices associated with idolatry (2:6; cf. 2:14-15).

An unwanted side effect of resisting assimilation is that the congregation lost the love it had at first (2:4). The Ephesian Christians faced the challenge of pursuing the way of Christian love without compromising the integrity of their faith. Christ warns them that unless this changes their lampstand will be removed, that is, they will lose their identity as a Christian church. This warning is coupled with the promise of eating from the tree of life that is in the paradise of God (2:7), which anticipates future life with God as depicted in 22:2.

Pergamum (2:12-17)

Christ begins his address to the Christians at Pergamum by recalling that he has the sharp two-edged sword, which connotes his power to judge (1:16; 2:12), and he declares that the congregation resides "where Satan's throne is" (2:13). This judgment falls upon a town that was one of Asia Minor's cultural and administrative centers. The city was built around a citadel hill that rose a thousand feet above the plains, dominating the surrounding region. Many of the city's public buildings were situated on terraces that were built into the side of the hill, and at its summit was an acropolis with a massive altar to Zeus. The city was the home of a renowned library, a temple to the emperor Augustus, and a shrine of Asclepius, the god of healing. Those seeking judgment in legal cases came before the Roman proconsul at Pergamum for hearings. It is possible that the epithet "Satan's throne" refers to one of the pagan temples or to the Roman presence in the city, although it can best be understood in more general terms as the power that threatens the church. The danger was most vividly shown by the death of the Christian named Antipas (2:13).

At the time Revelation was written, such violence does not seem to have been the primary concern. Instead, the church is reproved for tolerating a teacher nicknamed "Balaam," who instructed people to "eat food sacrificed to idols and practice fornication" (2:14). In the Old Testament, "Balaam" was a soothsayer that King Balak of Moab hired to put a curse on the people of Israel. After a humorous series of incidents, in which Balaam's donkey saw an angel and began talking, Balaam ended up blessing rather than cursing Israel (Numbers 22–24). Immediately afterward, however, the Israelites joined in the pagan practices of the people of Moab, worshiping the god Baal and engaging in sexual relations with the women of Moab (Num. 25:1-18), and Balaam was said to have drawn the people into these practices of idolatry and fornication (Num. 31:16). Calling one of the teachers at Pergamum "Balaam" warned the congregation about what the teacher was doing.

The question of eating meat that had been offered to idols had to do with the extent to which Christians could conform or assimilate into pagan society. The issue arose because much of the meat in Pergamum and other places came from animals that were offered to Greco-Roman deities. There were several circumstances in which Christians had to decide whether they could legitimately eat meat from pagan sacrifices.

One situation would arise when meat that had been offered during the civic festivals was distributed to the populace. Public celebrations were an important part of life in ancient cities. Festivals were held to honor various gods, to commemorate occasions in the life of the emperor and his family, and to celebrate victories in battle and other events. The festal processions that made their way through a city could include local dignitaries and perhaps the provincial high priest adorned with a crown and purple robes. Participants bore incense and images of the emperor and local deities. Oxen draped with garlands were led along by the procession to the place of slaughter. Portions of the animals would be offered to a god or gods, and the remainder of the meat would be distributed to people in the community. Afterward, athletic and musical competitions often began. Such festivities, which attracted visitors from around the region, were paid for by the government officials, local organizations, and sometimes by the emperor himself (Josephus, *Jewish War* 7.16). Social pressure made it natural for Christians to want to partake in such celebrations. Some found it acceptable to do so, but others objected that eating food that had been offered to pagan gods violated Christian principles.

A related situation concerned purchasing meat in the market. Some communities had shrines where sacrifices were offered frequently. Meat that was not consumed by the worshipers was offered for sale to the public. Those who sought meat for use in their homes had to decide whether they should purchase it on the open market and ignore the fact that the animals were probably slaughtered in honor of a god, or whether they should refrain from consuming such meat in order to avoid supporting institutions that were devoted to false worship (1 Cor. 10:25-30).

Finally, some Christians may have faced the question of eating meat in one of the banquet rooms that were associated with pagan gods (1 Cor. 8:10). The dining rooms in the temples devoted to Greco-Roman deities would comfortably hold seven to ten people, who would share a common meal at which the god was apparently assumed to be present. Social and trade associations in cities like Pergamum often had a patron deity, and their meetings often had a religious component. Christians who associated with non-Christians in social and commercial life faced the question about the limits of their ability to participate in the activities of these associations, including meals eaten at the sanctuary of a pagan god or in honor of a pagan god. "At stake here was the question of assimilation: What pagan customs could Christians adopt for the sake of economic survival, commercial gain, or simple sociability?" (A. Y. Collins, *Crisis*, 88).

Revelation does not indicate what arguments a teacher like "Balaam" might have used to persuade Christians to eat meat, but they might have been similar to those that some of the Christians at Corinth used to justify eating meat offered to idols. Paul's comments assume that they argued that as Christians they knew that there is only one true God, and that the deities represented by idols could not be true gods. The conclusion that the Corinthians drew was that if idolatry is truly a sham, then the sacrifices made to the idols have no true religious significance, and those who eat of such meat need not worry that they are actually worshiping another god (cf. 1 Cor. 8:1-13).

Readers are warned that unless they repent, Christ will come and make war against his opponents with the sword of his mouth, that is, he will battle them with his word (Rev. 2:16). Coupled with this threat is a cryptic promise, which says that those who persevere in faith will be given some of the "hidden manna," apparently anticipating the messianic feast at the end of time (19:9). The significance of the white stone that they receive is unclear, although since a mysterious name characterizes Christ (19:12), the stone seems to connect the faithful with Christ's victory.

Thyatira (2:18-29)

Christ identifies himself in terms of his fiery eyes and feet of bronze to the Christians in Thyatira, a town located in a broad valley that was bounded by gently rising hills southeast of Pergamum. An important commercial center, Thyatira was the home of many trade guilds, including associations of potters, tailors, leather workers, shoemakers, linen workers, bakers, coppersmiths, dyers, and wool merchants. The city's commercial character is evident in that the woman named Lydia, whom Paul met in Philippi, was a merchant from Thyatira who dealt in purple cloth (Acts 16:14).

The message to the church at Thyatira commends the Christians for their love — in contrast to the church at Ephesus that lacked love (Rev. 2:4) — as well as for their faith, service, and endurance (2:19). Nevertheless, they are rebuked for tolerating a self-identified prophet who was teaching Christians to "practice fornication and to eat meat sacrificed to idols" (2:20). The woman is nicknamed "Jezebel" to associate her with the infamous queen of Israel who had promoted pagan worship in the days of Elijah and Elisha. The original Queen Jezebel was not a prophet, but supported four hundred and fifty prophets devoted to the god Baal and another four hundred prophets devoted to the goddess Asherah (1 Kings 18:19). At the same time, she violently opposed the prophets of God (1 Kings 18:4). For a time Queen Jezebel seemed to succeed in spreading her pagan "harlotries and sorceries" (2 Kings 9:22), but through the activities of the prophets Elijah and Elisha she came to a gruesome end.

The woman at Thyatira was like the Old Testament Jezebel in that she was teaching people to accommodate pagan religious practices in the manner described in connection with Pergamum. The charge that Jezebel, like Balaam, was teaching people to "practice fornication" could mean that she advocated sexual license (Rev. 21:8; 22:15), but in this context the author probably uses a sexual metaphor for religious infidelity, since "fornication" is closely linked to eating idol meat (2:14, 20, 21). Accordingly, those who "commit adultery" with Jezebel are those who accept her teachings (2:22). The metaphor has precedent in the Old Testament, where Israel's relationship to God is compared to the exclusive relationship that one has in a marriage, while association with pagan cults is fornication (Hos. 1:2). The metaphor also has social and economic dimensions, since Revelation links fornication to the accumulation of wealth through the cultivation of good relations with Babylon the harlot (Rev. 17:2; 18:3, 9).

John seeks to reinforce resistance to the teaching of Jezebel through a parody of her teachings. One might assume that she was claiming to teach "the deep things of God," but the message in Revelation sarcastically mimics the saying by calling her teachings "the deep things of Satan" (2:24). Like Paul, who considered the worship of idols to be demonic (1 Cor. 10:19-21), John connects idolatry with Satan. The power of idolatry was seductive at Thyatira, but John insists that Satan's power was behind the killing of the Christian witness Antipas at Pergamum, and that the devil was the force that threatened Christians with imprisonment at Smyrna (Rev. 2:10-13). The promise that is offered to these Christians includes sharing in Christ's rule over the nations (2:26-28; 20:4; 22:5), as well as receiving the "morning star," who is Christ himself (22:16).

The Problem of Persecution

More overt hostility was experienced by the congregations at Smyrna and Philadelphia. Modern readers often assume that all persecutions of Christians in the first centuries after Christ were massive campaigns that the imperial government carried out against Christians throughout the Roman Empire. Scenes come to mind in which Roman troops go door to door in the Christian quarter of a city, dragging the faithful from their homes in order to throw them to the lions in the nearest Roman stadium. There is, however, little evidence that such systematic persecution was happening when Revelation was written. In the first century, persecutions were generally instigated by members of the local populace rather than by the imperial government, and they were local rather than empire wide in scope.

Smyrna (2:8-11)

Christ speaks as the one "who was dead and came to life" when giving encouragement to the Christians at Smyrna, who were suffering from "affliction" and "poverty" (2:8-9). This condition might suggest that the congregation was comprised of those who were already poor when they became Christians, but the mention of affliction might indicate that their poverty was due at least in part to harassment from non-Christians (cf. Heb. 10:32-34). Smyrna as a whole was not poor but elegant and prosperous. The city stretched down the slopes of a mountain onto the plain that adjoined the harbor that brought commerce to the region. The product of careful urban planning, Smyrna's streets were laid out in straight lines, paved with stone, and bordered by graceful porticoes. The city boasted temples to the emperors Augustus and Tiberius. As a cultural center, it had a good library and a shrine to the poet Homer. The Christian community was poor by comparison, although John declares that in Christ's eyes they are "rich" in faith (Rev. 2:9).

Hostility toward Christians was shown first in "the slander of those who say that they are Jews and are not" (2:9). This comment shows that the conflict was a family fight that had to do with questions about who were the true Jews. John insists that those who denounced the Christian community were not true Jews, implying that he and others who professed faith in Jesus were the legitimate representatives of Israel's tradition. Determining who belonged to the Jewish community was an important matter because Jewish people received certain types of legal protection. Many non-Jews viewed Jews with contempt and charged that they hated humanity because they refused to honor any god except their own and did not participate in forms of civic life that included pagan religious rites. Nevertheless, Jews were exempted from participating in the cult of the emperor and similar rites because their peculiar beliefs were part of their ancestral tradition (Tacitus, *Histories* 5.5).

Christians were, for some time, viewed as a subgroup within the Jewish community, and many shared the Jewish aversion to pagan practices. When the Jewish community attempted to define its boundaries more sharply, however, those who called Jesus "Lord" (17:14) and "Son of God" (2:18) were sometimes excluded. At an informal level, "slander" dishonored Christians; and by robbing them of the social esteem that most people need, it could pressure them into giving up beliefs that differed from those of the wider Jewish community. When slander failed to do this, it could also help to dissuade others from adopting Christian beliefs at the risk of losing a favorable standing in the eyes of others. Finally, however, slander could serve as a public denunciation of Christians before the local authorities who could imprison and perhaps kill them. The intensity shown in castigating the Jewish opponents as a "synagogue of Satan" (2:9) arose in a situation where slander meant depriving Christians of the protection of Judaism, making them vulnerable to a loss of life or freedom (Schüssler-Fiorenza, *Revelation,* 54-55).

Denunciations had to be made before civil authorities for them to lead to imprisonment. For local magistrates to take action, the charges needed to depict Christians as a threat to the social order (Acts 16:20-21; 18:14-15). Like Jews, Christians who refused to participate in civic activities and social commerce that compromised their religious convictions were considered to show "hatred against humankind" (Tacitus, *Annals* 15.44.2). People generally tolerated the Jews' peculiar religious beliefs and practices because they were part of the tradition that Jews inherited from their ancestors, but when Christians separated from the Jewish community, they could no longer claim that their perceived aloofness was simply a part of the tradition. Christians were accused of promoting "a new and mischievous superstition" (Suetonius, *Nero* 16).

As a result of denunciations, John warns that "the devil is about to throw some of you into prison so that you may be tested, and for ten days you will have affliction" (Rev. 2:10). Prisoners in city jails lived in squalor and cramped space. Stone walls, often without windows, created a dark, suffocating enclosure. During the day prisoners wore a collar and a manacle on one hand, while at night they slept on the ground with their legs in stocks so they could not stretch them out. Rations were scant and could be withheld by the jailer. In antiquity, people were not sentenced to prison terms as they are in modern times. People were put into prison in order to force them to obey the authorities, to hold them in custody until their cases came up for trial, or to confine them until they were executed.

The exhortation to be "faithful until death" implies that Christians could be executed because of their faith (2:10), as Antipas was killed at Pergamum (2:13). The Romans did not have a manual with procedures on how to deal with Christians, but a good example of what happened is indicated in a letter by Pliny, a Roman official who worked in Asia Minor not long after Revelation was written. Pliny said that after Christians were denounced to him, he "asked them in person if they are Christians, and if they admit it, I repeat the question a second and a third time, with a warning of the punishment awaiting them. If they persist, I order them to be led away for execution; for, whatever the nature of their admission, I am convinced that their stubbornness and unshakable obstinacy ought not to go unpunished" (Pliny, *Letters* 10.96.3-4). The message to the Christians at Smyrna does not promise escape from affliction and death, but does say that the faithful will not be harmed by "the second death" (Rev. 2:11), which means that they will not be condemned at the last judgment (20:14).

Philadelphia (3:7-13)

The city of Philadelphia was situated in a rich agricultural area. After being devastated by an earthquake in A.D. 17, the city was rebuilt with Roman assistance, and the city showed its appreciation for the emperor by calling itself "Neocaesarea." Later it adopted the family name of the emperor Vespasian (A.D. 69-79), calling itself "Philadelphia Flavia." The congregation had "but little power" (3:8), which suggests that it was rather small and poor. Like the Christians at Smyrna, those at Philadelphia were apparently denounced by members of a local synagogue (3:9). Despite the opposition, members of the congregation refused to deny Christ. The situation was perhaps not as severe as at Smyrna, however, because the message does not warn about imminent imprisonment or death.

Christ identifies himself as the one "who has the key of David, who opens and no one will shut, who shuts and no one opens" (3:7). This paraphrases Isa. 22:22, which speaks of the servant who has the key to the king's house. The sense is that Christ is the one who is able to admit people into the kingdom of God. Because of their relationship with the doorkeeper, Christ has set before the Christians at Philadelphia "an open door that no one is able to shut" (Rev. 3:8). This assures them that even though their adversaries seek to exclude them, Christ has opened the way into the presence of God for them. In the eyes of society they may be outsiders, but through Christ they are insiders. Promising that those who persevere in faith will be pillars in the temple of God and bear the name of the New Jerusalem points to final salvation (3:12; 21:2).

3. The Problem of Complacency

The situations of the congregations at Sardis and Laodicea differ significantly from those of the churches considered above. What is remarkable in the messages to these remaining congregations is the *absence* of any evident threat. No mention is made of Jewish accusers or the prospect of imprisonment; nothing is said about pseudo-apostles, false prophets, or Nicolatians encouraging them to be more hospitable to the pagan practices. To all appearances these congregations would seem to be thriving. Yet the messages to the Christians at Sardis and Laodicea are almost wholly negative. The dangers to these congregations come not from overt hostility but from the kind of comfortable conditions that lead to complacency. They may not be threatened by society's judgment, but they are threatened by Christ's judgment.

Sardis (3:1-6)

Christ identifies himself as the bearer of the seven spirits of God when speaking to the congregation at Sardis, which was one of the premier cities of Asia Minor. In earlier times Sardis gained a reputation for wealth from the gold that was said to have been found in a nearby river, while in the first century A.D. Sardis prospered from commerce and the fertility of the surrounding region. The oldest part of the city was built on a steep citadel hill that gave the impression of being an impregnable fortress (although it was twice captured by surprise attack). Temples to the goddess Artemis and to Caesar Augustus were among the city's religious sites. Devastated by the earthquake of A.D. 17, Sardis was rebuilt with Roman help and sought the honor of building a new temple for the imperial cult. The Jewish community at Sardis was apparently prosperous and influential, with its own place of worship and legal rights to a supply of ritually clean food (Josephus, *Antiquities* 14.259-61).

The message to Sardis contrasts appearances with reality. When John says that the congregation has "the name of being alive" (Rev. 3:1), he refers to the way that the Christian community appears in the eyes of other people. A good reputation means that other people view the congregation favorably. Thus if "death" is commonly associated with poverty and affliction (cf. 2:9-10), a reputation for being "alive" implies that the Sardis congregation enjoyed prosperity and an absence of affliction. The message to the congregation challenges this perception by declaring that in the eyes of the risen Christ the congregation is "dead" (3:1), for in terms of faith they are "at the point of death" (3:2).

There are several issues at Sardis. A lack of vigilance is indicated by repeated calls to "wake up" (3:2, 3). The Christians are like members of a household, who settle comfortably to sleep, unaware that an intruder might come. In their case the most dangerous intruder will not be an agent sent to arrest them, but Christ himself. For Christ warns: "I will come like a thief, and you will not know what hour I will come to you" (3:3; cf. 16:15; Matt. 24:43; Luke 12:39; 1 Thess. 5:2; 2 Pet. 3:10). Christ comes to rob them of the complacency that they mistake for true security. A second issue is that they seem content with incomplete obedience to Christ, which is a form of self-deception. Many consider the congregation to be "alive," but measured against the standard of unwavering faithfulness to God, their efforts are far from complete (Rev. 3:2). Caird provocatively calls the church at Sardis "the perfect model of inoffensive Christianity" (*A Commentary,* 48). Third, many in Sardis have "soiled their clothes" (3:4). Uncleanness was a common image for sin, although sin can be understood in various ways. Revelation identifies Christ as the one in whose blood people have "washed their robes and made them white" (7:14). Sin and uncleanness include whatever compromises relationships with God and Christ.

Promises are given to the Christians at Sardis along with the warnings. One is that those who persevere will walk with the risen Christ, "dressed in white" (3:4-5; cf. 4:4; 6:11; 7:9, 13). White robes, which connoted purity, were worn on festival occasions, during sacred ceremonies, and by Roman generals who celebrated victories. Christ also promises that those who persevere will not have their names blotted out of the book of life (3:5). The book of life is a way of speaking about citizenship in the kingdom of God. Later John will speak of people's names being written in the book of life from the foundation of the world (13:8; 17:8). People are placed in the book as an act of divine grace; they cannot obtain access to the book by their own efforts. The comment that "I will not blot your name out of the book of life" (3:5) is primarily a promise. Some cities blotted the names of those who were executed out of the citizenship rolls (Dio Chrysostom, *Discourses* 31.84-85). Christ assures the Christians that those who "conquer" — which can include being condemned by others in society — will not lose their citizenship in the kingdom of God on that account. On the contrary, Christ will confess their names before God, overturning the negative judgment of human courts.

Laodicea (3:14-22)

Christ introduces himself as "the faithful and true witness" to the congregation at Laodicea, which seemed not to know the truth about itself. The message sharply contrasts appearance and reality. A Laodicean would say, "I am rich, I have prospered, and I need nothing" (3:17). Their confidence is based on their prosperity, and in the rebuke that follows, Christ's message seems to play on common sources of civic pride. Laodicea had enough wealth or "gold" to refuse Roman offers of help for the rebuilding of the city after an earthquake in A.D. 60. Yet when Christ challenges them to "buy from me gold refined by fire so that you may be rich" (3:18), he alludes to the heat of social opposition to Christianity, promising that those who persevere can hope for a heavenly crown of gold. Laodicea was known for the production of fine dark wool, which was used in high-quality textiles. Christ, however, says that in his eyes the pretensions of the people are stripped away so that they stand before him "naked." The white robes that connote purification of sin and the victory of faithfulness come from Christ, not from the local textile factory (3:17-18). Laodicea had an important medical school that was located in an area known for its eye salve. Since the Laodiceans do not see their condition in relation to Christ, they are blind. The salve that enables them to see comes from Christ, whose message reveals the truth to them (3:17-18; Hemer, *Letters,* 178-209).

Along with undercutting the pride of the Laodiceans, the message chides the congregation because its works are "neither cold nor hot" (3:15). Accordingly, Christ says that he is about to spit them out of his mouth (3:16). Some detect a comparison to the local water supply. The nearby town of Hieropolis was known for its springs of hot water, while good cold water could be obtained in Colossae. Water that came by aqueduct to Laodicea would have been tepid and unappealing by the time of its arrival.

The promise given to the Laodicean Christians is given in the form of an announcement: Christ is standing at the door and knocking, which suggests that he is in some way an outsider to the congregation that one would expect to bear his name. Nevertheless, Christ is persistent, and he promises that when they open the door, he will eat with them. This is accompanied by the promise that those who conquer will have a place upon Christ's own throne (3:21; 22:5).

The messages to the seven churches establish a context in which readers of Revelation can ponder the meaning of the visions that will unfold in the next chapters. We have seen that those who were first addressed by the book faced issues ranging from persecution, to assimilation, to the complacency that arises from prosperity. Now we will ask how the scenes of the heavenly throne room, the four horsemen, and other visions can help to awaken the complacent, to strengthen the persecuted, and to bring those tempted to assimilate to a renewed sense of faithfulness. The promises that were made at the end of each message are not forgotten in the visions that follow, but point us to the final chapters of Revelation, when the faithful find everlasting life in the New Jerusalem. In the meantime, however, surprises await those who are willing to hear John's message.

Chapter 3

THE SCROLL UNSEALED

Revelation 4–7

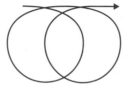

A divine voice beckons John to come through heaven's open door, opening the second cycle of visions. The voice is not a new one but the same trumpet-like voice that introduced the messages to the churches (1:10; 4:1). Similarly, the visions in this second cycle do not raise new issues but deal with the issues of faithfulness that emerged in the messages to the churches. As the previous cycle concluded, Christ stood knocking at the door, waiting for the Christian community to open to him (3:20); but before readers can respond, a new cycle begins as John is shown a door that already stands open (4:1). The contrast is provocative: as Christ asks the community to open their door to him, he opens heaven's door to them through John's prose. Moreover, having heard that those who conquered would sit with Christ on the throne, just as Christ conquered and sat down on God's throne (3:21), readers are now given a glimpse of the fulfillment of Christ's promise. They are shown a vision of God's throne (4:2) and a vision of Christ, who conquered through faithful suffering (5:5-6).

The visions in Revelation 4–5 center readers on God and Christ. Those who ponder these two chapters discover the heart of the book, for here its essential revelation is to be found. Through the images of the throne and the Lamb, readers learn how God's will is done through the crucified and risen Christ. Many readers miss the importance of this passage. Seeking to learn "what must take place after this" (4:1), they quickly move to the seven seals in chapter 6, where portents of disaster loom large. When John sees "what must take place after this," however, the first vision consists not of disaster but of worship. As a stone cast into a pool creates waves that move outward, the presence of God on the throne creates waves of praise that begin with the four creatures beside the throne, then surge outward to a circle of elders, to myriads of angels, and finally to every creature in heaven and on earth and under the earth, so that all creation joins in giving praises to God and the Lamb.

The visions in Revelation 4–7 can be called a "cycle" because they begin and end with worship in the heavenly throne room. The four living creatures, the elders, and the angelic hosts that sing praises to God in chapter 4 see the Lamb receive a scroll that is sealed with seven seals in chapter 5. As the Lamb opens the first six seals in chapter 6, threatening visions relentlessly erode readers' sense of security, pressing them to join with all who cry out, "Who is able to stand?" (6:17). As if in response, John tells readers about the redeemed who are able to stand in the heavenly throne room, where they join the four creatures, the elders, and the angelic hosts in offering songs of praise to God and the Lamb (7:10-12). Only then is the seventh seal opened, bringing reverent silence (8:1). The cycle begins in the presence of God and the Lamb and returns to the presence of God and the Lamb.

The Sovereign God (4:1-11)

Readers can best sense the force of the majestic scene that opens this cycle by taking it as a whole. John passes through the door into heaven to find himself in a majestic throne hall, where God the sovereign presides over the celestial court. As the seer enters the hall, his eyes are drawn to the throne, where the presence of God radiates in gem-like splendor. A polished pavement stretches out before the throne like the waters of a crystal sea, and the flames of the seven torches burning before the throne illumine the hall. Flashes of lightning issue from the throne, followed by low rumbles of thunder that rise and crash. Four strange courtiers attend the sovereign. Their faces resemble a human being, a lion, an ox, and an eagle. All have six wings and are covered with eyes. The heavenly sovereign is also attended by twenty-four regal figures, who wear crowns and sit on thrones. The voices of the creatures soar above the thunder, as they sing praise to the Almighty, and their song is picked up by the other attendants, who rise from their thrones to bow before God's throne, casting their crowns before him.

God is central to this vision. His presence is the radiant point around which the galaxy of other heavenly beings revolves, yet his appearance eludes direct description. John describes the heavenly court in a manner reminiscent of Ezekiel, who saw the throne of God together with lightning, a rainbow, a crystal sea, and four creatures. But where Ezekiel said that above the throne was "the appearance of a man" (Ezek. 1:26), John pauses, willing only to say that God's presence was like the radiance of precious stones (Rev. 4:3). The thunder and lightning that issue from the throne add to the display of God's power, yet the dangers inherent in these phenomena also prevent people from approaching too closely (cf. Exod. 19:16). John respects the differences between the human and the divine, between the creature and the Creator. His portrayal of the throne room preserves the mystery and transcendence of God, so that readers recognize that God is not merely a human being writ large.

The actions that occur in the heavenly throne room show that in the proper order of things, all creation is oriented toward its Creator. Human beings are not at the center, much as they like to think that they are. God is central, and the second ring of beings consists of four creatures, only one of whom has a human face. The others resemble a lion, an ox, and an eagle (cf. Ezek. 1:10), and all have six wings (Isa. 6:2).[1] Representing the entire created order, these creatures lead all liv-

---

1. Beginning in the late second century A.D., Christian writers identified the four creatures in the heavenly throne room with the four gospel writers. Those who read Revelation at the end of the first century would not have understood the creatures in this way since it was only later that Christians agreed that there were to be only four authoritative gospels. Over the centuries, however, the use of these images for the gospels has become commonplace. Interpreters have not always agreed on which creature represents which gospel, but the most common view is as follows: Matthew's gospel has the human face because it begins with a genealogy that

ing things in worship of their Creator. They voice one of the primary forms of awareness of God, which is that God is supremely "holy" (Rev. 4:8). God's holiness is his "otherness." It is the numinous quality of power and purity that sets God apart from all other beings, so that those who recognize God's holiness also recognize their own powerlessness and impurity (Isa. 6:3-5). The four creatures begin their song by acclaiming God "holy" (Rev. 4:8), but they add their "Amen" only when every creature in heaven and on earth and under the earth and in the sea offers its praises at the end of the scene (5:14; Bauckham, *Theology*, 32-33).

The next ring of heavenly figures consists of the twenty-four elders that look like kings (4:4). Interpreters have tried to determine whether they represent the twelve sons of Jacob and the twelve apostles, or a group of priestly figures, or another type of heavenly being. John, however, simply calls them "elders," leaving most questions about their identity unanswered. The term "elder," which is *presbyteros* in Greek, was often used for the leaders of Jewish (Luke 7:3; 9:22) and Christian communities (Acts 14:23; Titus 1:5; James 5:14; 1 Pet. 5:1-2; 3 John 1). By looking at the elders, the readers in the seven congregations can see the outcome of Christ's promises concerning the faithful. Earlier, Christ promised that the faithful would wear white robes (Rev. 3:5), that they would be given crowns (2:10), and that they would have a place on Christ's throne (3:21). This vision underscores the promise by depicting a group of elders clothed in white robes, wearing crowns, and sitting on thrones.

The twenty-four elders take up the song of praise that the four creatures began and now speak of the dependence of all creation upon God. In a threefold way the four creatures proclaimed God's infinite existence by calling him the one who "was and is and is to come" (4:8). Now in a threefold way the twenty-four elders voice finite creation's dependence upon the Eternal One by confessing that God created all things, that it was by God's will that they came into being, and that it was by God's power that they were created (4:11). The actions of the el-

---

traces Jesus' human origins. Mark is identified with the lion because it begins by calling Jesus the "son of God," referring to his royal power. Luke is the ox, since his gospel begins in the temple where sacrifices were made. John is the eagle, since his soaring introduction of Jesus as the Word of God points to his heavenly origin.

ders match their words. Instead of celebrating their own reign, they direct attention to God's reign. Their thrones and their crowns are theirs not by right, but as gifts from God. Therefore, the elders honor the Giver and dispel any illusion that they themselves possess ultimate authority by leaving their thrones and prostrating themselves before God, and by removing the crowns from their heads and casting them down before God's throne (4:10).

The heavenly throne is the vantage point from which John wants readers to look out upon the world of human affairs. Popular culture in the world of the seven churches gravitated toward human centers of power. Public appearances of the emperor often featured him sitting on a throne and accompanied by a crowd of friends, advisors, and attendants. When the emperor traveled, communities would send representatives, sometimes dressed in white, to greet him and present him with golden crowns to show their recognition of his sovereignty. Those who approached the throne would prostrate themselves, sometimes even bowing down before the throne when the emperor was absent (Aune, "Influence").

Toward the end of the first century, the emperor Domitian apparently demanded that people address him as "Lord and God" (Suetonius, *Domitian* 13.2), but such blatant compulsion seems to have been an exception. Emperors preferred to cultivate the impression that people sang their praises because their virtues were universally recognized and made them worthy of such honors. A throne of admirers could keep up a thunder of applause day and night, referring to the emperor and even to lesser kings as "gods" (Acts 12:22; Tacitus, *Annals* 14.15). Flatterers would lavish the title "Lord and God" on the emperor not so much out of coercion, but in the hope of winning his favor and advancing their social positions (Martial, *Epigrams* 5.8; 7.34; 10.72). By giving readers a glimpse of God's heavenly court, John presses Christians in the seven churches to see such popular displays of power as garish imitations of the true sovereignty that belongs to the Creator, who alone is truly worthy of being called "Lord and God" (Rev. 4:11).

The vision of God's court also sets the stage for the drama that will follow, in which kaleidoscopic cycles of images unmask the pretensions of powers that seek to take God's place so that readers can see how the forces of evil infiltrate political, economic, and social life. God's throne remains the true seat of power throughout Revelation

(6:16; 7:9-11, 15, 17; 8:3; 12:5; 14:3; 16:17; 19:4-5; 20:11-12; 21:5; 22:1, 3). Yet John also speaks of the "throne" of Satan, who exercises power through agents that deceive people and perpetrate violence against the faithful, including Antipas and other Christians (2:13; 13:2; 16:10). In contrast to the creatures around the throne, the forces of evil that are represented by the dragon and the beast refuse to acknowledge God's power. Paradoxically, the twenty-four elders gracefully surrender their crowns and thrones to God while they remain in heaven, but the dragon doggedly retains its crowns as it is driven out of heaven toward final defeat (12:7-9).

How would the vision of the heavenly throne room strike members of the seven churches? Since the situations of the readers varied, their responses to the vision would probably have varied also. First, Christians facing the threat of persecution might have found the vision reassuring, since it shows that God reigns despite the hostility that they receive from human beings. Power ultimately rests in the hands of the Creator, not their accusers. Second, those seeking to accommodate pagan culture would probably have been uneasy with the vision, for if God reigns, then compromising one's convictions for the sake of social and economic ease warrants the censure they received in Revelation 2–3. In allying themselves with the non-Christian world, they distance themselves from the heavenly court. Third, the complacent and self-satisfied would probably have found the vision disturbing, for in comparison to the splendor of God's presence, their pride in wealth and prestige is shown to be an act of self-deception. But whether the vision is initially assuring or disturbing, it is designed to attract all types of readers to the heavenly chorus, where they too might join in singing praises to God and the Lamb.

The Lamb Who Was Slain (5:1-14)

John's eyes are drawn to the right hand of God, which holds a scroll that has been sealed with seven seals (5:1). Mentioning the scroll creates a sense of expectancy, since the document presumably contains some sort of divine decree (Ezek. 2:9-10). The seven seals on the scroll — like the seals that were placed on royal decrees, wills, and other official documents — imply that its contents are valid. A seal in John's time consisted of a piece of wax that was placed on the edge of the scroll and imprinted with the ring of the person who sent the text. The seal ensured that the scroll truly declared the will of its author and that no one had altered the text. Only a person who had been properly authorized was to break the seals and open the scroll. Strangely, the seven seals protect the contents of God's scroll, but they also indicate that God has willed things that have not been fully carried out. The heavens may resound with choruses of praise to God, but Revelation 2–3 indicated that this was not true on earth. How will God's "will be done on earth as it is in heaven" (Matt. 6:10)?

An angel's voice intrudes in the celestial scene by crying out, "Who is worthy to open the scroll and break its seals?" (Rev. 5:2). A search is made throughout the realm of heaven, throughout the earth, and even in the regions under the earth, but the result is wholly negative. No created being can be found who is worthy to open the scroll. This again underscores the differences between creatures and their Creator. All creatures prove to be inadequate for the carrying out of God's purposes. When the question is asked, "Who is worthy?" the response at this point is simply "no one" (5:3). When John hears this, he weeps (5:4). His tears show that he does not share the perspective of those on earth who say, "I am rich, I have prospered, and I need nothing" (3:17). Rather, he weeps as one who could add his voice to those who suffer, asking "how long will it be" until God's just purposes are accomplished (6:10)?

The answer that John receives uses images that play on the difference between what is heard and what is seen. John *hears* one of the elders say that "the Lion of the tribe of Judah, the Root of David, has conquered so that he can open the scroll and its seven seals" (5:5). The image of a lion, which connotes power and majesty, is identified with Judah, the tribe from which kings came in the Old Testament. The book of Genesis said that "Judah is a lion's whelp" and that the "scepter shall not depart from Judah, nor the ruler's staff from between his feet, until tribute comes to him, and the obedience of the peoples is his" (Gen. 49:9-10). Messianic expectations were shaped by memories of King David, who came from the tribe of Judah. David was a warrior who fought like a lion and "conquered" neighboring peoples to establish the kingdom of Israel. Isaiah looked for a righteous king to come from the "root" of David's line, a leader who would be filled with God's

Spirit and subdue the wicked so that the earth would be full of the knowledge of the Lord (Isa. 11:1-10).

What John actually *sees,* however, is not a lion but "a Lamb, standing as if it had been slaughtered" (Rev. 5:6). The vision of the slaughtered Lamb is startling given the expectation that a lion would appear. People commonly assume that lions exhibit strength while lambs display weakness, and that a lion conquers by inflicting death on others, while the Lamb is said to have conquered by enduring death himself. Clearly, the portrayal of the slaughtered Lamb as a conqueror challenges ordinary modes of thinking. What John *hears* about the Lion recalls promises from the Old Testament, and what he *sees* in the Lamb reflects the crucifixion of Christ. Both images point to the same reality. According to the Old Testament, God promised to send a powerful and righteous ruler. These promises are not rejected but fulfilled through the slaughtered yet living Lamb, who is not a hapless victim but a figure of royal strength. The "horn" was a symbol of royal power (Ps. 132:17), and the Lamb has seven horns (Rev. 5:6). The messianic king was to bear the Spirit of God, which was to manifest itself in seven ways (Isa. 11:1-3a), and the Lamb's seven eyes represent God's sevenfold Spirit (Rev. 5:6). Conversely, Christ's death might appear to be a defeat, but in reality it is a victory, for through it he brings people of all nations into the kingdom of God (5:9-10).

This scene is a good place to ask again why Revelation communicates through symbolic images rather than in a more direct way. The Lamb will be the dominant image for Christ throughout the remainder of the book. The image of the Lamb can hardly be said to conceal Christ's identity, as if John had written in a code to keep his message from being understood. The opening lines of the book identified Jesus Christ as the faithful witness, whose blood frees people from their sins and makes of them a kingdom of priests (1:5-6). John could have been as direct here if he had chosen to do so. Rather than concealing meaning, the images reveal meaning by evoking associations in the minds of the readers.

A slaughtered lamb was commonly associated with sacrifice, which was a form of purposeful death. The image would have prompted many readers to think of the Passover (1 Cor. 5:7; John 1:29; 1 Pet. 1:19). The Passover sacrifice commemorated the way that God liberated Israel from slavery and made of them "a priestly kingdom and a holy nation"

(Exod. 12:3, 27; 19:6). The heavenly chorus in Revelation underscores these associations by declaring that the blood of the slaughtered Lamb ransomed people for God and made them to be a kingdom and priests (Rev. 5:9-10). Other associations may have come from the sense that the "blood" of a sacrificial victim made atonement for sin (Lev. 17:11). Still others may have recalled Isaiah's references to the servant of the Lord, who was compared to "a lamb that is led to the slaughter," yet "through him the will of the Lord shall prosper" (Isa. 53:7, 10). According to Revelation, the Lamb who was slaughtered was the agent through whom God's purposes would be carried out.

The four creatures and twenty-four elders who bowed before God's throne (Rev. 4:10) now make a remarkable shift by bowing down before the Lamb (5:8). The harps that were traditionally used to praise God (Ps. 150:3) now sound praises to the Lamb, and the bowls of incense that signified prayer to God (Ps. 141:2) are now placed before the Lamb (Rev. 5:8). If a "new song" was a fitting way to celebrate God's rule over the earth (Ps. 96:1), a "new song" is now sung to the Lamb; and the heavenly chorus that acclaimed God "worthy" (Rev. 4:11) now acclaims Christ "worthy" (5:9). Yet despite the shift in focus, the Lamb does not usurp God's place, for all that the Lamb has accomplished ultimately serves God's purposes. His death ransoms people "for God" (5:9) and brings them into a kingdom where they are priests who "serve our God" (5:10).

The song of praise to the Lamb shows that from John's perspective Christ's position does not reflect the deification of human power and practices. When human beings "conquer," they do so by inflicting death and damage on their adversaries. In John's time, the Roman armies had extended the borders of the empire through such conquest, capturing people of many tribes, languages, and nations. Captives taken in war typically became slaves, who were relegated to the lowest stratum of society. They were not considered citizens and did not perform the sacred duties that free people performed. In subsequent chapters, the beast will be shown to conquer in precisely this oppressive fashion (13:7-8).

At each point, the Lamb works differently. The Lamb conquers by faithfully enduring death, and the result of his conquest is that people of every tribe, language, and nation are brought into new relationship with God. They are not degraded to the status of chattels, but are elevated to membership in God's kingdom. Rather than being excluded from sacred service, they carry out sacred service to God. The dignity of being a priestly kingdom, which God gave to the tribes of Israel (Exod. 19:16; Isa. 61:6), is extended to people of all tribes of the earth through the work of the Lamb. God's kingdom is not yet visible to the eye, but his people can be confident that they "will reign" (future tense) when God's purposes for the world are made complete in the new heavens and new earth (Rev. 5:10; 22:5). Until that time, knowledge of belonging to God's kingdom offers a basis upon which to resist giving up in despair to the powers that oppose the reign of God.

The scene climaxes as the seer's gaze stretches beyond the inner circle of creatures and elders to behold the incalculable number of angels that surround them. The chorus of the song declared that God was "worthy" to "receive glory and honor and power" (4:11), but as the myriads of angels add their voices they ascribe "power and wealth and wisdom and might and honor and glory and blessing" to the slaughtered Lamb, who is "worthy" (5:12). The Lamb does not replace God, but is extolled along with God, for through him the songs of praise that were formerly confined to heaven are now extended to earth, so that every creature in heaven and on earth and under the earth, and all that is in the sea give "blessing and honor and glory and might" to God and the Lamb together (5:13). As all creation joins in such praise, the four living creatures that began the song add their "Amen" (5:14). This is God's will for the world.

The vision invites those in the seven churches to join in the cosmic song of praise; but despite the joyous quality of the scene, readers in the seven churches will be shown that adding one's voice to the chorus can be a costly venture. As further visions unfold, readers learn that many derive their wealth not from God — to whom all power and riches belong — but from "Babylon," where the beast and not the Lamb is honored, and where human beings are sold rather than freed (18:13). Babylon's claims will prove false, and those who place their trust in her wealth and glory will mourn (18:15-19), so that the sound of lamentation over Babylon's downfall in Revelation 18 forms a counterpart to the celebration of Christ's victory in Revelation 4–5. That, however, is to get ahead of the story. Readers live during the time when the power of God and the powers opposed to God are still in conflict. Therefore, the question is whether they will join with those who sing praises to the Lamb, or whether they will refuse to do so, and later join in the laments of those who have sought their security elsewhere.

The First Six Seals (6:1-17)

As the Lamb opens each seal on the scroll that he received from God, the voice of one of the four living creatures who stand beside the throne shouts "Come!" In response, a series of four horsemen gallop before John's eyes, warning of conquest, violence, hardship, and death. After the horsemen vanish, a vision of martyrs appears, followed by a specter of destruction and divine wrath that threatens all of humanity.

Readers do well to ask themselves what they expect from these visions. Many are fascinated with the seven seals because they think that the text issues predictions about a series of events that will occur in the future. They assume that if they can match the visions with events in the newspaper, they will be able to tell when the end of the world will come. According to this approach, we will know that we have arrived at the first seal when we see some world power embarking on the path of conquest. We will know when we have arrived at the second seal when the threat of violence spreads. As violence leads to economic hardship, we will find ourselves at the third seal, and so forth until God's wrath is poured out and the kingdom of God arrives with the opening of the sixth and seventh seals.

"Prediction" is not the right word for these visions, however, because they depict threats that do not fall neatly on a time line. Virtually everyone understands that the four horsemen have a symbolic or representative quality. We realize that the text is not telling us to expect the end times to begin when we see a solitary figure with a bow in his hand riding a white horse through the streets of our city, but recognize that the visions stand for larger realities. The text makes clear that the horsemen represent conquest, violence, economic hardship, and death. These were genuine threats for people in the first century and they have remained threats for people in subsequent centuries, which is why attempts to predict the onset of the end times on the basis of these visions have consistently failed. The dangers that they depict cannot be confined to any one period: waves of conquest, outbreaks of violence, and periods of economic hardship have occurred repeatedly in human history, and death finally comes to all.

The principal purpose of the visions in Revelation 6 is to awaken a sense of uneasiness in readers by vividly identifying threats to their well-being. The four horsemen are designed to shatter the illusion that people can find true security in the borders of a nation or empire, in a flourishing economy, or in their own health. Subsequent visions promise that God will not allow injustice to continue forever — which is assuring to the victims, but disturbing to the perpetrators — and warn that no place on earth and no position of power or wealth will protect people from the judgment of God and the Lamb. Those who grasp the way that these visions relentlessly undercut human pretensions will find themselves asking the final question in the chapter: "Who is able to stand?" (6:17). Those who have been moved to ask this question are rightly prepared for the visions that follow in chapter 7.

Albrecht Dürer's woodcut of the four horsemen shows how these threats work on readers. The first horseman with his bow appears in the background of the picture, furthest away from the viewers. This placement is suggestive because fear of conquest by a foreign power is often furthest away from readers' minds. If the first horseman awakens a sense of distant uneasiness, the second horseman brings the threat a step closer by pointing to the violence that people perpetrate on "one another" (6:4). Danger is not limited to external invasion, but can also come from internal conflict. The third horseman brings the threat still closer by depicting economic insecurity, as he grasps scales like those used in commerce. This horseman is the largest and most prominent in Dürer's picture, suggesting that economic difficulties loom largest in most people's minds. The fourth horseman, who represents death, is in the lower foreground of the picture, together with the bizarre creature that represents Hades. Viewers' eyes often overlook the figure of death as their attention is drawn to the large horseman representing economic uncertainties; but death is the threat that sits in the lap of each viewer. No one escapes it.

The visions of the four horsemen have captured the imaginations of people for centuries, but certain aspects of the imagery would have been most apparent to people in the seven churches addressed by Revelation. The first horseman, who is armed with a bow, was an apt figure to represent conquest since horses were commonly used in warfare, and various armies had bowmen, some of whom belonged to the cavalry (Judith 2:15). The most famous mounted bowmen of John's time, however, came from Parthia, the region that lay beyond the Roman Empire's eastern frontier. The Parthian forces, which featured mounted archers, repeatedly drove back the Roman army in 53 B.C., 36 B.C., and

The Four Horsemen (Rev. 6:1-8)
by Albrecht Dürer

A.D. 62, bringing Roman imperial expansion to a halt. The Parthians were a nagging reminder about the limits of the security that Rome — the region's most powerful empire — could provide. The implication was that the Christians who partook of the sacrifices offered to the deified emperors and other Roman gods (Rev. 2:14, 20) were compromising their convictions to placate powers that were not supreme, but vulnerable to invasion by outside forces. Those who were sure that they needed nothing more than the prosperity provided by the empire (3:17) were deluding themselves.

The second horseman, who wields a great sword, "was permitted to take peace from the earth, so that people would slaughter one another" (6:4). Where the first rider represented the threats to security that come from outside one's borders, the second rider stands for the threat of violence that can erupt within one's own society. The vision is written in a way that disturbs one of the premier attitudes that the Romans tried to inculcate in people, namely, that the world should be grateful to them for providing peace. Orators were effusive in their praise of the *Pax Romana* or Roman Peace, lauding it as the source of unprecedented prosperity. As regional conflicts were contained, new roads were built and ships plied the seas. Merchants expanded commerce to include the glittering array of items mentioned later in Revelation: "cargo of gold, silver, jewels, and pearls, fine linen, purple, silk and scarlet, all kinds of scented wood," ivory, bronze and iron, spices, flour, livestock, and slaves (18:11-13). Many accepted the deaths of people like Antipas (2:13) and the oppressive steps taken against other Christians (2:10) as measures needed to preserve the peace. Yet the second rider warns against being lulled into complacency by comfortable conditions that pass for peace (3:1), for such peace can be removed.

The third horseman holds a pair of scales, like those used in commerce, and issues a threat of economic hardship (6:5-6). The rider does not decree an utter famine, but speaks of wheat and barley being purchased at high prices, while oil and wine continue to be available. Nevertheless, these conditions would have been harsh on the poor. If a denarius was a day's wage for a laborer, then it would cost an entire day's pay to buy one quart of wheat or three quarts of barley. These quantities of grain might be enough to keep a small family alive, but there would be no money left to buy any oil or wine. The flourishing Roman economic system was celebrated for its ability to make grain and other foodstuffs widely available (18:13), but the specter of crop failures and food shortages — like those that periodically plagued Asia Minor and other places — is a vivid reminder about the limits of any economic system to guarantee prosperity.

The fourth horseman, who sits astride a sickly green horse, represents death (6:8). This rider holds nothing in his hands, but is followed by "Hades," the Greek name for the realm of the dead. Dürer's woodcut depicts Hades as a strange creature with an enormous mouth because the Old Testament sometimes personified Hades ("Sheol" in Hebrew) by saying that it had a voracious appetite and opened its mouth wide to devour the powerful (Isa. 5:14). Death's tools include the violence that people perpetrate by the sword, the famines that break out due to crop failures and other causes, the diseases and plagues that rob people of health and life, and the wild beasts like wolves and hyenas, whose teeth tear the vulnerable (Rev. 6:8). Thus the specter of death heightens and expands the threats represented by the previous horsemen, hemming readers in with forces that ultimately reach beyond human control.

Where is God in all of this? In one sense God does not exactly inflict these plagues on the world, since the four horsemen are the powers that are directly responsible for the threat. Yet it is also clear that these threatening powers do not operate independently of God. Each horseman appears only after the Lamb has broken a seal on the scroll that he received from God and only after one of the living creatures that stand beside God's throne has given the command: "Come!" The first horseman "was given" the crown of victory, implying that his power to conquer came from God (6:2), and the second horseman "was permitted" to take peace from the earth, presumably by God, and he "was given" a sword to accomplish the task (6:4). When the third horseman appears, the voice that announces high prices for grain comes from "a voice in the midst of the four living creatures" in the heavenly throne room (6:6). The fourth horsemen was "given authority," apparently by God, to inflict death (6:8). There are, to be sure, indications of divine restraint, since the voice from the throne room limits the severity of the food shortage (6:6) and death is not allowed to range freely, but is confined to only one fourth of the earth (6:8). Nevertheless, God constitutes a threat.

We will see in subsequent chapters that visions like these do not attempt to explain why there is evil in the world. John is keenly aware that threats to human life cannot always be ascribed to God because a number of forces are at work in the world. It is true that God creates both "weal and woe" (Isa. 45:7), that God can "kill and make alive," and that he can "wound and heal" (Deut. 32:39). At the same time, the world is also the arena in which Satan operates and human sin wreaks havoc. In many of Revelation's visions carnage is created by the beast and its allies, who are not agents of God but opponents of God. Therefore, because multiple forces are at work, people cannot always tell whether what they perceive to be a threat comes from God, from Satan, or from human sin.

Instead of offering an explanation for evil, visions like those in Revelation 6 address listeners as a form of proclamation that is designed to bring repentance and faith. The visions are designed to unsettle complacent readers, like those at Sardis and Laodicea, who may be lulled into a false sense of security by social and economic conditions that are favorable to them, reminding them that power ultimately belongs to God. At the same time, the visions give the oppressed incentive to persevere in the confidence that the conditions that allow for their oppression will not continue forever. John's visions of the horsemen are similar to those described by the prophet Zechariah. When Zechariah heard a divine horseman report that "the whole earth remains at peace," an angel demanded to know how long God would allow this condition to continue, because ongoing peace simply gave the powerful the luxury of oppressing the people of God (Zech. 1:11-12; 6:1-8). For change to come, God would need to disturb the peace.

The opening of the fifth and sixth seals results in a jarring pair of scenes that challenge ordinary perceptions of peace and security: the martyrs rest in heaven (Rev. 6:9-11) and the remainder of humanity is disturbed on earth (6:12-17). These visions press readers to give up the idea that they can remain neutral, asking them whether they identify with the martyrs or with the rest of humanity. There is no middle ground. At the same time, the text shows that heavenly perceptions of the two groups are the opposite of earthly perceptions. From an earthly point of view, the story of the martyrs would seem to show that faith leads to suffering and loss. The conclusion one would draw from this is that faith should be given up in order to gain greater security on earth. The visions reverse this perception by showing that the faithful who have suffered on earth ultimately find rest and reward in heaven, while the rest of humanity, who appear secure on earth, will ultimately be disturbed by the judgment that falls from heaven.

The vision of the martyrs under the altar is designed to awaken the readers' willingness to identify with those who have suffered for the faith. By the time Revelation was written, Antipas had been killed at Pergamum (Rev. 2:13). Other sources tell that Stephen and James had been slain in Jerusalem (Acts 7:58-60; 12:1-2), and that Nero had brutally murdered Christians in Rome by crucifying some of them, having others torn by dogs, and burning still others to death (Tacitus, *Annals* 15.44). The martyrs utter a cry that has appeared on the lips of the afflicted throughout the generations: "How long will it be before you judge and avenge our blood on the inhabitants of the earth?" (Rev. 6:10; Zech. 1:12; Ps. 79:5-10). Some modern readers are bothered by the martyrs' cry for justice, arguing that it does not measure up to the standard of turning the other cheek and loving one's enemies, as Jesus taught; but the plea for justice cannot be easily dismissed. The martyrs suffered not because they were sinners but because they were faithful. One rightly asks: Does God care? Does genuine love turn a blind eye while the wicked shed the blood of the innocent? Or is mercy another name for indifference?

The martyrs receive a divine response, but one that raises as many questions as it answers — at least at this point in the story. The good news is that each is given a "white robe," which connotes purity, victory, and celebration (Rev. 6:11). Despite the hostility they received on earth, the gift shows that the martyrs are valued in God's eyes. Moreover, the martyrs are given a place under God's own altar, which suggests that their deaths were not meaningless tragedies but sacrifices that ultimately serve God's purposes. The strange news is that they are to remain at rest until the number of their fellow Christians, who are to die for the faith, has been completed (6:11). Perhaps this is good news because it means that God does envision an end to the suffering, but one wonders why more martyrs need to be added to the rolls. No answer is given here. Readers are left with the question. Only in Revelation 11 is John shown how the witness that Christians give in and through their affliction leads others to repent and to give glory to God (see chapter 4 below).

The opening of the sixth seal results in the earth and sky quaking, the sun becoming dark and the moon turning to blood, as the stars fall and the sky vanishes (6:12-14). These portents echo prophetic warnings about the coming day of divine wrath, showing how the creation itself responds to the will of its Creator (Isa. 34:4; Joel 2:30-31; Amos 8:9). The vision challenges the idea that readers might attain a kind of security by compromising their faith in order to blend into the beliefs of the general populace, as some of those addressed by Revelation were inclined to do. The martyrs in the previous vision fell under human judgment because of their faith, and they paid for it with their lives. Accordingly, one might think that a better alternative would be to give up one's faith in order to maintain one's standing in the eyes of society. The sixth vision, however, shows that those who assimilate into the general society in order to escape its judgment actually open themselves to judgment before the throne of God. Seeking refuge with the rich and powerful at the expense of one's faith is ultimately futile, for the sixth seal shows the wealthy and influential seeking refuge from God and the Lamb by calling the mountains and hills to fall on them.

When the mass of humanity finally cries out, "Who is able to stand?" (Rev. 6:17), readers might expect the answer to be "No one," for all seem doomed to destruction under God's wrath. Yet that is in fact not the case, for the next chapter shows that there are some who are able to stand before God and the Lamb, not by their social position, but by grace.

The Redeemed: 144,000 and a Great Multitude (7:1-17)

"Who can stand" before the judgment of God and the Lamb (6:17)? An answer is given when John sees a vision of the redeemed "standing" before the throne singing praises to God and the Lamb (7:9). This festive scene of a vast crowd dressed in white, waving palm branches and shouting acclamations, interrupts the torrent of disasters that broke loose at the opening of the first six seals. Although the opening of the sixth seal produced catastrophes in the heavens and convulsions on the earth, four angels hold back the collapse of the created order by restraining the winds that threaten to devastate the world (7:1-3). Earlier, an angel's voice halted the choruses of heavenly praises so that someone worthy to open the seals could be identified (5:2). Now an angel's voice halts the onslaught of earthly destruction until the servants of

God can be identified (7:3). Previously, the "seals" on God's scroll were broken so that terrors could be unleashed, but here the terrors are kept at bay so that "seals" can be placed on the foreheads of God's people (7:2-3).

The word "seal" in this context suggests a number of different meanings. On one level it means that people belong to God. Elsewhere the redeemed are said to bear the names of God and the Lamb on their foreheads, which is where the seal is placed (14:1; 22:4). It is possible that being sealed with the names of God and Christ was done in a formal sense through Christian baptism, although Revelation does not make this explicit. On another level, sealing indicates protection. There are instances where bearing the seal protects the faithful from the plagues that afflict unbelievers (9:4; cf. Ezek. 9:4-6), but it does not mean that the people of God are spared suffering of all sorts. They are presumably vulnerable to the threats depicted by the first six seals, and later visions warn that powers hostile to God will persecute and kill the saints (Rev. 6:9-11; 11:7; 12:11; 13:7-10). The seal does not ward off suffering altogether, but it does shield people from the wrath of God and the Lamb (6:16-17). Those who bear the names of God and Christ are protected through tribulation so that they can stand in time of judgment and join in the celebration of God's victory (7:10).

The redeemed are identified as a group of 144,000 people from the twelve tribes of Israel (7:4-8). The use of this particular number has fascinated many readers of Revelation. Groups like the Davidians and Jehovah's Witnesses have understood that gathering a group of 144,000 prior to Christ's second coming is part of their evangelistic task, although they have not assumed that the members of this select group must be physical descendants of the twelve tribes. Other forms of premillennialism do expect the 144,000 to be ethnic Jews who convert to Christianity during the great future tribulation, while the "great multitude" depicted in 7:9-17 will be the non-Jews who convert to Christianity during this same period (see chapter 1 above). Although many are intrigued with these theories, it is unwise to take the number in a literal sense. When John later says that the New Jerusalem is a cube that measures 12,000 stadia or about 1500 miles on each side, most readers quickly realize that he is not giving the precise dimensions of the heavenly city, but is using numbers to symbolize the city's perfection (21:16). Similarly, when John speaks of 12,000 being gathered from each of the twelve tribes, for a total of 144,000, the numbers symbolize completeness.

More importantly, this passage uses two different images for the same reality. The redeemed are identified as an assembly of 144,000 in 7:4-8 and as a "great multitude" in 7:9-17, but both refer to the same group. On one level, to be sure, the images appear to contrast, since the first refers to a definite number of people who come from the twelve tribes of Israel, while the second refers to a group that cannot be numbered, who come from every tribe and nation. Nevertheless, this vision makes the same contrast between hearing and seeing that was used in 5:5-6 where John *heard* that the "Lion of the tribe of Judah, the Root of David," had conquered, but he *saw* a Lamb that had been slaughtered. The reference to the Lion of Judah and the Root of David recall Old Testament promises concerning a messianic king, and the vision of the slain Lamb shows that these promises are realized through the death of Christ. In exactly the same way, John *hears* (7:4) about the redeemed who come from the twelve tribes, which recalls Old Testament promises concerning God's preservation of Israel; but when he actually *sees* (7:9) the realization of the promise, he encounters a countless multitude coming from every tribe and nation (Bauckham, *Theology,* 76-77).

Just as references to the Lion and the Lamb enable readers to consider the same person (Christ) from two different perspectives, the references to the 144,000 and to the great multitude allow readers to see the same community (Christ's followers) from two different perspectives. The community of faith encompasses people from many tribes, nations, and languages (7:9-17), yet this same community represents the fulfillment of God's promises concerning the preservation of Israel (7:4-8). If the promises concerning "the Lion of Judah" are not negated but fulfilled through the blood of the Lamb (5:5-6), the promises concerning "the tribe of Judah" (7:5) and the other tribes are not negated but fulfilled through the multitudes that are redeemed by the blood of the Lamb (7:14).

The Lamb "conquers" through his death, and his followers celebrate his triumph by waving palm branches — traditional symbols of victory (1 Macc. 13:51) — in their hands (Rev. 7:9). The chorus of praise that was first heard at the beginning of this vision cycle is now repeated, as the four living creatures, the elders, and the angels who encircle the throne again ascribe "Blessing and glory and wisdom and thanksgiving and honor and power and might" to God forever (7:12; cf. 5:11, 13).

The torrent of threats that appeared at the end of Revelation 6 gives way to a cascade of promises at the end of Revelation 7. Virtually all of the language in 7:15-17 echoes what was said through Israel's prophets. According to Ezek. 37:27, God said that he would make his dwelling or "tabernacle" with his people, and Rev. 7:15 repeats that the one who is seated on the throne will "tabernacle over them." According to Isa. 49:10, God promised that the redeemed "shall not hunger or thirst, neither scorching wind nor sun shall strike them down, for he who has pity on them will lead them, and by springs of living water will guide them." Revelation 7:16-17 declares that these promises are fulfilled by the Lamb at the center of the throne, who is the shepherd that guards them against hunger, thirst, sun, and heat, and guides them to springs of the water of life. Finally, Isa. 25:8 said that "the Lord God will wipe away the tears from all faces," and Rev. 7:17 repeats that "God will wipe away every tear from their eyes."

The chorus of echoes of Old Testament promises creates a resounding affirmation of the faithfulness of God. The words spoken through the prophets are not forgotten but given new life through the blood of the Lamb. If the threats in Revelation 6 take away the readers' confidence in the security provided by nation, community, economic prosperity, and health; and if they warn that positions of wealth and influence ultimately fail to shield people from the wrath of God; the visions in Revelation 7 call readers to be confident that God will be true. Instead of identifying with the multitudes who call upon the mountains and hills to shelter them from God and the Lamb (6:16-17), listeners are invited to seek the shelter that God and the Lamb provide (7:15-17). If God brought Christ, the Lamb, through death to a place on the heavenly throne, readers can persevere in faith, confident that God will bring all of his people through tribulation to a place in his court.

At the opening of the seventh seal (8:1), the echoes of celestial praise fade into reverent silence. The quiet, which lasts for half an hour, offers a respite from disaster and celebration, allowing readers to "Be still and know that I am God" (Ps. 46:10). Rather than serving as an anticlimax to this cycle of visions, the silence adds suspense to the drama. The earth has been shaken by the mere opening of the seals that

91

bound the scroll of God. Therefore, one might expect even more terrible and wonderful things to occur now that the scroll is opened so that it can be read. The next cycle of visions will show whether this is to be the case.

Chapter 4

TRUMPETS OF TERROR AND HOPE

Revelation 8–11

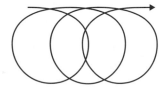

Seven trumpets are blown in succession, creating the third cycle of visions in Revelation. At the conclusion of the previous cycle, a graceful silence lingered in heaven's chambers after the voices in the celestial chorus had sounded the "Amen" in their praises of God and the Lamb (7:12; 8:1). Rather than allowing readers to bask in quietude, however, John directs attention to seven angels, who are given seven trumpets, whose sound will break the stillness and signal an onslaught of new visions even more terrible than those that have gone before (8:2). With each successive scene, disaster strikes earth, sea, and sky, until demonic hordes of locusts and cavalry torment humanity amid clouds of fire, smoke, and sulfur (8:7–9:21). The cycle is all the more ominous because the destruction unfolds in a relentlessly measured way. The effect is something like an orchestral performance in which the strings scrape dissonant chords while woodwinds shriek, trumpets blare, and cymbals crash in what seems to be wild discord — except that all the players move to the steady beat that is set by the conductor's hand: one, two, three, four. . . .

As the terrors crescendo to unbearable levels after the fifth and sixth trumpets, the wicked persist in their refusal to repent (9:20-21), so that the audience might well expect the seventh trumpet to signal the arrival of God's catastrophic judgment with earsplitting finality. But the last trumpet does not sound and the end does not come. Instead, there is an interlude, just as there was an interlude before the end of the previous cycle of visions. Following the same stylized pattern, the accounts of the seven seals and the seven trumpets begin with six threatening visions, shift to an interlude, then conclude with the seventh item in the series. In the series of seven seals, the interlude interrupted the specter of judgment to show the faithful in heaven, giving glory to God and the Lamb (7:1-17). Now, in the series of seven trumpets, the interlude interrupts the specter of judgment to show how the testimony of the faithful who suffer on earth helps move others to give glory to God (10:1–11:13).

The contrast between conditions before and after the interlude is striking. After the first six trumpets, many die and "the rest" persist in sin and false worship (9:20); but after God's witnesses have suffered faithfully and been raised, and judgment has fallen upon a part of humanity, "the rest" do what they have not done before by giving glory to God (11:13). Thus the interlude culminates not with universal destruction, but with a lessening of judgment and an occurrence of conversion. As inhabitants of the earth give glory to God, the seventh trumpet sounds and heavenly voices announce that "the kingdom of the world has become the kingdom of our Lord and of his Christ, and he shall reign forever and ever" (11:15). Readers find themselves again in the heavenly throne room where the twenty-four elders fall on their faces before God and sing thanks to him, just as they have done again and again (11:16-18; cf. 4:11; 5:8-14; 7:11-12).

The First Six Trumpets (8:2–9:21)

Trumpets serve as the motif that runs throughout this cycle of visions. The cycle begins in the heavenly throne room as seven angels are given seven trumpets (8:2), a gesture that helps to create a sense of anticipation because trumpets had different functions. On the field of battle, armies used trumpets to signal the beginning of an attack (2 Chron. 13:12), while people in threatened cities sounded trumpets to warn inhabitants that an assault was coming (Amos 3:6). Accordingly, the first six trumpets signal successive waves of destruction, some of which are created by grotesque and demonic armies. In the festive setting of worship, however, the sound of the trumpet was heard as an offering of praise to God (2 Chron. 5:13). Fittingly, the seventh trumpet heralds the resumption of the heavenly chorus of worship and praise.

Before the seven angels blow the trumpets, John directs attention to the heavenly altar where another angel is given incense to offer with the prayers of the saints (Rev. 8:3-5). John does not explain what the saints are praying for, but gives the impression that they pray for deliverance and justice. Earlier, incense carried the prayers of the saints before the Lamb, who was worthy to break the seals on the heavenly scroll so that God's purposes would be brought to completion (5:8). Later, the martyrs cried, "Sovereign Lord, holy and true, how long will it be before you judge and avenge our blood on the inhabitants of the earth?" (6:10). Now the trumpet visions offer a response of sorts, for as prayers and incense rise from the altar in heaven, an angel scoops fire from the altar and hurls it to earth.

The effects of coals from the altar being cast upon the earth are felt most directly in the first four trumpets, which form a group of visions in which a third of the earth, sea, fresh water, and heavenly bodies are afflicted (8:6-13). The highly stylized pattern is similar to that of the previous cycle, where the first four seals constituted a group of four horsemen (6:1-8). As coals from the heavenly altar are thrown down, fire mixed with hail creates a storm that scorches a third of the earth, devastating a third of the trees and all the green grass. At the second trumpet something like a mountain ablaze with fire is hurled into the sea, turning a third of its waters to blood (8:8). The third trumpet continues the theme of heavenly fire as a star falls upon the earth, burning like a torch (8:10). The star is called "Wormwood," the name of a plant that is extremely bitter to the taste. Where previous trumpets brought devastation on land and sea, this trumpet makes the fresh water of the world's rivers and springs bitter and deadly (8:11). The fourth trumpet completes this part of the sequence by turning to the heavenly bodies (8:12). A third of the sun, moon, and stars are afflicted, so that a third of their light is darkened.

Reading this chapter in context raises troubling questions about God. In Revelation 4–5, readers were given a positive vision in which

One of the Seven Angels with the Trumpets (Rev. 8:1-13)
by Albrecht Dürer

God was acclaimed as the Creator of the world. Those chapters depicted a harmonious universe in which the creatures and elders around the throne gave praise to God for bringing all things into being (4:11). The heavenly song of praise was taken up by "every creature in heaven and on earth and under the earth and in the sea, and all that is in them," so that every living thing glorified God and the Lamb (5:13). In Revelation 8, however, readers are given a negative vision that shows destruction rather than creation. Instead of heaven, earth, and sea resounding with songs of blessing to God for his power of creation, we see heaven, earth, and sea suffering the brunt of divine destruction (8:7-12). Readers might rightly ask why God would threaten to devastate the world that he made.

One clue to understanding these ominous visions is to consider what they do *not* do. The scenes do not unfold as simple predictions of a sequence of future disasters. We noted in the previous chapter that the threats represented by the seals in Revelation 6 — conquest, violence, economic hardship, and death — do not fall neatly on a time line, but are visionary messages that are designed to remove the readers' sense of security. After the sixth seal is opened, the sun becomes black, the moon becomes like blood, the stars fall, and the sky vanishes, which seems like a decisive end to the heavenly bodies (6:12-17); yet by Revelation 8, the sky and the heavenly bodies are back again so that they can become dark all over again in the new cycle of threats (8:7-12). Similarly, John clearly says that "all the green grass" is burned up in 8:7, yet in 9:4 the grass is apparently back again, because the demonic locust plague is told not to harm it. The peculiar way that the heavenly lights vanish then reappear and the grass suffers destruction only to return so that it can be protected is an important part of Revelation's manner of communication. These inconsistencies disrupt attempts to take the visions as a linear sequence of events that will unfold in a neat step-by-step fashion at some point in the future. Revelation gives the appearance of a sequence by numbering the visions according to trumpets one, two, three, and four, only to confuse the sequence by including details that do not fit the pattern.

The visions in Revelation 8–9 do not convey information that allows readers to discern how soon the end of time will come, but they do issue warnings that are designed to bring repentance. That repentance is the goal becomes clear when John points out how, despite the ominous events that he describes, the wicked "did not repent of the works of their hands or give up worshiping demons and idols" (9:20). Again, "they did not repent of their murders or their sorceries or their fornication or their thefts" (9:21). Although the language might seem stereotypical, it speaks to issues confronting Christians in the seven churches that were first addressed by Revelation. Prior to Rev. 9:20-21, the call to "repent" was directed to people associated with the congregations that were battling complacency, tendencies to assimilate into pagan culture, and lovelessness (2:5, 16, 21, 22; 3:3, 19). Revelation 2–3 rebukes those who favor an easy tolerance of idolatry, which is identified with immorality, the demonic, and the murder of Christians (2:13-14, 20-21, 24). If repentance involves "waking up" (3:2-3), the nightmarish visions signaled by the seven trumpets help to startle readers out of their drowsy complacency to a new awareness of the consequences of sin and evil.

Recognizing that repentance is the proper response to these visions helps to explain the stylized way that the passage strips away the readers' sense of security. Note that judgment does not immediately fall upon sinners, but afflicts the world around them, hemming them in with dangers in earth, sea, and sky. The first trumpet unleashes fire and hail — like the plagues that afflicted the Egyptians (Exod. 9:13-35) — which leads to a loss of vegetation on earth (Rev. 8:7). The second trumpet turns the sea into blood — again like a plague on Egypt (Exod. 7:17) — with a loss of sea creatures and ships (Rev. 8:9). In Revelation, ships are associated with the riches that the ungodly accumulate by trafficking with "Babylon," the symbol of greed, arrogance, and bloodshed (18:15-20). Thus the loss of ships means economic loss. The third trumpet brings "wormwood" and partially poisoned water (8:11), which recalls how Jeremiah said that God would make the ungodly "eat wormwood and give them poisoned water to drink" because of their idolatry (Jer. 23:15). The fourth trumpet begins to enclose the world in darkness, again recalling a plague that preceded Israel's liberation from Egypt (Exod. 10:21-29).

The mounting threats show that it is an illusion to think that one can find security apart from God and the Lamb. Revelation presses readers to identify with those who belong to the Lamb, rather than allying themselves with the world that stands apart from the Lamb. Neutrality is not an option. Consider the contrasting way in which "blood" is used in Revelation 7–8. On the one hand, the redeemed are washed in the blood of the Lamb (Rev. 7:14). On the other hand, the world that has shed the blood of the saints (6:10) is spattered with blood that falls from heaven with fire and hail, later finding itself awash in the blood of judgment, as a third of the sea is stained red (8:7, 9). The followers of the Lamb are promised a future in which they will not suffer from scorching heat (7:16), although the unfaithful will be threatened with fire from heaven (8:7, 8, 10). The Lamb will guide people to the springs of the water of life (7:17), whereas those who prefer not to drink his life-giving water will find that the springs of the earth will become bitter and deadly (8:11). Those who follow the Lamb will not be struck by the sun (7:16), but judgment means that the sun itself will be struck, along with the moon and stars (8:12).

The eerie screech of an eagle declares "Woe, woe, woe to the inhabitants of the earth, at the blasts of the other trumpets that the three angels are about to blow" (8:13).[1] In the wake of this ominous message, the fifth trumpet tightens the circle of threats still further (9:1-12). The first four trumpets hemmed people in on all sides, as disasters struck earth, sea, and sky; but now danger comes from yet another direction, from beneath the earth itself. Earlier, smoke ascended before God from the altar in heaven (8:4), and now smoke comes up from the shaft of the bottomless pit to engulf the world in its fumes (9:1-2). The text has a surreal quality that makes it impossible to situate in time and space — one would be hard-pressed to locate the shaft of the bottomless pit on a map — but the repulsive images that appear effectively display the horrors of falling under God's wrath.

The passage makes a sharp contrast between the inhabitants of the earth, who experience the brunt of divine judgment (8:13), and those that bear the seal or name of God, who are not harmed (9:4). When the contrast is posed so starkly, most readers would presumably want to identify with those who bear the seal of God, not with the inhabitants of the earth. For readers seeking to cope with day-to-day life in the seven churches depicted in Revelation 2-3, however, the contrast was not so clear. A number of the congregations seemed inclined to compromise their Christian commitments to identify more fully with the pagan world around them in the hope of avoiding negative judgments against them by others in society. The trumpets challenge such tenden-

---

1. The eagle in Dürer's woodcut on p. 96 uses "Ve, ve, ve" for the three woes.

cies by showing a reversed picture, in which the faithful are not endangered but protected, and the wider society is not in the position of passing judgment but of receiving judgment. Therefore, the text shows that those who hope to secure themselves by assimilating into the pagan culture are deceiving themselves.

Revelation depicts life under two forms of rule. The vision of the heavenly throne room in Revelation 4–5 showed a rightly ordered universe, in which creatures offered praise to their Creator and to the Lamb, who are worthy of power. But in Revelation 9, grotesque figures create a demonic parody of the created order, showing what conditions are like under the lordship of the king of the underworld, whose names Abaddon and Apollyon mean Destruction and Destroyer (9:11). Each of the winged creatures that attended the Creator had its own distinct face, one with a human face and another with the face of a lion, etc.; but the winged beings that accompany the Destroyer have a hideous collage of traits: lions' teeth protrude from human faces, while in front their chests are plated with iron and in back they have tails like scorpions. Where the elders in the heavenly throne room cast their crowns before God as they raised a harmonious song of praise (4:10-11), the demonic locusts continue to wear crowns on their heads as they raise a pounding and clanking roar, like chariots going into battle.

The judgment depicted here is not direct divine punishment, but a revelation of what it would mean for God to hand over the world to other powers. The horde of locusts that emerges from the hellish smoke is a plague reminiscent of the locusts that fell upon the Egyptians before the exodus (Exod. 10:1-20) and of the locusts that the prophet Joel took as a portent of the day of the Lord's judgment (Joel 1–2). Unlike natural locusts, which attack plants and leave people alone, these locusts reverse the pattern by attacking people and leaving plants alone; and where natural locusts destroy with their mouths, these locusts inflict pain with their tails (Rev. 9:3-5, 10). The result of their fiendish work is that the inhabitants of the earth no longer seek to embrace life and to escape the pain of death, but seek to embrace death and to escape the pain of life (9:6).

The sixth trumpet brings another vision with the same nightmarish quality as the previous one (9:13-19). A voice from the golden altar in heaven gives the command that four angels, who have been restrained at the river Euphrates, should be unleashed. For readers of

John's time, the Euphrates lay on the eastern frontier of the Roman Empire, where the Parthians posed a threat to the social and political order that had created peace and prosperity for many under Roman rule. Unlike the mounted bowman that appeared in 6:2, however, this vision goes beyond ordinary forms of conquest. John speaks of a cavalry force of two hundred million, whose destructive power comes primarily from the horses, who have the heads of lions and breathe lethal fire, smoke, and sulfur from their nostrils. These bizarre creatures also have serpent-like heads on the ends of their tails. Now the death that people sought during the locust plague in 9:6 is brought about as one-third of humanity dies (9:18).

The horrors that John depicts do not move the surviving inhabitants of the earth to repent (9:20-21), which in one sense is astonishing. Given the torrent of plagues that engulfs them, one might assume that the natural response would be to turn to God for deliverance from destruction. In another sense, however, their refusal to repent has its own peculiar logic, since those who are surrounded by evils might think that accommodating evil is the most natural way to survive. For example, when the fifth trumpet sounded, demonic hordes from the underworld swarmed over the earth with seemingly unstoppable force (9:1-11); and here the inhabitants of the earth respond to the onslaught not by opposing the demons but by "worshiping demons" through the practice of idolatry (9:20; cf. 1 Cor. 10:20). When the sixth trumpet sounded, the fire, smoke, and sulfur that spewed from the nostrils of millions of horrific cavalry left a third of humanity dead (Rev. 9:13-19); and in the midst of such murderous circumstances, people continue to carry out murders themselves (9:21). A cloud of smoke has wafted up from the gate of the underworld, spreading its hellish vapors over the earth (9:1-2). Therefore, it is perhaps not surprising that those who breathe the fog and filthy air mutter the incantations used in sorcery (9:21). If the trumpets were designed to bring repentance, they failed to do so. For repentance to occur, a different approach will need to be taken.

Judgment Interrupted (10:1-11)

The mounting specter of God's final catastrophic judgment upon the world seems to continue into Revelation 10, only to be interrupted by a voice from heaven. In the wake of humanity's refusal to repent, an angel descends, cloaked with cloud and rainbow, his face blazing like the sun and his legs burning like fire. With one foot placed on the sea and the other on the land, his fearsome appearance initially gives the impression that the end has come. His voice resounds like thunder, and in response, seven more thunders roar out what one would imagine to be the decisive negative verdict on the godless, which would unleash a last, devastating series of punishments upon the earth. But a voice from heaven interrupts the waves of terror by telling John, "Seal up what the seven thunders have said, and do not write it down" (10:4). The message of thunder is to remain sealed and unspoken. Like the rainbow that adorns him, the angel signals at least a temporary halt in the storm's fury.

The angel holds in his hand an open scroll (10:2) that can best be understood as the scroll that the Lamb received from God in 5:7, the scroll whose seals were opened in 6:1–8:1. One "mighty angel" drew attention to the scroll in God's hand in 5:2 and "another mighty angel" now brings the open scroll to John (10:1-2). Many assume that the contents of the scroll that the Lamb received from God were disclosed by the visions that appeared as the Lamb broke each of the seven seals, but this is almost certainly not the case. It seems more plausible to think that the message on the scroll is revealed after all of its seals are broken so that the document can be unrolled and read. Revelation tells how the seals on the scroll in God's hand were broken by the Lamb so that an angel can now give the open scroll to John. This procedure follows the sequence that John described at the beginning of the book, where he said that his message came from God, who gave it to Jesus, who in turn sent it through an angel, who finally gave it to John (1:1).

If the warning judgments represented by the seals and trumpets in 6:1–9:21 were preparatory visions that were designed to move people to repentance, the angel's words continue to reverse the impression that God's purposes are ultimately destructive rather than saving. In the wake of visions that depict disasters in earth, sea, and sky, the angel with the scroll raises his right hand and swears an oath by the God "who lives forever and ever, who created heaven and what is in it, the earth and what is in it, and the sea and what is in it" (10:6). The angel's words echo the praises offered to the Creator by the chorus in the heavenly throne room (4:11) and the song that living things in earth, sea, and sky came to share through the work of the Lamb (5:13). According to the angel, God's fundamental identity is that of Creator, not destroyer.

The angel also declares that when the seventh angel blows his trumpet, "the mystery of God will be fulfilled, as he announced to his servants the prophets" (10:7). The Greek word that is commonly translated "announced" is *euangelizein,* which means to speak good news. It is related to the word *euangelion* or "gospel." Therefore, when the seventh trumpet blows and readers learn that "the kingdom of the world has become the kingdom of our Lord and of his Christ" (Rev. 11:15), they encounter "good news." This message is consistent with the prophetic visions Israel's prophets spoke concerning the coming of God's kingdom (Isa. 2:1-4; Mic. 4:1-5; Zech. 14:16). Accordingly, when John depicts the accomplishment of God's purposes in its fullest form in Rev. 21:1-22:5, he describes the New Jerusalem in language taken from Isaiah, Ezekiel, Zechariah, and other prophetic writings. The element of "mystery" pertains not so much to the goal of God's saving purposes as it does to the means by which God will attain the goal. Therefore, the visions in Revelation 11 will disclose to readers how the suffering of God's servants mysteriously helps to bring about the conversion of the ungodly (cf. Rom. 16:25-26).

The angel gives the open scroll to John to eat (Rev. 10:9-10), so that after John has taken the message into himself, he will be able to reveal its contents (cf. Ezek. 2:8–3:3). The angel tells John, "You must prophesy again about many peoples and nations and languages and kings" (Rev. 10:11). Readers have already learned that the Lamb's blood "ransomed for God saints from every tribe and language and people and nation" (5:9) and that this diverse group joins in celebration in the presence of God (7:9). But if God's witnesses come *from* every nation, they also bear a message that pertains *to* every nation. John will speak of the community of faith being oppressed and of God's witnesses offering testimony at the cost of their own lives. Although John will warn that members of "peoples and tribes and languages and nations" will oppose the faithful and fall prey to evil powers (11:10; 13:7), he will also call those of "every nation and tribe and language and people" to worship and give glory to God (14:6-7). Although Revelation warns that judgment will fall upon the ungodly, it extends hope that the saints will rejoice when people from "all nations" come to worship God after his judgments have been revealed (15:4; Bauckham, *Theology,* 83-84).

The visions that encapsulate the message of the scroll show that the suffering and witness of the followers of the Lamb will play a role in bringing inhabitants of the earth to repentance, so that many will give glory to God (11:13). If readers were inclined to make a simple contrast between the inhabitants of the earth, who suffer under divine judgment, and the people of God, who are spared (9:4), they will soon realize that the situation is more complex. John will continue to make a sharp distinction between faithfulness to God and idolatry, but he will also caution that the faithful will suffer as they bear witness to the truth. Not surprisingly, John experiences the message as both sweet and bitter (10:10). The message of the scroll is sweet to the extent that it promises protection for the faithful as God carries out his just and saving purposes, but it is bitter in that ultimately the accomplishment of these purposes involves the suffering of God's people and the deaths of his witnesses.

Suffering, Witness, and Conversion (11:1-14)

The angel promises that there "will be no more delay, but in the days when the seventh angel is to blow his trumpet, the mystery of God will be fulfilled" (10:6-7). This heightens the sense of expectation that the end will come immediately, yet the seventh trumpet does not blow. Instead, the interlude continues with a vision that contains a summary of John's message. In brief, almost cryptic form, this section introduces the beast that rises from the abyss to make war on the saints (11:7). The conflict between the beast and the people of God will be described at length in Revelation 12–19, but here John offers readers a summary of the message. The visions in Revelation 11 serve as an overture to the last half of the book.

Community of Faith as Oppressed Temple (11:1-2)

John is given a rod with which to measure the temple, the altar, and those who worship there; but he is told not to measure the temple's outer court, for that is to be given over to the nations who will trample the holy city for forty-two months (11:1-2). There is already a shift in that it is not the godless inhabitants of the world who suffer, as it was under the fifth trumpet; it is rather the people of God who are oppressed.

The way people understand this vision is shaped in large part by the assumptions that they make about Revelation itself. Those who assume that Revelation makes direct predictions of future events commonly take this passage literally, as a reference to a new temple being built in Jerusalem. In contrast, those who find that Revelation communicates with readers through symbolic language interpret the temple as a symbol of the Christian community. We will consider each interpretation in turn.

Literalistic interpretations of the places that are mentioned in 11:1-2 note that the first Jerusalem temple was destroyed by the Babylonians in 587 B.C. and the second temple was razed by the Romans in A.D. 70. Therefore, if Revelation makes direct predictions of future events, the passage must mean that the temple will be rebuilt. Those who worship in the "temple" are assumed to be Jews, and the reference to the "altar" is taken to mean that the sacrifices prescribed by Jewish Law will be resumed, after having been discontinued when the second temple was destroyed. Along with the rebuilding of the temple is the prospect of the "holy city," Jerusalem, being overrun by Gentile nations for forty-two months. Many who follow this approach comb news reports from the Middle East for signs that the prophecy is coming to pass (see pp. 19-26 above).

Literalistic interpretations of the time mentioned in 11:1-2 also maintain that these events will unfold during the first half of a seven-year period of tribulation that will occur before Christ's second coming. The belief that the tribulation will last for precisely seven years is based on the reference to such a period in Dan. 9:27. Proponents of this idea argue that Revelation, like Daniel, divides the period into two equal parts, each lasting for forty-two months (Rev. 11:2; 13:5), which is the same as 1260 days (11:3; 12:6) or three and a half "times" or years (12:14). During the first half of the tribulation they expect the threats against Jerusalem to increase, and during the second half, they anticipate the Antichrist to extend his power until he is defeated during the battle of Armageddon at the end of the seven-year period.

A very different and more plausible understanding of the places mentioned in this passage takes the "temple" and the "holy city" as metaphors for the Christian community. The vision of God's "temple" being oppressed does not have to do with a location hundreds of miles removed from the Christians in Asia Minor, who were first addressed by Revelation. The vision calls readers to faithfulness in their own conflicted contexts. The pervasive use of symbolic language in previous visions — the Lamb is Christ, a mounted bowman represents conquest, etc. — prepares readers in a general way to discern the symbolism in 11:1-2. Moreover, even though John was commanded to "measure" the temple, the altar, and the worshipers, the text shows no interest in the physical dimensions of the sanctuary. The importance of the command is in what it signifies: the preservation of true service to God.

More specific preparation to understand the symbolism was given in 3:12, where Christ promised that the faithful would be made into pillars in the "temple" of God and that they would be named for God's own "city." A "temple" that has human beings as its pillars is not a building made of stone, but is a community of people. Moreover, the temple is the place where priests serve, and according to 1:6 and 5:10, all who have been cleansed by the blood of the Lamb are priests. The "temple" is a suitable way to describe their priestly community. Similarly, to say that the faithful will be called the "city" of God shows that the "holy city" is an apt metaphor for the holy community, the assembly of the faithful. Referring to the church as a "temple" is not unique to Revelation, since it was an important metaphor among Christians of John's time (1 Cor. 3:16; 2 Cor. 6:16; Eph. 2:20; 1 Pet. 2:5). John develops this common metaphor in visionary form.

Taking the "temple" and "holy city" as metaphors for the Christian community also fits the immediate context, where God's faithful witnesses are called "lampstands" (Rev. 11:3-4). Both the first and second temples included lampstands among their principal furnishings (1 Kings 7:49; Josephus, *Jewish War* 5.217). If the "temple" in Rev. 11:2 represents the Christian community, it makes sense to use the image of the lampstand for Christian witnesses. John prepared readers to take the imagery in this way by explaining that lampstands symbolize Christian congregations in 1:20, and he makes clear that the lampstands are human beings by referring to their prophetic testimony and deaths in 11:4-10.

Like the references to places, the three-and-a-half-year time span mentioned in this passage can best be taken in a symbolic way. John can invoke this time period because it was identified with oppression in Daniel (Dan. 7:25; 9:27; 12:7), but the context helps to show that it cannot be taken in strictly chronological terms. The broad context of the book regularly refers to periods of time in non-literal ways. For example, when John says that the allies of the beast receive power for "one hour" (Rev. 17:12), it is difficult to believe that he is predicting a future political alliance that will last for precisely sixty minutes. Moreover, John connects the three-and-a-half-year period with multiple images that do not fall into a temporal sequence. In 11:1-2, the span is depicted as a time when the community of faith or "temple" is threatened; in 12:6 and 12:14 it is the time when the woman who represents the people of God flees to the wilderness to escape Satan the dragon; and in 13:5 it is the period in which the beast, who is the dragon's agent, oppresses the saints. Together the various three-and-one-half-year periods depicted in these chapters add up to more than seven years, indicating that they represent overlapping realities.

The figure of three and a half was a common way to speak about a limited period of affliction. According to 1 Kings 18:1, Elijah called a drought that lasted into a third year, but in tradition the period was said to have lasted for three and a half years (Luke 4:25; James 5:17). John plays on the number by shifting from speaking about three and a half *years* of oppression to speaking about three and a half *days* during which God's witnesses lie dead before the eyes of the inhabitants of the world (Rev. 11:9, 11). Forms of the number three and a half help to identify a time of oppression in these chapters, but the ever-changing ways in which this period is depicted caution against taking it in a strictly chronological sense.

In summary, the vision of the temple in 11:1-2 represents the Christian community being preserved despite threats by the unbelieving world to overwhelm it. The inner part of the sanctuary, which is kept safe from the nations, is the community in which true worship continues. The comment about the outer court being given over to the nations cautions that God will allow a part of the community to come under the sway of the pagan world. The seven churches addressed by Revelation were already aware of this possibility, as some contended with groups and individuals who encouraged the faithful to compromise their convictions by assimilating more readily into pagan culture (2:14-15, 20-25), and others experienced overt hostility from non-

Christians (2:8-11; 3:8-9). Nevertheless, John is told to "measure" the temple, that is, to mark out a holy sphere in the confidence that God will preserve a place for the faithful despite these threats.

Two Witnesses (11:3-14)

The threat of the community being overwhelmed by the non-Christian world does not mean that the faithful retreat. Instead, John depicts two "witnesses" prophesying during the period when the "temple" or community of faith is oppressed. The character of their message is indicated by the sackcloth that they wear, which indicates that they are calling people to repentance. Wearing sackcloth was a sign of mourning and penitence, since those who understood themselves to be under judgment had reason to humble themselves before God (Job 42:6; Dan. 9:3; Jonah 3:6; Matt. 11:21). This form of witness suits a context in which the plagues that occurred under the first six trumpets failed to bring humankind to repentance (Rev. 9:20-21). These witnesses indicate that the opportunity for repentance is still available even as the community is besieged.

The two witnesses represent the community of faithful Christians. The witnesses are depicted as lampstands, and in 1:20 the lampstands represented Christian congregations. Although the vision specifically refers to "two" witnesses, the implication is not that faithful Christians will be found in only two places. Rather, the imagery fits the practice of providing two witnesses to sustain a truth claim in court (Deut. 19:15). The term "witness" suggests that the faithful are bound to speak the truth in disputed situations, like the witnesses that testify in a courtroom. Moreover, to be "witnesses" means to continue the legacy of the crucified and risen Jesus, who has already been called God's faithful "witness" (Rev. 1:5; 3:14). John has already applied the title "witness" to the Christian named Antipas, who was slain for his faith (2:13; cf. 17:6), and the two "witnesses" depicted in 11:3-13 extend the role of faithful witnessing to the faithful more broadly.

As figures that stand for the faithful generally, the two witnesses encompass the traits of individuals from many periods in the history of God's people. Calling them olive trees and lampstands recalls how Joshua the high priest and Zerubbabel the governor — who led Israel during the time of Persian domination — were depicted as olive trees whose oil supplied a golden lampstand (11:4; Zech. 3:1-4:14). The faithful of John's time embody these traits during a time of Roman domination, when they constitute a "kingdom" that recognizes the sovereignty of God, and serve as faithful "priests" to the Creator of heaven and earth (Rev. 1:6; 5:10). The speech of the two witnesses can be compared to fire pouring from their mouths, which was a trait of the prophet Jeremiah, who bore witness during the time that the Babylonians besieged Jerusalem and its temple (Jer. 5:14; Rev. 11:5).

Other elements reinforce the impression that the witnesses encompass traits from the people of God in many periods of time. They are like the prophet Elijah, who called fire from heaven and shut up the heavens so that rain would not fall during a period in which rulers promoted the worship of false gods among the people (Rev. 11:5-6; 1 Kings 17:1; 18:38; 2 Kings 1:10). They are also like Moses, who had power to turn water into blood and to send plagues upon the earth while Israel was in bondage in Egypt (Rev. 11:6; Exod. 7:17-21). Although there were traditions that Moses and Elijah were to return before the Day of the Lord, both witnesses encompass all the traits mentioned above.

The final element of their witness is their faithfulness to the point of death, following the way of Jesus (Rev. 11:7-10). Elijah was said to have been taken directly to heaven, so that he did not experience death (2 Kings 2:11), but the witnesses depicted here share in the fate of those prophets who were slain for speaking the word of God, and in the fate of Jesus, who was crucified (Matt. 23:30-31, 37; Acts 7:52). Their forceful prophesying in the face of opposition culminates not in the annihilation of their opponents, but in their own martyrdom. Their faithfulness does not lend protection from death, for they are subjected to the dreaded fate of being denied burial (Rev. 11:9). Vindication only comes later, after death. In this they follow Jesus, who was crucified and later raised to heavenly glory.

The deaths of these witnesses are parabolic of the fate of the faithful in many times and places. Although John says that the witnesses are killed in "the great city" where Jesus was crucified (11:7-8), the passage cannot be limited to one place on earth. The scene has a surreal quality in which places have more to do with characteristics of good and evil than with specific locations. The adversary of the faithful is a beast that

109

comes from the bottomless pit (11:7). The entry to the pit cannot be located on a map, but it refers to the origin of evil powers, as in 9:1-2. When John refers to the place where Jesus was crucified, he does not mention the name of Jerusalem. Instead, he identifies the place as Sodom and Egypt (11:8), evoking memories of the infamous sins of Sodom that warranted the destruction of the city by fire (Gen. 18:20; 19:24) and of Egypt's oppression of the people of Israel (Exod. 1:8-14).

The city where the faithful are killed is called "the great city" (Rev. 11:8), which can refer to the whole realm in which oppression takes place. In kaleidoscopic fashion, the title "great city" is here associated with Jerusalem, Sodom, and Egypt. Elsewhere it refers to Babylon (14:8; 16:19; 17:18; 18:10, 16, 18, 19, 21), which in turn is another name for Rome, the city built on seven hills (17:9), the city that is glutted with "the blood of the prophets and saints, and of *all who have been slaughtered on the earth*" (18:24). Those who gaze upon the bodies of the witnesses are not simply the residents of Jerusalem, but "members of the peoples and tribes and languages and nations" (11:9), and the deaths of the faithful are known and celebrated by "the inhabitants of the earth" (11:10). The parabolic quality of the scene will be emphasized later, when the heavenly chorus says that "the nations" raged (11:18).

The passage has to do with the witness of the faithful to the world and of their ultimate vindication through resurrection from the dead. After their dead bodies have served as a spectacle to the world, the breath of life enters them, and they stand on their feet, like the dry bones that Ezekiel saw coming back to life (Rev. 11:11; Ezek. 37:5, 10). Like Christ, they are taken up to heaven (Rev. 11:12). The song of praise that resounds at the end of this chapter shows that the resurrection of these witnesses represents the resurrection of all the faithful. The vision shows readers what the heavenly chorus means when it declares that the time has come "for judging the dead" and "for rewarding your servants, the prophets and saints and all who fear your name, both small and great" (11:18). In this passage we see an image of the suffering and vindication of the people of God.

In the end, judgment does fall upon the nations, but its force is blunted. John says that an earthquake occurred "and a tenth of the city fell; seven thousand people were killed in the earthquake" (11:13). The progression toward total judgment, which seemed unstoppable in the series of visions that were recounted in Revelation 8–9, is now reversed.

Each of those visions spoke of disaster falling upon a third of the earth, culminating with the specter of death for a third of humanity (9:18). At the end of Revelation 11, however, destruction falls on only one-tenth of the city, which means that nine-tenths of the people are spared. To sense the magnitude of the change, consider how this reverses a broader biblical pattern. Isaiah warned that God's judgment would fall so widely that only a tenth would survive it, and that even that tenth would be burned again (Isa. 6:13). Similarly, Amos warned that when God's judgment came, nine-tenths would meet destruction (Amos 5:3). In Revelation, however, the opposite is true, for nine-tenths are saved and only one tenth is destroyed (Bauckham, *Theology*, 87).

After the earth experienced the horrors of the first six trumpets, people stubbornly persisted in idolatry and refused to repent (Rev. 9:20-21), but here nine-tenths of the people give glory to God, which is what the heavenly chorus did with their songs of praise (4:11; 5:13; 7:12). The witness, death, and vindication of the community of faith accomplish what the prospect of judgment alone does not do. It brings people of many tribes, languages, and nations to fear God and to give him glory. Note that in the days of Elijah — whose legacy is carried on by the two witnesses, as noted above — all but seven thousand people embraced idolatry (1 Kings 19:18). In Revelation, however, the situation is reversed, for all but seven thousand now give glory to God (Rev. 11:13). The conversion of the nations, rather than their destruction, is God's will for the world (14:7). The glimpse of the fulfillment of God's purposes that is given here is developed more fully in the final chapters of Revelation, where kings and nations again give glory to God and the Lamb in the greatest of all cities, the New Jerusalem (21:24-26).

The Kingdom of the Lord (11:15-19)

John prefaces the blowing of the seventh trumpet with the warning that "woe" is coming; but in predictably unpredictable fashion he follows that warning of woe with a song of celebration rather than a lament. John raises readers' expectations by announcements of things to come, but as soon as he establishes a pattern, he alters it so that readers cannot be confident of their own abilities to anticipate what God will do next. Earlier, John said that three "woes" would come, one at the sound of each remaining trumpet (8:13). When the fifth trumpet blew and a horde of locusts appeared, John indicated that the first "woe" had occurred (9:12). Therefore, when the sixth trumpet leads to the deaths of a third of humanity, readers might expect John to announce that the second "woe" has occurred, but John does not do so. Instead, he strangely delays the announcement of the second "woe" until a lesser judgment has occurred and humanity gives glory to God (11:13-14).

When John warns that "the third woe is coming very soon" (11:14), readers might expect it to occur when the angel blows the seventh and final trumpet, but again John surprises them. Instead of hearing about destruction, as one would expect after a warning of "woe," readers learn that "the kingdom of the world has become the kingdom of our Lord and of his Christ" (11:15). The page is flooded with yet another vision of the twenty-four elders worshiping God and singing a song of praise to him, as they have done in previous scenes of heavenly worship (4:9-11; 5:8-14; 7:11-12). Previously, God has been acclaimed as the one "who was and is and is to come" (4:8). Here, however, only the past and present tenses are used, as they speak to God as "you . . . who are and who were" (11:17). The omission of the future tense suggests that the end has arrived.

So should the end be understood as "woe" (11:14) or as a celebration of God's reign (11:15)? The answer to the question will depend on the reader's perspective. On the one hand, those who are willing to acknowledge God's sovereignty, as the twenty-four elders do by stepping down from their thrones and bowing before God, will hear the news of God's reign as a reason to rejoice (11:16-17). On the other hand, if God reigns, this will be woeful for those who seek to take God's place. The coming of God's kingdom brings "woe" to the nations who rage against him, for their position will be lost, and it brings "woe" to those who oppress the servants of God, for God will give those servants the reward that is due to the faithful (11:18).

God's kingdom does not bring the destruction of the world, but the destruction of "those who destroy the earth" (11:18). This announcement puts on notice the evil forces that have already been unleashed as well as those that will appear in subsequent chapters. The Creator opposes the "Destroyer" that emerged from the shaft that leads to the underworld (9:1, 11), the dragon that is cast down to earth (12:9), and the beast who allies himself with other powers to oppress the people of God (11:7; 13:1-18; 17:1-18). The victory of God that is announced here will be depicted at greater length in Revelation's final chapters. The coming of God's kingdom does not simply mean that people are plucked from the mire of this world to find safety in heaven. The Creator seeks the liberation of the world itself from the forces that hold it captive (Rom. 8:18-25).

The opening of the heavenly temple and the appearing of the ark of the covenant are a vivid way to convey the continuing sense of threat and hope that attend God's reign (Rev. 11:19). The ark of the covenant was a gold-plated box in which the people of Israel enshrined the tablets of the law that summarized their covenant relationship with God. Since Moses was said to have patterned the ark after a heavenly original (Exod. 25:9-10), many assumed that one would find an ark in heaven even though the earthly ark was apparently lost when the first temple was destroyed by the Babylonians in 587 B.C. The ark was associated with the presence of God. Concealed in the inner chamber of the sanctuary, it was the place where God met with the representatives of the people (Exod. 25:22).

The appearance of the ark in Rev. 11:19 is a signal that people should be prepared to meet God, but such a meeting can bring either blessing or judgment. The penitent can hope to find favor with God, but those who oppose God can expect to encounter his judgment. In former times, the ark of the covenant brought the presence of God into battle against Israel's enemies (Josh. 6:13); and here it marks the beginning of a new series of battles against those who oppose God and the coming of his kingdom. God's temple is open. The Almighty is not confined there. The lightning, thunder, earthquake, and hail portend disaster for his adversaries (Rev. 11:19).

Chapter 5

THE BEAST AND THE LAMB

Revelation 12–15

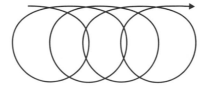

Act I of Revelation concluded with the blowing of the seventh trumpet and the announcement that "the kingdom of the world has become the kingdom of our Lord and of his Christ" (11:15). The cycle of devastating plagues had ended, God's slain witnesses had returned to life, judgment had fallen on a part of humanity, and the rest ascribed glory to God. The twenty-four elders, who regularly appeared in scenes of heavenly celebration, returned to the stage singing praises to God for taking the royal power that was rightfully his (11:16). But as the chorus of praise resounded in the celestial halls, an ominous undertone could be heard, indicating that the end of Act I was not the end of the drama, for the time had come to "destroy those who destroy the earth" (11:18).

As the curtain rises on Act II, the audience prepares for a renewed attack of divine powers that will culminate in the final destruction of the forces of evil. There have already been intimations of the direction that the story will take. In the visions of the temple under siege and of the two witnesses giving testimony at the cost of their own lives, Christian readers could see how their own communities were called to bear witness to God's truth in the face of social opposition and threat. A mysterious beast ascended from the smoke of the bottomless pit just long enough to slaughter God's witnesses before vanishing as quickly as it came (11:7); but it will soon be back so that readers can see more starkly the powers that oppose the faithful. The previous chapter showed that God's witnesses did not suffer in vain, for God vindicated them and brought many to repentance; but the sinister presence of the beast and other powers must be brought to an end.

A few program notes on Act II can help anticipate the story that will unfold in Revelation 12–22. The drama that spans the last half of the book traces the defeat of Satan, who is cast down from heaven to earth, and from earth to the abyss. In the course of the action, Satan seeks to operate through other agents, including two beasts and a harlot, but God and the Lamb eventually thwart the efforts of these "destroyers of the earth." The progression of the plot continues to follow shorter cycles of visions that convey warnings and promises of blessing, but the overall sequence of events is highly stylized and can be outlined as follows:

> Satan thrown from heaven to earth (Rev. 12)
>   beast and false prophet conquer (Rev. 13)
>   harlot rides on the beast (Rev. 17)
>   harlot destroyed by the beast (Rev. 17)
>   beast and false prophet conquered (Rev. 19)
> Satan thrown from earth into the abyss (Rev. 20)

The outline shows how John systematically introduces Satan, the beast and false prophet, and finally the harlot into the drama, and how in reverse order he describes the defeats of the harlot, the beast and false prophet, and finally Satan himself. The last piece in the sequence occurs almost as an anticlimax when the Devil is momentarily released, only to be cast into the lake of fire (20:7-10).

The story of the triumph of God over evil unfolds on a cosmic scale. Ordinary limitations of time and space do not apply, for the warring parties traverse a battlefield that stretches from the heights of heaven to the abyss beneath the earth. A woman appears in the sky with her feet above the moon and stars encircling her head, yet she flees from heaven to seek refuge on earth (12:1, 6). Her adversary the dragon has a serpentine tail that sweeps across the vastness of the night sky, brushing myriads of stars down to the ground (12:4). Angelic warriors grapple with the dragon and his henchmen in the skies, sending them tumbling from space to earth where the battle continues (12:7-12). The dragon angrily dusts itself off in order to embark on a new chase scene, and the woman who once stood above the moon sprouts wings so that she can fly away from the dragon (12:13-14). In what modern audiences would consider a feat of animation, a river gushes out of the dragon's mouth, while the earth opens a mouth of its own in order to swallow the river (12:15-16).

Modern readers may find the cosmic drama played out in Revelation 12–22 to be something like a movie that thrills audiences with special effects, as heroes and villains traverse the galaxies in battles for control of the universe. Such a comparison to modern popular culture does not trivialize Revelation, but actually offers a way to understand what the book is doing. John's audience lived within a wider culture that had its own heroes and image makers, its rumors and stereotypes, its rituals and graffiti. Christians faced the continual challenge of discerning how far they could go in embracing non-Christian practices, and at what point they needed to resist. The description of the seven churches in Revelation 2–3 shows that Christian nonconformists were sometimes treated violently by non-Christians; but a more insidious threat was the power of popular culture to seduce Christians into compromising their convictions and relaxing into complacency (see chapter 2 above). John grapples with the icons of the popular culture of his day in order to unmask them, so that when readers see the realities that lie behind the facades, they might better resist compromise and persevere in faith.

Revelation 12–15 consists of a short cycle of visions within the longer drama. The visions depict a messianic war that extends from Christ's incarnation (12:5) to his second coming (14:14-20). Readers of John's time and readers of our own time live in between these two events. All who look back to Christ's first coming and await his second coming find themselves called to endure amid competing claims upon their loyalties (13:10; 14:12). The struggle is intense, but in the end John brings readers back to the heavenly throne room, where the saints who have overcome the beast sing praises to God and the Lamb as they have at the end of previous cycles (15:1-4).

The Woman, Michael, and the Dragon (12:1-18)

Stories of the battle between the forces of good and evil help to win the audience's loyalties to the side of good and to alienate them from evil. In one such story that circulated in John's time, the antagonist was a fierce dragon named Python and the protagonist was a woman named Leto, who was the mother of the god Apollo. When Leto became pregnant by the god Zeus, the dragon pursued her in order to kill her and her child. The north wind rescued Leto by carrying her away, so that she eventually found refuge on the island of Delos, which lay in the Aegean Sea. There the woman gave birth to Apollo and Artemis. Four days later, Apollo set off in pursuit of the dragon, soon slaying the creature to avenge his mother.

Roman emperors were able to put the tale to good use by associating themselves with Apollo, whose defeat of the evil dragon was said to have ushered in an age of peace and prosperity. Citizens of the empire could be expected to identify the woman in the story with the goddess Roma, who was the queen of heaven. Her son would be the Roman emperor, who overcame the forces of evil and chaos so that light and peace could flood the world. Caesar Augustus was hailed as a new Apollo, for his reign was said to mark the beginning of a new golden age. The emperor Nero liked to present himself in the guise of Apollo, his image on coins bearing the radiant beams from his head that were Apollo's trademark.

When John tells about a pregnant woman and a dragon in Revelation 12, Christians in the seven churches would have heard echoes of the familiar story of Leto, but they would also find that John's version reverses the usual implications of the tale, so that in his version the woman in labor is not a pagan goddess, but the people of God; the child is not the emperor but Christ; and the dragon represents the forces that oppose Christ and threaten his church. In the end, a story that was used to celebrate the popular culture is now transformed in a way that helps readers resist being assimilated to that culture.

The Dragon Threatens the Woman and Child (12:1-6)

The story begins when John sees a "sign" emerging in heaven, almost like a constellation coming to life in the evening sky. As John looks at the heavens, he sees the figure of a woman, who is clothed with the sun and has the moon under her feet. The twelve stars around her head form a crown, which is the symbol of victory and rule (4:4, 10). The woman is pregnant and cries out in labor pains as she prepares to give birth to the child who is "to rule all the nations with a rod of iron" (12:5). The description of the child is taken from Psalm 2, which speaks of the Lord's anointed one or "messiah," who is called the Son of God, the one who will be given the nations as his heritage. The Hebrew version of the psalm says that the anointed one will "break" the nations with a rod of iron, but the Greek version says that he will "rule" or literally "shepherd" the nations with his iron rod (Ps. 2:9). This image threatens the opponents of God, for it points to their demise (Rev. 2:27; 19:15); yet the same image is encouraging for the people of God, for Christ "shepherds" them by leading them to living water (7:17).

As John continues to look at the heavens, a fiery red dragon appears among the stars. People envisioned a dragon as a grotesque reptile with four legs and a long tail that writhed like a serpent (12:9; Isa. 27:1). The terrifying monster in John's vision has seven heads and ten horns, and it is so huge that its twitching tail sends down showers of stars that empty a third of the sky of light. The reason for the dragon's hatred of the woman and her child is not stated, but is evident in its appearance: the seven diadems on the monster's head show that it aspires to reign. The woman who wears a crown of stars and the child who is to rule the nations are the dragon's rivals, and he must destroy them. By communicating in this way, John can expect readers to identify with the woman and child, and to be repulsed by a monster that wants to make a meal out of a newborn. The effect is that readers who identify with the child identify with Christ, and set themselves against the powers that seek to destroy the Messiah.

The dragon's threat against the woman and her child backfires. Instead of destroying his rivals, the monster's crude attempt to devour the child results in the child being enthroned in heaven while the woman escapes to a place of refuge. Christian readers of Revelation would recognize that John's vision points to Christ's deliverance from death and to his exaltation to heavenly reign through his resurrection. Although this visionary account moves directly from birth to enthronement without mentioning the crucifixion (cf. Rom. 1:3-4), Jesus' death is presupposed rather than forgotten. John clearly assumes that his readers know that the Messiah died (Rev. 1:5, 7, 18; 5:6, 9, 12) and he will soon emphasize the saving effect of Jesus' blood (12:11). This vision is not designed to repeat what readers already know, but to stress that Christ's death was not a triumph for evil, appearances notwithstanding. The dragon threatened Christ, but in the end it is Christ and not the dragon that ends up on the throne (5:6; 7:17; 12:5).

Michael and the Dragon (12:7-12)

Christ's enthronement does not usher in a period of peace and tranquility, but becomes the catalyst for an epic battle in heaven. Christ is the one who is to "rule all the nations" (12:5), but his rule does not come unopposed. With the exalted Christ on the throne, the angelic figure Michael mounts a massive attack on the dragon that sought to destroy Christ. Michael is the angelic "prince" who defeats the powers that oppose Israel (Dan. 10:13, 21); he is the heavenly "protector" of God's people (Dan. 12:1) and opponent of the Devil (Jude 9). Much of the lore about Michael the archangel comes from sources outside the Bible, but Revelation assumes that readers are familiar with this commander of the angels. Moreover, since Michael fights on behalf of God's people, those who understand themselves to be people of God can assume that Michael fights on their behalf.

Michael's assault defeats the dragon, who now is explicitly identified as the Devil and Satan, and this defeat dramatically limits the area in which Satan can operate. Instead of being able to work in heaven, denouncing the saints before God (Rev. 12:10), Satan is banished from heaven so that he must restrict his operations to the earth. Although modern readers sometimes assume that this passage refers to Satan's fall from heaven at the dawn of time, this is not the case.[1] Revelation 12

---

1. The idea that Satan was originally one of God's angels, who rebelled and fell from heaven at the dawn of time, is a composite picture that is pieced together from various passages in Scripture. Isaiah 14:12-15 speaks of the Day Star being cast down to Sheol for arrogantly trying to rule over God. Jude 6 refers to the angels that did not keep to their proper place, who are now kept in chains in deep darkness. The serpent that tempted Eve is not identified as Satan in Genesis 3, but later passages do speak of sin and death entering the world through Satan (Wis. 2:24). On the other hand, Isa. 27:1 speaks of a future defeat of a great dragon, and Luke 10:18-19 says that Jesus saw Satan falling like lightning as his followers cast out demons.

Michael Battling Satan the Dragon (Rev. 12:7-9)
by Albrecht Dürer

depicts a battle that takes place as a consequence of Christ's resurrection and enthronement (12:5, 11). Note that Michael's triumph over Satan does not mean that Satan is sent from heaven to earth for the first time, for Satan was about the business of deceiving "the whole world" long before his battle with Michael (12:9). As John envisions the situation, Satan had access to earth and heaven before his war with Michael, but Satan loses a massive amount of territory as a result of the war, for he no longer has access to heaven. The Devil's ferocity stems in large part from being hemmed in.

Voices from heaven announce the meaning of the heavenly battle, much as the chorus that stands at the side of the stage in a Greek play helps the audience interpret the action. The chorus declares that with the enthronement of Christ and the expulsion of Satan the dragon, salvation has come (12:10). Two dimensions of salvation receive special attention.

First, Satan's expulsion from heaven means that he no longer is in a position to denounce the saints before God (12:10). The Hebrew word *satan* means "adversary," and the Old Testament pictured Satan as the member of God's heavenly court who accused people of sin. For example, God considered Job to be righteous, but Satan insisted that Job was not truly good (Job 1:6-12; 2:1-6). Similarly, Zechariah saw a vision in which a high priest appeared in filthy clothing, and Satan stood by to denounce him; but God refused to heed Satan and took away the priest's guilt, clothing him in clean festive garments (Zech. 3:1-5). Similarly, Revelation announces that all the people of God are priests who have been cleansed by the blood of the Lamb, so that they can be clothed in white garments (Rev. 1:5-6; 5:9-10; 7:9-14). By portraying Christ as the slaughtered Lamb, Revelation reinforces the idea that Christ's death is the sacrifice that purifies people from sin. Satan's expulsion from heaven shows that Christ's blood effectively "conquers" the Devil (12:11), because it means that he no longer has any business denouncing the saints whom Christ has cleansed (cf. Rom. 8:33-34).

Second, the heavenly voices seek to reverse ordinary perceptions of the faithful who suffer on earth. Earlier in Revelation, John spoke of the forces of Satan threatening the church, imprisoning believers, and killing the faithful (Rev. 2:10, 13). Therefore, Christian readers might conclude that the deaths of the faithful constituted victories for the Devil. But throughout Revelation, true conquering and true victory are accomplished through faith. Those who remain faithful, even to death, and who refuse to give up their commitments "conquer" Satan, because they do not submit to his will (12:11). In the eyes of the world, Christians who lose their lives in order to remain true to the Christian faith suffer a tremendous defeat; but in the eyes of heaven, they are triumphant because they share in the victory of the crucified and risen Lamb.

Finally, the story of Satan's expulsion from heaven offers readers incentive to persevere, despite the ongoing threat of evil. From an earthly perspective, evil can seem so pervasive as to be unstoppable. Where the wicked prosper and the righteous suffer, the Devil seems to reign. From a heavenly perspective, however, evil rages on earth not because it is so powerful, but because it is so vulnerable. Revelation likens Satan to a rogue animal that the forces of God have corralled, driving it off the expansive plains of heaven into the fenced-in area of earth. The beast rampages within its newly limited circumstances, seeking to do as much damage as possible during the short time that remains until the company of heaven slips the noose around its head, binds its legs, and chains it up so that it can do no further damage (12:11; 20:2). Those who think that Satan rages because he is invincible will give up in despair, but those who recognize that Satan rages on earth because he has already lost heaven and is now desperate have reason to resist him, confident that God will prevail.

The Dragon Pursues the Woman and Her Children (12:13-17)

The final scene in this chapter resumes the story of the woman who escaped from the dragon to find refuge in the wilderness (12:6). We now learn that the woman represents the people of God. At the beginning of the chapter, the woman was shown to be the mother of the Messiah, who is to rule the nations (12:5), so that Christian readers might naturally identify her with Mary, the mother of Jesus. By the end of the chapter, however, it becomes clear that the woman is the mother of all believers, for she has many "children," namely all those "who keep the commandments of God and hold the testimony of Jesus" (12:17). The woman encompasses the story of Israel, from whom the Messiah was born, as well as the story of the church, which was persecuted after Jesus' death and resurrection. In 11:1-2, the people of God were symbolized by the temple, which was threatened by hostile forces and yet preserved during a three-and-a-half-year period. In 12:1-17, John tells the same story all over again by depicting the people of God as a woman, who is threatened by a dragon and yet preserved for three and a half years. Different images are used in each passage, but the message is the same.

John's visionary account of the threat against the woman and the woman's preservation uses imagery that encompasses many moments in the story of God's people. This allows the story to apply to people in many times and places. Eve, the mother of all the living, was warned that she would find pain in childbearing; and the woman in Revelation indeed cries out in the agony of giving birth (Gen. 3:16; Rev. 12:2). Although Eve fell prey to the wiles of "that ancient serpent" who deceived her, God promised that her offspring would bruise the serpent's head (Gen. 3:15). This occurred through the triumph of the Lamb and the saints over Satan the serpent (Rev. 12:11).

Other aspects of the woman's story recall Israel's exodus and sojourn in the wilderness. The people of Israel fled through the sea to escape destruction at the hand of pharaoh, their pursuer. At that time God, who is able to "divide the sea" and to "break the heads of the dragons" (Ps. 74:12-15), carried the people as if on "eagles' wings" to a place of refuge in the wilderness (Exod. 19:4). There he nourished them with manna throughout the years of their wandering (Deut. 8:3). Similarly, the woman in Revelation is delivered from the dragon, who unleashes a torrent of water against her, and she is given eagle's wings to carry her into the wilderness, where she is "nourished" as God nourished Israel (Rev. 12:6, 14-16).

Still other aspects of the passage bring the drama closer to the situation of the readers. After the exodus, the people of Israel continued to experience periods of threat from the king of Egypt, whom the prophet Ezekiel identified as a dragon (Ezek. 29:3; 32:2). Later, the armies of Babylon threatened and finally captured Jerusalem, so that the Babylonian king could be likened to a dragon that filled its belly on the people of God (Jer. 51:34). Daniel spoke of fearsome creatures with ten horns, like the dragon in Rev. 12:3 (Dan. 7:7), and the book of Isaiah speaks of Zion, the city of God, in labor and giving birth to a son, as a sign of deliverance (Isa. 66:7-9). After using evocative imagery that can be connected to many Old Testament passages, John concludes the vision by tying it to the experiences of Christians, who are threatened because they "hold the testimony of Jesus" (Rev. 12:17). In the story of the woman, readers can see their story within the story of God's people generally.

The Two Beasts (13:1-18)

The cosmic battle between the forces of Satan and the allies of God and the Lamb, which was vividly described in Revelation 12, continues without pause in Revelation 13, where the dragon operates through henchmen that appear as a beast from the sea and a beast from the land. Sensationalistic interpreters commonly give little attention to the richly symbolic stories of the woman, the child, Michael, and the dragon in Revelation 12. Instead, they fix attention on Revelation's portrayal of the beasts in Revelation 13, assuming that the passage offers coded predictions about events that will take place in the modern world. We will consider this approach below, but first we will work through the visions of the beasts, asking how they continue the story that began in the previous chapter. The woman's conflict with the dragon in Revelation 12 did not offer simple predictions of future events, but conveyed a message for the people of God in many times and places. The visions of the beasts do the same thing. By continuing the story of the dragon, they continue warning readers across the generations about the power of evil, calling them to renewed faithfulness and endurance (12:10).

The Beast from the Sea (13:1-10)

Before the beasts appear, Satan stands on the shore of the sea as if to conjure up a new and terrible specter of evil (12:18). The horrific beast that comes up from the water bears a striking resemblance to Satan the dragon. Readers have no difficulty seeing through the beast's disguise, for like the dragon, this creature has seven heads and ten horns. Significantly, however, the beast wears ten diadems, whereas the dragon wore only seven (12:3; 13:1). The implication is that the dragon's desire to gain sovereignty has only been heightened following his expulsion from heaven. Terrible in appearance, the beast has a leopard's body, a bear's feet, and a lion's mouth (13:2). Although the beast has received a death blow on one of its heads, it has recovered, giving the impression that it is invincible.

The masses are enthralled by this grotesque creature, following it as if bewitched (13:3). The crowds ask two questions that prompt readers to contemplate what they are seeing. First, they ask, "Who is like the beast?" (13:4). The crowds would presumably respond to their own question by saying, "No one is like the beast. The beast is incomparable." John, however, has prepared his readers to answer the question differently. Readers can discern that in some ways the beast is like Satan, but in a perverse way the beast tries to disguise itself as Christ, as we will see. Second, they ask as they behold the beast, "Who can fight against it?" Again, the crowds would presumably respond by saying, "No one can fight against the beast. The beast is invincible." And again John has prepared readers to answer differently, for readers learned in the previous chapter that the armies of heaven have already defeated the dragon in heaven, and that Satan is conquered by the blood of the Lamb and by the testimony of the saints. Readers know that if the allies of God and the Lamb can fight against the dragon, they can surely fight against the beast.

The beast is the demonic counterpart to the Lamb. Revelation uses these two images to represent the emissaries of Satan and God. Earlier, we observed that John did not portray Christ as a Lamb in order to conceal Christ's identity, as if he were writing Revelation in secret code. Instead, John refers to the Lamb in order to reveal something about the saving power of Christ's self-sacrifice (see chapter 3 above). In the same way, John refers to the beast in order to reveal something about the destructive power of evil, not to conceal the beast's identity. Describing Christ as the Lamb helps attract readers to the innocent victim who suffered for their sakes, while portraying the agent of evil as a horrible beast helps repulse readers from all that this evil figure represents.

Many of the beast's features are hideous distortions of those of the Lamb. Christians believed that the God enthroned in heaven sent Christ into the world as the Lamb who suffered and died for others. In a perverse counterpart to this story, the Devil who is kicked out of heaven sends a beast into the world to make others suffer and die. In previous chapters, readers learned that the Lamb shares the power, the throne, and the authority of God (5:6, 12, 13; 12:5, 10); now they learn that the beast shares the power, the throne, and the authority of Satan the dragon (13:2). When John was in the heavenly throne room, he saw a Lamb that was standing as if it had been "slaughtered," and he heard the saints singing their praises to the Lamb that had been "slaughtered" and yet was alive (5:6, 9, 12). Now, however, he sees a living beast with a head that had been "slaughtered" and healed (13:3). Although English translations vary, the same Greek word for "slaughter" *(sphazein)* is used for both the Lamb and the beast. The outcome of the Lamb's work is that the world worships God the Creator (5:10, 13), but the outcome of the beast's work is that the world worships Satan the destroyer (13:4).

John depicts a conflict between God and Satan in which neutrality is not possible. Readers have learned that the Lamb "conquers" by faithfully enduring death for the sake of others (5:5-6; 12:11), and now they learn that the beast "conquers" by inflicting war and death upon others (13:7). The Lamb suffered in order to free people of "every tribe and language and people and nation" so that they could serve God as a kingdom of priests (5:9-10). The beast, however, works to oppress people of "every tribe and people and language and nation," so that they bow down before it as their master (13:7-8). Readers find themselves called to side with God and the Lamb against evil.

The portrayal of the beast draws together traits of oppressive powers from various times and places, creating a composite picture of evil. In this Revelation 13 follows the pattern of Revelation 12, where the woman and the dragon combined elements from different periods of Israel's history with the experience of Christians in John's time. The physical features of the beast recall Daniel 7, which spoke of a series of empires arising before the kingdom of God arrived. Daniel envisioned four successive kingdoms as four great beasts coming out of the sea. The first looked like a lion, the second like a bear, the third like a leopard, and the fourth had ten horns (Dan. 7:1-8). Revelation draws all these features into a single beast (Rev. 13:1-2). The fourth beast in Daniel had a horn that spoke arrogantly, made war on the saints, and had power for a period of three and a half years (Dan. 7:21, 25). In Revelation, the beast itself does all these things (Rev. 13:5-7). By replacing four individual beasts with one great beast, Revelation indicates that the threats presented by four successive empires are part of one great threat.

Revelation's description of the beast also draws on the popular culture of John's time, helping to connect the reality of evil to the readers' experience. Many features of the beast correspond to traits of Rome and its emperors, as John will make clear in 17:9, where he connects the beast with the kings of the city built on seven hills. As the leaders of a powerful empire that extended from Asia to Europe and North Africa, the Roman emperors had authority over people of many tribes, tongues, and nations (13:7). Admirers praised the emperors with what some considered "blasphemous names" (13:1), addressing them as "lord" and "son of god," as "savior" and even as "god" (Tacitus, *Annals* 14.15; Martial, *Epigrams* 5.8). In contrast, John would insist that such titles belong to God and the Lamb (Rev. 2:18; 4:11).

The supreme embodiment of hostility to Christians was the emperor Nero. When the finishing touches were put onto the image of the beast, Nero sat for the portrait. John's readers would have remembered that Nero ruthlessly "made war on the saints" (13:7), condemning some to be torn apart by wild dogs, others to be crucified, and still others to be burned alive (Tacitus, *Annals* 15.44). The end of Nero's life also gave a perverse credibility to the portrayal of a beast that was slain and yet lived (Rev. 13:3, 12, 14). Nero killed himself by putting a dagger to his own throat (Suetonius, *Nero* 49.2), but rumors arose that Nero was still alive and in hiding, so that he would return one day to avenge his enemies. Modern readers might be familiar with this phenomenon from the tabloids, which sometimes report rumors that a dead celebrity is really living incognito somewhere. In John's time popular fascination with Nero was fed by the occasional appearances of Nero impersonators (Suetonius, *Nero* 57; Tacitus, *Histories* 2.8). By combining the threats represented by the four empires in Daniel 7 with images reminiscent of Nero, the beast exemplifies the threats that confront the people of God in many generations.

Courage for "endurance and faith" in the face of such threats comes from the confidence that one belongs to the Lamb, or as Revelation puts it, that one's name has been written in "the book of life of the Lamb that was slaughtered" (Rev. 13:8). The references to the book of life would be misunderstood if taken to mean that those who fall into sin must be among those who have been excluded from God's "book."

Revelation does not view human life in such a deterministic way, but emphasizes the importance of repentance for those inside and outside of the church (2:5, 16, 21, 22; 3:3, 19; 9:20, 21). Mentioning the book of life reminds readers that people belong to God by the grace of God. Revelation does not suggest that people are placed in the book of life when they achieve a passing score on a spiritual endurance test. Since God claims people "from the foundation of the world" (13:8; 17:8), being placed in the book is an act of pure grace on God's part. Therefore, Revelation does not call readers to endure in the hope of some day being listed among the redeemed, but urges readers to persevere because God has already claimed them and does not want them to fall away.

Belonging to God does not bring exemption from suffering. The warning about being subjected to captivity (13:10) is a reminder that God's people — like the Lamb — will find that suffering is part of the life of faith. Moreover, since the beast operates by inflicting suffering and death on others, readers are warned not to adopt the same tactics (13:10). People "conquer" the beast not by inflicting more damage than the beast does, but by following an alternative course of faithful endurance and resistance to idolatry and oppression that has been set by the Lamb (12:11).

The Beast from the Land (13:11-18)

John's characterization of the powers of God and the powers of evil continues as he introduces the beast from the land, who is the third member of what amounts to a demonic "trinity." On one side of the conflict are God, the Lamb who brings people to worship God, and the Spirit that speaks through the prophets. On the other side of the conflict are Satan, the beast from the sea who brings people to serve Satan, and the beast from the land, who functions as a false prophet. We noted above that the beast from the sea, who was slaughtered and yet lives, presents itself as a perverse imitation of Christ; yet the beast's true character emerges as it oppresses people and brings them to worship Satan the dragon rather than God. In a similar way, the beast from the land imitates Christ in that it has "two horns like a lamb"; but again its true character appears in speech that is like that of a dragon — the emblem of Satan — and in deeds that bring people to serve the first beast rather than Christ the Lamb (13:11).

129

John understands the second beast to be a false prophet (16:13; 19:20; 20:10), who poses a contrast to the two prophetic witnesses depicted in 11:3-13. We saw in the last chapter that the two witnesses carried on the tradition of Moses, who performed signs like turning water to blood and bringing plagues upon the land (Rev. 11:6; Deut. 34:11). Now we find that a false prophet can perform similar signs (Rev. 13:13). Like the two witnesses who carried on the tradition of Elijah by overcoming their adversaries with fire (Rev. 11:5; 1 Kings 18:38; 2 Kings 1:12), the false prophet also calls down fire from heaven (Rev. 13:13). Nevertheless, appearances are deceiving. Signs do not prove that someone is a true prophet. The touchstone for true prophecy is whether it moves people to worship the true God or a false god. Regardless of the number of signs performed, one who directs people to worship a false god is not a true prophet (cf. Deut. 13:1-11; 1 John 4:1-6).

John lampoons the beast from the land by declaring that its solemn demands that people should make an image of the beast that was slaughtered and yet lives are mere acts of deception (Rev. 13:14). The beast from the land may create an impressive spectacle for gullible audiences by performing signs and wonders, but all of the hype is simply smoke and mirrors that induces people to worship an object made by human hands. John stood in a tradition that considered idol worship to be absurd. The book of Isaiah contains a rollicking satire in which a pagan craftsman uses half of a tree for cooking fuel and the other half to make the image of a god. The craftsman cooks his supper over the fire that he kindles with half of the tree's wood, then he turns around and worships the image that he fashioned from the other half of the wood. Like Isaiah, John would consider it ridiculous to cry out to an image that cannot hear or see, "Save me, for you are my God!" (Isa. 44:9-20)

The false prophet in Revelation 13 seeks to overcome the impression that idols are merely lifeless objects by contriving to "give breath to the image of the beast so that the beast could even speak" (Rev. 13:15). For someone like John, fabricating a talking statue is a feat worthy of the hokum that one expects to find at a sideshow in a traveling circus. A good illustration from antiquity is a religious huckster named Alexander, who created a shrine in which he installed an image with an artificial head, whose hinged jaws could be raised and lowered by means of a system of cords. A small tube was inserted into the back of the head so that as the jaws moved, someone behind the scenes could talk through the tube and create the illusion that the idol was speaking (Lucian, *Alexander the False Prophet* 26).

John's satirical portrayal of the beast may be entertaining, but his goal is utterly serious, since he wields humor as a weapon in the struggle for truth and commitment. To most observers, the beast would seem to be all-powerful, because it could kill those who refused to submit to its will (Rev. 13:15). Readers like those at Smyrna understood that such threats were real, since they faced the prospect of imprisonment and death for their faith (2:10). Satire, however, is a weapon that the powerless can wield against the powerful. It alters perceptions, transforming an object of fear into an object of ridicule. Those who can laugh at something begin to rise above it, making it easier to resist. Some of John's readers found the proponents of false religious claims to be intriguing or innocuous, while others found them to be intimidating. John seeks to startle both types of readers into a renewed willingness to resist compromise by showing that such claims are absurd.

The vision does not allow readers the luxury of remaining neutral. If an angel places God's name as a seal on the foreheads of the worshipers of God (7:2-4; 14:1), the beast from the land places the name of the beast from the sea on the foreheads or right hands of the worshipers of the beast (13:16; 14:9, 11; 16:2; 19:20; 20:4). Every person belongs to someone. The only question is whether one bears the name of the true God or the name of a counterfeit god. Readers cannot assume that the seal or the mark will be visible to the eye, any more than they can expect to see two visible horns protruding from the head of a false prophet (13:11) — would that detection of falsehood were so easy! Instead, the presence of the seal or the mark is evident in the commitments of the persons who bear them.

John brings the question of commitment into the workaday world by referring to a situation in which "no one can buy or sell who does not have the mark" or name of the beast (13:17). The faith of many of the Christians in the seven churches may have been more severely — though perhaps more subtly — challenged by economic pressures than by overt threats of violence. The discussion of the seven churches in chapter 2 above considered how social and economic factors would have promoted complacency and Christian assimilation to pagan culture. Those who sought to advance themselves socially and economi-

131

cally would have wanted to participate in the local trade guilds, although the social life of these guilds often included rituals and meals in honor of a pagan deity. Business contracts typically went to those who were on good terms with Roman authorities, including those who were involved in the deaths of Christians (18:15-19, 24). As sales were made, people used coins that bore the images of Rome's gods and emperors. Thus each transaction that used such coins was a reminder that people were advancing themselves economically by relying on political powers that did not recognize the true God.

Before John offers readers an alternative to submitting to the beast, he piques their curiosity by linking the name of the beast to the number 666 (13:18). In one sense it may be sufficient to note that the triple six connotes imperfection. Previously in Revelation, completeness and blessing have been associated with the number seven. The seventh seal brings reverent silence (8:1) and the seventh trumpet announces the kingdom of God (11:15). The number six, however, has more to do with imperfection and judgment, for the sixth seal and the sixth trumpet unleashed visions of wrath and devastation (6:12-17; 9:13-19). Following this pattern, the number 666 implies that the beast signifies unfulfillment and destruction.

Yet John goes further by inviting readers to "calculate the number of the beast, for it is the number of a person" (13:18). The text apparently assumes that readers are familiar with *gematria,* which is the practice of adding up the numerical values of the letters in a word. In antiquity, the letters of the alphabet had numerical values ascribed to them, so that a = 1, b = 2, etc. By explaining that 666 is "the number of a person," John implies that 666 is the sum of the values of the letters in a person's name. The practice was not uncommon. On the level of street culture, for example, a graffiti artist at Pompeii used a number for the name of his beloved when he scrawled on the wall: "I love her whose number is 545." On the level of religious writing, Christian authors delighted in showing that the name "Jesus" in Greek letters added up to 888 (*Sibylline Oracles* 1.324-29).

The problem is that it may be easy to calculate the number if one already knows the name, since all one has to do is add up the values of the letters; but it is extremely difficult to determine the name on the basis of a number, since many different letter combinations can yield the same total. With a little ingenuity, people in every generation seem capable of finding an adversary who can in some way be linked to the number. Candidates for 666 stretch from medieval popes to modern tyrants like Hitler.[2] Therefore, when reading this cryptic text, it is crucial to keep two things in mind. First, we must ask what the number might have communicated to the Christians of the seven churches that were first addressed by Revelation. Since John wrote in order to be understood by them, we must consider what meaning they might have seen in this number. Second, we must ask how the number fits into its literary context. John does not mention the number until he has described the beast in some detail, so that the number does not provide new information, but reinforces what readers have already learned.

Given the allusions to Nero in Revelation 13, it seems likely that 666 corresponds to *Nerōn Kaisar,* which is the Hebrew form of the name Nero Caesar.[3] Although John wrote in Greek, he explicitly says that he uses Hebrew names for "Abaddon," which is the one who brings destruction (9:11), and for "Armageddon," the gathering point for the adversaries of God (16:16). By the time Revelation was written, Nero was dead, but John portrays the beast as a Nero figure in order to underscore the threat that it poses. John sought to startle the Christians who thought that the best way to get along in pagan society was to accommodate its practices under the assumption that it was all quite harmless. Through his imagery John warns, "'Beware, it is Nero all over

2. On the numerical values of Pope Benedictus see p. 10 above. More recently, some noted that the three names of Ronald Wilson Reagan each had six letters, creating a 666. Alternatively, the word "computer" can be made to equal 666 if a = 6, b = 12, c = 18 and so forth. Thus c = 18, o = 90, m = 78, p = 96, u = 126, t = 120, e = 30, and r = 108. (See Boyer, *When Time Shall Be No More,* 283). More tongue in cheek, even Barney the dinosaur, who appears on a popular children's show, has been shown to have antichrist potential. Start with "CUTE PURPLE DINOSAUR," then change the U's to V's and extract all the Roman numerals in the phrase (CVVLDIV). Convert these to Arabic numerals (100 5 5 50 500 1 5) and add them up. The result is 666 (Clouse, Hosack, and Pierard, *New Millennium Manual,* 171).

3. When written in Hebrew letters the name is *nrōn qsr.* The calculation is as follows: nun (50) + resh (200) + waw (6) + nun (50) + qof (100) + samech (60) + resh (200) = 666. Some copyists changed the number to 616, as noted in the footnotes in many Bibles. This variant apparently assumes that the name should be spelled "Nero" rather than "Neron." By dropping the final "n," the total of the value of the letters is reduced by 50, yielding 616 rather than 666. In either case, the name of Nero works.

again,' just as one might say of a new dictatorial anti-Semitism that many might see as innocuous, 'Beware, it's Hitler all over again'" (Boring, *Revelation*, 164).

Some modern readers attempt to find the vision of the beasts being played out in events that are reported in the newspaper. The usual assumption is that Revelation predicts the coming of a tyrant who will achieve world dominance by forming a coalition of European or world nations. The formation of the European Common Market and other steps toward European economic unity, or attempts to strengthen the United Nations have been taken as signs that the beast's power is on the rise. The future dictator and his supporters are expected to promote one world religion and to use computer technology to control the global economy. Since all who participate will have to be marked with a number, some warn that social security numbers, credit card numbers, or the international product code numbers point to the beast's activity.[4]

Proponents of this scenario skillfully play on fears of being overwhelmed by life in the modern world, and often try to gain credibility by claiming to offer a strictly literal understanding of the Bible. This, however, is not the case. Those who insist that Revelation literally predicts the rise of a future world dictator eventually recognize that Revelation speaks symbolically, not literally. Note that they do not expect the dictator to have seven heads or ten horns, or to have the body of a leopard, or to look like a lamb, even though Revelation pictures him this way. The question is not whether to read the text symbolically, but *how* to read its symbolism. The issue is whether the visions of the beasts in Revelation 13 function as coded predictions concerning figures that will appear at the end of time, or whether the passage depicts threats that affect people of many times and places.

Historical interpretations of the beasts, which differ from the futuristic interpretations in many ways, rightly seek to understand how the imagery would have communicated to readers in the seven churches. Yet some historical interpretations resemble their futuristic counterparts in that they assume that the imagery functions as a code. The difference is that historical interpretations assume that the code

---

4. For example, see Hal Lindsey's description of "The Future Fuehrer" in *The Late Great Planet Earth,* chapter 8; and the way Tim LaHaye and Jerry B. Jenkins portray the Antichrist, Nicolae Carpathia, in *Left Behind,* 413-15, 426, 435-36.

points to figures in the first century rather than to figures in the twenty-first century. Accordingly, the beast from the sea represents Rome, while the beast from the land stands for the local Asian supporters of Rome. Some identify the beast from the land with the political leaders in Asia Minor who enforced imperial policies, and others argue that the beast must be the priest or college of priests that promoted the imperial cult. Since the beast from the land was a false prophet, still others prefer to link the beast's activities to false prophets like "Balaam" and "Jezebel," who had infiltrated the Christian communities (2:14, 20).

The fact that interpreters find it difficult to limit the beast from the land to any one figure in John's time or our time is not a problem. Rather, it shows that the imagery depicts threats that cannot be limited to a single time and place. On the one hand, the portrayal of the two beasts does not convey coded information that will allow readers to know when the end of time has come. On the other hand, the visions may have called first-century readers to resist Roman practices, but the text cannot be reduced to a political tract. Rather, the visions give readers a way to discern the presence of evil as they issue "a call for the endurance and faith of the saints" (13:10). Instead of then asking when the beast will appear, we might better ask when the beast's presence is *not* apparent. When is idolatry *not* a threat? When do the followers of the Lamb *not* experience pressures to give up their commitments? "Endurance" and "faith" constituted the path that John and his first-century readers were already called to follow (1:9; 2:2, 3, 19; 3:10), and it has been the path for those who have come after them. The summons to persevere is not simply a message for a generation living in the first century or at the end of time; it is a message for all generations that are confronted with idolatry and violence.

Judgment, Blessing, and Endurance (14:1-20)

John's visions press readers to see themselves in the middle of a conflict between the powers of God and evil in which neutrality is not possible. The visions that unfold in this chapter provide glimpses of the outcome of the conflict, giving readers incentive to persevere in the confidence that God will not abandon the faithful or allow evil finally to triumph.

The Redeemed on Mount Zion (14:1-5)

The story of the cosmic battle has thus far shown how one of Satan's agents, the great seven-headed beast, dominates the seas (13:1), while another insidious beast dominates the land (13:11). In contrast to the satanic beasts, however, the Lamb of God holds the high ground, Mount Zion, where the company of the redeemed gathers (14:1). The name "Mount Zion" has positive connotations as the place where the faithful gather in safety (Isa. 24:23; Joel 3:21) to worship the God who creates and delivers them (Ps. 146:10). Although Mount Zion traditionally referred to a location in Jerusalem, here it refers to heaven, where the saints sing before God's heavenly throne (Rev. 14:3; cf. 4:2). The redeemed, who are pictured as a group of 144,000, are the whole people of God, not merely one part of it, as we have already seen in the discussion of 7:4-8 (see chapter 3 above). The sense that the 144,000 represent the whole people of God continues here, where the "redeemed" sing a "new song" before God (14:3). The comment reminds readers that they already know that the "new song" praises the Lamb who has "redeemed" people "from every tribe and language and people and nation" to serve God (5:9-10).

John insists that no one can remain uncommitted in the conflict between God and evil. Either one bears the mark and name of the beast (13:16-18) or one bears the seal and name of God and the Lamb (14:1). John did not make such a sharp distinction because the alternatives were obvious to his readers, but because the alternatives were not obvious. A number of the Christians in the seven churches to which John wrote seemed willing to compromise their Christian commitments in order to assimilate into the surrounding culture (2:14, 20). Many in those Asian cities would have found it ridiculous to profess exclusive loyalty to God and the Lamb when one could be much more comfortable by joining in the practices of the wider society. John's visions offer the opposite perspective by seeking to show that it is absurd to join in society's misguided veneration of oppressive powers when one could join in celebration of the true Lord of heaven and earth.

The followers of the Lamb are depicted as holy warriors who have "not defiled themselves with women" (14:4). Traditionally, abstaining from sexual relations was expected of soldiers in battle (Deut. 23:9-10;

136

1 Sam. 21:5). John invokes this idea in his description of a war of religious commitments. Earlier, his references to "fornication" (Rev. 2:14, 20-21), "adultery" (2:22), and becoming unclean (3:4) had to do with engaging in idolatrous practices. Later, the notion of sexual infidelity will be connected to the violence, oppression, and greed fostered by Babylon the harlot (17:1-6; 18:3, 9). Here, the "virgins" are those who follow the Lamb and reject the practices associated with God's adversaries. John did not consider sexual relations to be inherently defiling or view women as especially unclean, since elsewhere he portrays the people of God as a woman who bears many children (12:17) and as a bride on her wedding day (19:7-9; 21:2, 9). The 144,000 chaste warriors (14:1-5) and the woman with many children (12:13-17) represent one and the same people of God (Schüssler-Fiorenza, *Revelation,* 88-89).

Shifting imagery yet again, John pictures the faithful as "first fruits" of the harvest (14:4). Traditionally, the first fruits were the first ripe sheaves of grain that were offered to God as a recognition of God's claim upon the whole harvest (Exod. 23:19). Briefly mentioning the first fruits suggests that the harvest was just beginning, setting the stage for Christ to continue the harvest of the earth in Rev. 14:14-16.

Messages of Three Angels (14:6-13)

Three angels now appear in quick succession. The first angel calls everyone to "Fear God and give him the glory, for the hour of his judgment has come; and worship him who made heaven and earth, the sea and the springs of water" (14:7). John shapes the way that people are to hear the angel's message by calling it an "eternal gospel," which means that he wants readers to receive it as good news for all generations (14:6). The message is good news or "gospel" because God wants those of "every nation and tribe and language and people" to join in giving glory to their Maker, adding their praises to those of the chorus that celebrates around God's throne (4:11; 5:13; 7:12). The angel's voice recalls how the torrent of judgments unleashed by the seven trumpets was interrupted before utter devastation occurred, so that the inhabitants of the earth could come to fear and glorify God (11:13). Conversion rather than destruction is God's desire. Powers of evil have overrun the earth, but God remains Lord. Beasts rise up from sea and land

(13:1, 11), but God made the sea and land, and will finally not surrender his world to the forces that terrorize it (14:7). The Creator has not abandoned the creation.

The second angel declares, "Fallen, fallen is Babylon the great!" (14:8). Since this is the first time that Babylon is mentioned in Revelation, the announcement may seem incongruous. The angel says that Babylon has "fallen" even though the city and its demise will not be described until Revelation 17–18. Nevertheless, the peculiar movement again reminds readers that Revelation does not narrate events in a chronological sequence. The angel's message is not a simple description, but a warning that is designed to affect readers' commitments. Knowing that Babylon is doomed to fall should make readers wary of placing any confidence in the city, even before they are told what Babylon is. In the Old Testament, Babylon was the power that destroyed the first temple in 587 B.C., and in later chapters John will extend the name "Babylon" to Rome, the power that destroyed the second temple in A.D. 70. We will see, however, that "Babylon" is more than a code name for Rome, for John creates a portrait of "Babylon" that encompasses threats against the people of God from many times and places.

The third angel issues one of the most gruesome warnings in Revelation (14:9-11). The warning begins appropriately by emphasizing that God's judgments are just. In 14:8 listeners heard that Babylon "made all nations drink the wine of the wrath of her fornication," and in 14:9-10 they hear that the allies of the beast will "drink the wine of God's wrath." In other words, those who join in the outrageous practices of the beast, which were described in the previous chapter, will receive judgment in return. God's justice is not capricious. It falls on the guilty, not on the victims whom they wronged. All of this seems right. The problem is that John goes on to speak of Christ and the angels watching over the eternal torment of the damned, who suffer the pain of fire and sulfur forever. As the smoke of their torment rises up before the hosts of heaven, it creates a ghastly counterpart to the prayers of the saints rising like clouds of incense before God's throne (5:8; 8:4; 14:11).

Modern readers respond in different ways to this vision of pitiless judgment, and not all of these responses are helpful. Some readily wield the specter of eternal condemnation as a weapon against their opponents. All too often those who do this assume that judgment must be intended for other people, but not for themselves. Yet self-righteousness is a form of self-deception that blinds people to their own sin. Ironically, those who refuse to show love fall under the judgment of Christ (2:4). In reaction to this, other modern readers dismiss John's vision of eternal torment as unchristian because of its pitiless vindictiveness. The idea is that since Jesus told people not to judge others (Matt. 7:1; Luke 6:37), we can assume that God will also refrain from judgment. The problem is that John's vision of judgment is not unique in the NT, and the same gospels that say "judge not" also warn about God condemning people to "the furnace of fire, where there will be weeping and gnashing of teeth" (Matt. 13:36-43, 47-50; Luke 16:19-31). Judgment is an integral part of the Christian message.

The vision of divine wrath is properly read as a warning. Warnings are not given in order to make people despair of grace, but to bring about change and to avert disaster. When a child unwittingly speeds on a bicycle toward a busy intersection, a parent will call out a warning about the coming catastrophe. The parent shouts because the cross traffic poses a real threat and because there is still hope of preserving the child's safety. The terrifying vision in Rev. 14:9-11 functions in the same way. John is compelled to write because the threat of divine judgment is real, and he is able to write because the hope of averting judgment is also real. To dismiss the reality of the danger or to close off the reality of hope distorts the message. In the end, the best response to the specter of judgment is not to explain it away, but to heed the angel's call for repentance (14:6-7) and to seek the mercy of God.

John couples his warning with the promise that those who die in the Lord will be "blessed" and find "rest" from their labors (14:13). The extravagant scenes of heavenly celebration in previous chapters offer readers a sense of what blessing and rest entail (14:3; cf. 4:1–5:14; 7:9-17; 11:15-17). What is significant here is how Revelation's warnings of judgment and promises of blessing work together. In one sense, each functions differently: warnings disturb readers (14:9-11) while the promises assure them (14:13). Nevertheless, both the warnings and the promises serve the same end, to encourage readers to persevere in faith (14:12). When visions that work so differently in some ways move readers toward the common goal of enduring faith, they have the effect for which they were designed.

Ingathering and Judgment (14:14-20)

The interplay between promise and warning continues in the last two visions of this chapter, which depict the ingathering of the saints and the judgment of the wicked. The first vision is a promising one in which the Son of Man comes on the clouds of heaven to gather in the harvest of earth (14:14-16). John has already identified the Son of Man as the risen Christ, who is present among the churches (1:12-20), and he has described the faithful in heaven as the "first fruits" of a much larger harvest that will be completed upon Christ's return (14:4). The image of the grain harvest had positive and even joyful connotations that early Christians associated with bringing people into the kingdom (Mark 4:29; John 4:35-38). When biblical texts refer to the harvest as a time of judgment in the negative sense, they speak of threshing the grain to remove the chaff, which is carried off by the wind or burned (Ps. 1:4; Matt. 3:12; 13:30; Luke 3:17), and of separating the good grain from the weeds (Matt. 13:30); but these threatening associations are not in view in Rev. 14:14-16, which describes only the final harvest of souls for God.

The negative side of judgment is depicted through the vision of gathering and pressing out grapes (14:17-20). Although harvesting grapes could be understood positively, it is clear that judgment is intended because the grapes are thrown into "the great wine press of the wrath of God" (14:19). Just as the redeemed in 14:4 are the "first fruits" of the people of God who are harvested in 14:14-16, the wicked, who made the earth drink the wine of Babylon's wrath in 14:8, now serve as the vintage that is trampled out by God's wrath in 14:17-20. The imagery recalls other biblical passages in which the wicked are trodden down like the grapes that are crushed under the feet of those who tread in a wine press (Joel 3:13; Isa. 63:3). In the spiraling visions of Revelation, this same scene will be played out again when Christ himself treads "the wine press of the fury of the wrath of God the Almighty" (Rev. 19:15). Revelation does not move in chronological sequence so as to enable readers to trace the outworking of God's purposes on a time line. Instead, Revelation repeats the vision of the wine press (14:17-20; 19:15), just as it repeats the announcement of Babylon's fall (14:8; 18:2) in order to underscore the reality of judgment.

At the conclusion of Revelation 14, readers are confronted with two possibilities: the hope of salvation that is represented by the grain harvest and the threat of judgment that is represented by the trampling of the grapes. The two alternatives are designed to bring clarity to a confusing situation in which people are confronted with contending truth claims. The agents of evil seek to influence the inhabitants of the world by deception and intimidation, but the angels of God call "every nation and tribe and language and people" to worship the Creator (14:6-7). Readers may be lulled into believing that evil is invincible or perhaps not evil at all, and that godliness brings only loss (13:4, 7); but John challenges this perception by pointing to the end of the story, in which earthly conditions are reversed, and the faithful are gathered together while the wicked are trodden down.

Lord of the Nations (15:1-4)

John underscores the urgency of endurance and hope by bringing readers back to the heavenly throne room, where those who have "conquered the beast and its image and the number of its name" stand beside the sea of glass with harps in their hands, singing praises to God (15:1-4). Mentioning the sea of glass and the harps takes readers back to 4:6, where the crystal sea stretched out before God's throne, and to 5:8-9, where the heavenly chorus raised a new song before the Lamb with harps (cf. 14:2-3). Referring to the redeemed as "those who conquered" recalls that the Lamb "conquered" by offering himself as a sacrifice to redeem others (5:5-6); that followers of the Lamb "conquered" by remaining faithful to God and to Christ at the cost of their lives (12:11); and that the Christians in the seven churches are called to "conquer" by remaining faithful to God and the Lamb (2:7, 11, 17, 26; 3:5, 12, 21). Repeating the visions of heavenly worship stresses that this is the future that Revelation wants for its readers. This is where God and the Lamb want people to be (4:8, 11; 5:9-14; 7:9-17; 11:15-18).

John calls what they sing "the song of Moses, the servant of the Lord, and the song of the Lamb" (15:3). The vivid imagery transforms the story of Israel's liberation from slavery in the time of Moses into the story of liberation through the Lamb, which reaches its consummation in the heavenly throne room. At the time of Moses, Israel was threatened by the pharaoh, preserved from destruction at the sea, and given refuge and nourishment in the desert. We have already seen how in Revelation 12, this is transformed into a story for many times and places as the woman, who represents God's people, is threatened by Satan the dragon, preserved from death by water, and given refuge and nourishment in the wilderness (12:1-6, 13-17). Now John takes up another element in the story. In Moses' time, those who were delivered from pharaoh sang a song beside the Red Sea (Exodus 15), and here those who have conquered the beast sing beside the fiery sea. A new element is that they sing a song that is identified with the Lamb as well as with Moses, because victory over evil occurs through the Lamb's blood (Rev. 5:5-10; 12:11).

Remarkably, the faithful do not sing about their own deliverance, but celebrate God's position as King of the nations. Instead of focusing on the destruction of Israel's enemies, as does the song of Moses in Exodus 15, the song in Revelation 15 focuses on the conversion of the peoples of the world. The lyrics begin, "Great and amazing are your deeds, Lord God the Almighty. Just and true are your ways, King of the nations" (15:3). Inspired by a number of Old Testament passages (Deut. 32:4; Ps. 86:8-10; 111:2; 139:14; 145:17; Jer. 10:6-7), the heavenly singers laud God's power and justice, asking, "Lord, who will not fear and glorify your name?" They answer their own question by announcing that "All nations will come and worship before you" (Rev. 15:4).

According to Revelation, God does not want the nations of the world to be lured into allying themselves with the powers of evil (13:7-8), but neither does he want the nations to be destroyed. Instead, God's desire is for the conversion of the nations, so that they join in the cosmic chorus of praise that is his will for the world (5:11-14). At the end of the previous cycle of visions, we considered how God eased the series of pitiless judgments that fell upon the earth, so that through the suffering, witness, and vindication of his people, the inhabitants of the world might repent and glorify God (11:13). In the current cycle of visions, an angel has called those of "every nation and tribe and language and people" to glorify God (14:6). Now the song of victory that concludes this cycle celebrates a favorable response to the angel's message, fixing before the reader's eyes the hope of the conversion of the world. The vision of hope in 15:2-4 does not mean that the end of ends has come, however, for even before the song of triumph has been sung, John warns that more plagues will occur (15:1). The spiraling pattern that has repeatedly taken readers through sequences of threats into scenes of heavenly celebration is about to do the same again.

Chapter 6

THE HARLOT AND THE BRIDE

Revelation 15–19

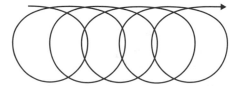

The fifth cycle of visions begins where the previous cycle ends, with a triumphant song of praise rising from the assembly of the faithful. As cascades of harp sounds flood the heavens, the saints sing the song of Moses and the Lamb, celebrating God's lordship over the nations. The followers of the Lamb sing beside a fiery sea of glass after conquering the beast, much as the people of Israel sang beside the sea after their liberation from pharaoh (15:2-4). Yet before the heavenly singers have finished, John warns that the end has not yet arrived, for the beast still rages on the earth (15:1). Therefore, just as God sent plagues upon pharaoh and his allies in order to liberate his people from bondage, God's angels send plagues upon the beast and his allies in order to liberate the world from his tyranny (16:1-21). A number of the plagues in this fifth cycle — painful sores, water turning to blood, darkness, frogs, and hail — are similar to the plagues that fell on Egypt, and their purpose is also similar: to move the ungodly to repent and to liberate the faithful from oppressive powers.

Up to this point in the drama, the leaders of the forces of evil have been Satan the dragon, the beast from the sea, and the false prophet, who is also known as the beast from the land. Now this vile company is joined by a fourth figure: Babylon the great harlot, who rides upon the seven-headed Beast (17:3). John pens a merciless parody of the city's wealth and power when he depicts a woman who, from a distance, might appear to be an elegant lady, for she is dressed in a purple and scarlet gown, and adorned with gold, jewels, and pearls. Yet with scathing satire, he points out that she sips sewage from the golden cup in her hand and clings to her grotesque mount in a drunken stupor. The vision of the harlot brings a turning point in the story of Satan's empire, for the beast that carries the harlot suddenly lashes out and destroys her, thereby eliminating one of God's adversaries. The next cycle of visions will bring the defeat of the beast itself (see the introduction to chapter 5 above).

Two sets of heavenly voices call out at the fall of Babylon, so that readers can see the meaning of her demise. First, an angel strikes up a kind of dirge over the city and declares, "Fallen, fallen is Babylon the great!" (18:2). He is joined by another heavenly voice that taunts the allies of Babylon by mimicking the woeful voices of the kings and merchants who reveled in the power and luxury that Babylon provided, until another angel interrupts their grieving by hurling a millstone into the sea as a sign of Babylon's doom. Afterward, a second group of voices lifts up a chorus of praise and thanks to God for bringing Babylon's arrogance, violence, and corrupting wealth to an end. As "Hallelujahs" spread throughout the heavens, the twenty-four elders and four living creatures, who so often lead the hosts of heaven and earth in praising God, bring the vision cycle to its climax by adding their "Amen," while the multitudes raise a thundering song of thanks that the Lord God Almighty reigns (19:1-8). The harlot has been vanquished. The bride is ready. The faithful await the coming marriage feast.

The Seven Bowls of Wrath (15:5–16:21)

Tent of Witness in Heaven (15:5-8)

Revelation's scenes of celebration and warning encircle each other like links on a chain. The festive vision of the saints singing praises to God and the Lamb (15:2-4), which concluded the previous cycle of visions, is bracketed by the specter of seven angels preparing to bring seven final plagues upon the earth. Although the angels are introduced in 15:1, the action begins when John's eyes are drawn to "the temple of the tent of witness in heaven" (15:5). Calling the heavenly sanctuary "the tent of witness" suggests that it corresponds to the pattern of the tent sanctuary that Moses saw on Mount Sinai (Exod. 25:9). According to the book of Exodus, the tent had two chambers that housed sacred furnishings, and the entrance to each chamber was veiled with a curtain or screen made of purple, blue, scarlet, and linen material.

When the curtain parts, a stately liturgical procession takes place. Seven angels appear, robed in the white linen that is suitable for priests (Rev. 15:6; Lev. 16:4), and they wear golden sashes across their chests, as did the Son of Man (Rev. 1:13). The angelic procession is met by one of the four living creatures who attend God's throne and lead the celestial court in songs of praise (4:8; 5:8). Whether this creature has the face of the lion, ox, eagle, or human being (4:6-7), John does not say. In a former vision, the living creatures bowed in the heavenly throne room, holding golden bowls full of incense in their hands; and as the smoke drifted up from the golden bowls, it bore the prayers of the saints before the Lamb (5:8). Now in this vision, a living creature again holds golden bowls, but the direction of the action is reversed. Instead of bearing the prayers that rise before the Lamb, the bowls bear the wrath that will be poured out upon the earth.

When the angels receive the bowls, the temple is filled with smoke from the glory and power of God, so that no one can enter it for a time (15:8). Similar manifestations of divine glory occurred when Moses dedicated the tent sanctuary in the wilderness (Exod. 40:34-38) and when Solomon dedicated the temple (1 Kings 8:10-11). But the fearsome display that John sees is more ominous than joyous, and one might best respond to it as Isaiah did, when he cried out "Woe is me for I am lost!" (Isa. 6:4-5). By casting up an impenetrable veil of smoke, God ensures that the angels who are to pour out the plagues upon the earth will not be able to turn back until their grim task is completed.

Seven Bowls of Wrath (16:1-21)

A voice from the temple commands the seven angels to pour out the seven bowls of wrath upon the earth (Rev. 16:1). The plagues that follow occur in the same stylized pattern that we noted in the series of trumpets in Revelation 8–9. In parallel fashion, the first four trumpets and the first four bowls bring plagues upon the earth, sea, inland waters, and sun (8:7-12; 16:2-9). The fifth trumpet and bowl deal with the destroyer and beast (9:1-11; 16:10-11), while the sixth trumpet and bowl portray hostile armies massing near the Euphrates River (9:13-19; 16:12-16). The repetitive character of the visions again shows that Revelation does not predict a neat sequence of events that will allow readers to discern where they are on God's timeline. Instead, the book repeats a similar message of warning in multiple ways.

Why repeat the warning visions? The visions are not simple descriptions of future events, but warnings that are designed to move the readers of Revelation to repentance and renewed commitment to the ways of God and the Lamb. Although the trumpet plagues warn of disasters that affect a third of the earth, and the bowl plagues portend more complete judgments on the worshipers of the beast, both series are designed to strip away the readers' sense of security by hemming them in with dangers in earth, sea, and sky. Each series, in its own way, focuses on the issue of whether people will repent or refuse to repent in the face of God's judgment (9:20-21; 16:9, 11, 21). When readers are moved to ask where their own deepest loyalties lie, the text has its proper effect.

The first angel pours a bowl of wrath on those who worship the image of the beast (16:2). The plague is not an indiscriminate deluge of destruction, but a manifestation of divine anger toward God's adversaries. The contents of the bowl affect the worshipers of the Beast who bear "the mark of the Beast" that identifies them with powers opposed to God. Earlier, John learned that those who worshiped the beast's image would be spared by the beast's allies, while those who refused to bow down would be killed (13:15). Since God vindicates those who resist the beast by bringing them to life in heaven (15:2), one might also expect God to punish those who worship the beast by bringing them to a gruesome death on earth. But this does not occur. Where John once saw "the mark of the beast," he now sees "a foul and painful sore" upon the beast's followers (16:2). The mark of the idolatry through which people accommodate evil and seek to escape affliction, is now matched by a sore that brings affliction. Painful though it is, however, the sore that God inflicts upon the followers of the beast is less severe than the death that the beast inflicted upon the followers of the Lamb. Like the sores that came upon the Egyptians before the exodus (Exod. 9:10-11), it presses people to repent of their oppressive practices (Rev. 16:9, 11).

The second angel pours a bowl of divine wrath into the sea, so that the waters are transformed into cold blood, like the blood of a dead person, and every living thing in the sea perishes (16:3). The result raises questions about divine justice. God created the sea and everything in it (14:7), and God's desire is that all creatures, including those that swarm the seas, should join in a cosmic song of praise to their Maker (5:13). So why should the sea and its creatures die? Revelation finally does not explain why innocent creatures or innocent people perish. Neither this passage nor any other passage provides an answer.

Instead, Revelation takes up a related question: Why do the ungodly survive? Why have God's judgments not annihilated those who oppress the faithful? On one level, the vision of the sea turning to blood warns that those who perpetuate injustice will bear the consequences of their deeds. The inhabitants of the earth have shed the blood of the saints (6:10), and now waves of bloody water wash up on their shores. The beast slew God's faithful witnesses, leaving their dead bodies in the streets (11:8-9), and now the sea itself assumes the quality of a corpse. The ungodly may not yet have perished, but this plague warns that God's justice will prevail. If God has spared them it is not because God is indifferent to evil, but that God has granted them the chance to repent — a point that will soon be made explicit (16:9, 11).

The third angel pours a bowl of wrath into the rivers and springs of water, which become as bloody as the sea (16:4). An angel announces that this plague carries out divine justice, declaring that since the wicked have "shed the blood of saints and prophets, you have given them blood to drink. It is what they deserve!" (16:6). At first glance, this seems to follow the biblical principle of retribution, in which wrongdoers are punished "eye for eye, tooth for tooth" (Exod. 21:24). And there is, to be sure, a poetic justice in that people who have shed streams of blood are now made to drink from blood-filled streams.

Yet is this truly a punishment commensurate with the crime? The full biblical principle states that people are to be punished "life for life" (Exod. 21:23). A similar passage insists, "Whoever sheds the blood of a human, by a human shall that person's blood be shed" (Gen. 9:6). Since Revelation agrees that "if you kill with the sword, with the sword you must be killed" (Rev. 13:10), we should expect the wicked to be slain in as pitiless a fashion as they slew the saints. Yet here they are not killed, but given blood to drink. There is a strange restraint in the justice of God. Earlier, the saints under the altar asked how long God would delay in avenging their blood upon the inhabitants of the earth (6:9-11). Here a voice from the altar suggests that the prayers of the saints have received an answer that does not entail a full retribution on the wicked, but a mitigated judgment that is declared to be "true and just" (16:7). The purpose of the plagues is not simple punishment. Rather, like the plague that turned the Nile River into blood before the exodus (Exod. 7:17-21), the plagues in Revelation are designed to bring repentance.

The issue of repentance is made evident after the fourth angel pours a bowl of wrath on the sun, so that the adversaries of God suffer from fierce heat (16:8). Like previous plagues, this one stops short of destroying the wicked, and John now focuses attention on the issue of how one responds to the plagues. Earlier visions have made clear that God wants people of all nations to fear him and give him glory (11:13; 14:7). This is the reason that judgments have been interrupted and messengers sent out to call people to repentance. The worshipers of the beast, however, refuse to repent and to glorify God (16:9). Their response makes clear that they have not simply been bullied into worshiping the beast in order to avoid affliction (cf. 13:16-17), because here they suffer affliction, yet still refuse to worship God. Moreover, they do not remain silently obstinate, but reveal their true loyalties by blaspheming God as the beast did (13:5-6).

The function of these visions is not primarily to predict the future, but to confront readers with two options: either one joins in giving God the glory, as the heavenly chorus does (4:11; 5:13; 7:12; 15:4), or one joins in blaspheming God, as the people do here. Readers who remain disinterested spectators miss the point of John's account of these plagues. John wrote down the visions for the sake of the readers, in order to turn them from idolatry and injustice. The sharp alternatives would strike readers in different ways. On the one hand, readers who experience pressure to renounce their Christian commitments find that the contrasts summon them to persevere in the face of opposition. Some local authorities may have demanded that Christians reject Christ in order to escape imprisonment and death (2:8-11; 3:8-9), but this vision reverses that perception by showing that those who blaspheme God fall under divine judgment. On the other hand, readers who accommodate pagan culture (2:12-28; 3:1-6, 14-22) find that the sharp alternatives press them to see that neutrality is not possible, for making their peace with the practices of the beast brings them into conflict with the Almighty.

The fifth angel pours a bowl of divine wrath "on the throne of the beast" with the result that the beast's kingdom is engulfed in darkness (16:10). Readers have already learned that the beast received its throne from Satan the dragon (13:2). Once in possession of this evil throne, the beast blasphemed God, slaughtered the saints, and demanded allegiance from people of every tribe and nation (13:5-8). If God is just — and this passage repeatedly declares that God is indeed just (16:5-7; cf. 15:3) — then God must keep the beast from further terrorizing the earth. What is remarkable is that God's angel does not destroy the beast's kingdom, but immerses it in darkness, like the darkness that engulfed Egypt before Israel's deliverance from bondage (Exod. 10:21). Once again, the plague presses people to repent and worship God. The vision makes clear that if they refuse to change, it is not because God has prevented it, but because they are firmly allied with the beast (Rev. 16:11). The question raised by this vision is whether the readers will follow the course set by the unrepentant, or whether they will show loyalty to God and the Lamb.

The sixth angel pours his bowl on the river Euphrates so that its water dries up (16:12). In the past, the waters of the Red Sea parted so that Moses could lead the people of Israel out of Egypt (Exod. 14:21-22), and the Jordan River parted so that Joshua could lead them into the Promised Land (Josh. 3:14-17); but here the waters of the Euphrates dry up "to prepare the way for the kings from the east" (Rev. 16:12). The vision evokes a sense of threat against the powers that oppressed the people of God in different periods (cf. Isa. 50:2; Nah. 1:4). Centuries before Revelation was written, the people of Judah were dominated by the Babylonians, but the Persians came from east of the Euphrates to conquer Babylon, allowing the Judean exiles to return home. In John's time, the dominant power belonged to the Romans, who were uneasy about attacks by the Parthians from east of the Euphrates. The imagery is not confined to one period of time, but evokes associations from different times in order to convey a warning about the vulnerability of the powers that oppress the people of God.

If the two plagues unleashed by the previous bowls brought a negative response from the followers of the beast, this bowl brings a negative response from the beast and its closest allies (Rev. 16:13). Rather than surrendering in light of their coming defeat, the adversaries of God intensify their opposition. Foul spirits that look like frogs — which were regarded as unclean and not to be put into the mouth — come out of the mouths of the dragon, the beast, and the false prophet, who was formerly depicted as the beast from the land (13:11). In a last-ditch effort to retain their control, these spirits lure the kings of the earth to a place called Armageddon, where they will be prepared for the final great battle on the Day of God Almighty (16:14-16).

Armageddon (16:16)

The word "Armageddon," in contemporary culture, has become almost synonymous with nuclear warfare and the annihilation of civilization. Popular treatments of Armageddon usually feature missiles with atomic warheads, squadrons of aircraft, and tank brigades colliding in the Middle East. The description of the great battle does not occur until 19:11-21 — a passage that strangely omits all references to tanks and missiles — so that we will reserve discussion of these points until the next chapter. Since the name "Armageddon" occurs only in 16:16, however, we will consider its significance here. Two questions are important.

First, is the name literal or symbolic? John says that "Armageddon" is a Hebrew term, and it seems to be based on the Hebrew word *har* or "mountain" and the name "Megiddo," which is a place in northern Israel. The name is peculiar, however, since Megiddo is actually located on a plain rather than a mountain. It is clear that when John addresses his readers, he uses the literal names of the towns in which they live: Ephesus, Smyrna, Pergamum, etc. (1:11). It is also clear that he uses Hebrew names symbolically when he nicknames his opponents Balak, Balaam, and Jezebel — figures associated with idolatry in the Old Testament (2:14, 20). John uses these symbolic names to tell readers something about the false teachers in their communities. In 9:11 he identifies a demonic angel by the symbolic Hebrew name "Abaddon" ("Destruction") and the Greek name "Apollyon" ("Destroyer"). When identifying places, John refrains from calling the place where Christ was crucified "Jerusalem," but refers to it symbolically as "Sodom" and "Egypt" (11:8). Finally, he symbolically extends the name "Babylon" (14:8; 16:19) to Rome, the city built on seven hills (17:9). Since John regularly uses Old Testament names in a symbolic rather than a literal sense, it seems evident that "Armageddon" should be taken symbolically rather than literally.

Second, what does the name signify? Old Testament references to Megiddo often link it to battles in which the adversaries of Israel are defeated. In Judges 5:19 Megiddo is associated with Deborah's victory over Israel's foes. The battle was won when God sent rain from heaven so that the Canaanite chariots were bogged down in the mud and the Canaanite army was routed. In 2 Chronicles 35:22 (cf. 2 Kings 9:27), King Josiah of Judah was killed near Megiddo. Although he was a good king, this text says that he was killed because he would not listen to the word of the Lord, so that his fate serves as a warning to all who refuse to heed God. Finally, Zech. 12:11 announces the coming day of the Lord's victory, mentioning Megiddo as the place where worshipers of a pagan god mourn. Taken together, the associations suggest that Megiddo is a place name that portends the coming destruction of the adversaries of God.

Before any battle takes place, however, the seventh angel tosses a bowl of wrath into the air, unleashing lightning, thunder, and hundred-pound hailstones (Rev. 16:17-21). A voice from God's throne declares, "It is done!" so that at last the judgment of God would appear to be complete. Earlier, an angel condemned Babylon, who made "all nations drink the wine of the wrath of her fornication" (14:8); and now God gives the city "the wine-cup of the fury of his wrath" (16:19). The world is struck by an earthquake more violent than any that have occurred since the creation of humankind. The earthquake shatters Babylon and the cities of the world collapse into rubble. The islands and the mountains of the world vanish. Yet the comment that concludes this scene of devastation does not focus on the annihilation of the wicked, but on their refusal to repent. Rather than surrendering to God, they continue to curse God, as they have done in the face of previous plagues (16:21). The question is, will Revelation's readers do the same?

John will probe the mystery of humanity's peculiar resistance to God and the nature of God's judgment by focusing on the city of "Babylon" in the next scene. His text does not move in a linear sequence, for even though Babylon is shattered by an earthquake in 16:19, John doubles back to describe the grandeur of the city in a personified form in Revelation 17. After depicting Babylon's destruction by fire in 17:16, further reasons for the city's downfall — arrogance, violence, and wealth — emerge in the laments of Revelation 18.

The Great Harlot (17:1-18)

One of the angels who poured the bowls of divine wrath on the earth shows John the judgment that will fall upon the great harlot (17:1). The vision that John now describes is a kind of counterpart to the story of the woman and the dragon that began Act II of Revelation. In the earlier vision, the people of God were personified as a woman clothed with the sun, giving birth to the Messiah who would rule all the nations. The woman and her child were pursued by a great seven-headed dragon, but the woman found refuge in the wilderness, and the dragon was cast down from heaven to earth, where it made war on the saints and deceived the nations through a seven-headed beast (12:1–13:10). Like the woman in that vision, John is now taken into the wilderness (17:3), which offers him a refuge from the lies of the dragon and the threats of the beast, allowing him to see this insidious power for what it is.

The women in Revelation 12 and 17 are portrayed in sharply contrasting ways in order to win the readers' allegiance to the persecuted woman, who represents the people of God, and to alienate them from the repulsive harlot, who represents the adversaries of God. The woman clothed with the sun is the mother of the Messiah and the faithful (12:5, 17), while the courtesan clothed with scarlet is "the mother of whores and of earth's abominations" (17:5). The first woman is pursued by a seven-headed monster, while the second woman happily rides a seven-headed monster and drinks the blood of the saints (17:6). Given this picture, there is little question but that readers will identify with the first woman and not with the harlot.

154

In practical terms, the message is that Christians may find themselves in difficult straits, like the woman who flees to the wilderness, outside the social mainstream; but if the other option is to cozy up with a debauched prostitute and her pet beast, readers might find that life outside the social mainstream is not so bad. John did not make such sharp contrasts because the distinction between good and evil was obvious to his readers. For many, the problem was precisely the opposite. John castigates those who seem unable to discern the difference between the true God and surrogate gods, or to distinguish faithfulness from unfaithfulness. Christians at Sardis and Laodicea had been lulled into complacency by their wealth (3:1-6, 14-22), while those at Pergamum and Thyatira seemed willing to accommodate the harlotry of pagan practices in the interest of social harmony (2:14, 20-22). The portrayal of the harlot is designed to unmask the seductive powers that dull the readers' perceptions, startling them into a keener awareness of what faith means.

Satirical Portrayal of the Harlot (17:1-6)

Satire runs throughout John's portrayal of the harlot, and modern readers may find that their most valuable preparation for understanding this imagery is their familiarity with the editorial pages of the newspaper. Consider how satire works in political cartoons. An artist will caricature political leaders by exaggerating a person's identifiable traits, so that one might have a bird-like nose, enormous ears, or an outlandish hairdo. Political groups are represented by a stock of stereotyped images. The United States is often pictured as Uncle Sam, who has a coat and striped trousers, a top hat adorned with stars and stripes, and a goatee sprouting from his chin. An elephant stands for the Republicans and a donkey for the Democrats. If the identity of any figure is in doubt, the artist will write its name on its picture.

Satirists show relationships between global or national powers in the way they depict action in their drawings. Uncle Sam might sit comfortably astride the Republican elephant or be trampled under the elephant's feet; he might lead the Democratic donkey by its nose or suffer a kick from the donkey's hooves. Each gesture shows a different type of relationship. Satire seeks to show readers something that they might not otherwise see, and its humorous elements contribute to its persuasive power. If people can be persuaded to think that what appears impressive is actually ridiculous, that what seems glamorous is really garish, and that what appears desirable is in fact ludicrous, they will be more ready to resist it.

John's satirical portrait of the great city works in a similar way. Instead of using a beautiful and dignified lady as its emblem, John pictures it as a debauched courtesan. Where one might wish to find a noble exemplar of virtue, she reels along in a drunken stupor. Instead of sitting astride an elegant steed, the harlot clings to the back of an outrageous seven-headed beast. In her hand she raises a golden cup that one would expect to be filled with the finest wine, but John tells his readers that it actually contains sewage of the vilest kind. The pretentious lady is in fact a contemptible buffoon. To make sure that readers can identify her, John writes the name "Babylon the Great" across her forehead, as a modern artist might do in a political cartoon.

The portrait of the harlot draws on a wealth of stock imagery. In the Old Testament, Israel's relationship to God was compared to a marriage in which God was the husband and Israel was the bride. By worshiping other gods, the people violated their marriage covenant with God and assumed the role of a prostitute, who embraced many lovers (Hos. 2:5; Jer. 2:20; 3:1-14; Ezek. 16:36). The unfaithful one might "dress in crimson" and deck herself "with ornaments of gold," but the prophets warned that all her primping would be in vain, for in the end her lovers would destroy her (Jer. 4:30), which is the fate of Babylon in Rev. 17:16.

Several ancient cities were described as prostitutes in the Old Testament, because their grandeur and wealth wooed the people of Israel into compromising their exclusive relationship to God. One of the cities that was "seated upon many waters" (Rev. 17:1) was Tyre, a city along the Mediterranean coast (Ezek. 27:3). Tyre was derided as a prostitute because of its willingness to do whatever was required to lure clients into its glittering network of sea trade (Isa. 23:17). Nineveh, the capital of Assyria, was built beside the Tigris River. Nineveh could show cruelty toward the nations it conquered, but it was also "the prostitute, gracefully alluring, mistress of sorcery, who enslaves nations through her debaucheries" (Nah. 3:4). King Ahaz of Judah was so taken with Assyrian art that he had an Assyrian-style altar built for the Jerusalem

The Harlot Riding the Seven-Headed Beast (Rev. 17:1-8)
by Albrecht Dürer

temple, even as he paid the Assyrians for the privilege of being their servant (2 Kings 16:5-16).

Memories of "Babylon the Great," the name inscribed on the Harlot's forehead, contribute even more directly to John's portrait of the city (Rev. 17:5). Built beside the Euphrates River and interlaced by canals, Babylon was enthroned "by mighty waters" (Jer. 51:13), like the harlot in Rev. 17:1. If the harlot held a cup in her hand and made the nations drunk (Rev. 17:2, 4), Jeremiah previously said that Babylon "was a golden cup in the Lord's hand, making all the earth drunken" with its mind-numbing power (Jer. 51:7; cf. Jer. 25:15-16). Nevertheless, in its run for success, Babylon eventually tripped and fell under divine judgment (Jer. 51:8). The same will be true of the harlot in Revelation.

Readers in John's time would readily have connected Babylon the harlot with Rome, the city set on seven hills (Rev. 17:9), whose power was both cruel and seductive. Babylon destroyed the first Jerusalem temple and Rome destroyed the second temple. The Romans also shed "the blood of the saints and the blood of the witnesses to Jesus" in the ruthless persecutions that took place under Nero and in other sporadic acts of violence (17:6); but that did not mean that all Christians considered Roman rule intolerable. The Roman Empire stretched across "many waters" from Europe to Asia (17:1), and sea trade flourished (18:11-19). Many "of the inhabitants of the earth" (17:2), including some Christians (3:17), became intoxicated with the prosperity that the Romans provided and were willing to commit fornication with the cult of the emperor (2:14, 20-22). In the most basic sense, however, "fornication" means not only "participation in the idolatrous worship of Roman gods, including Caesar, but accepting Rome as the point of orientation for life in this world, that is, making Rome herself a god" (Boring, *Revelation,* 180).

John pens a satirical portrait that incorporates Roman symbols, but caricatures them in order to break the spell with which the great city bewitches the nations. Artistic representations of the goddess Roma, who personified Roman power for the Greek world, sometimes depict her as a noble woman draped in battle dress, reclining on the seven hills of Rome. Her foot stretches out to the Tiber River that flows in front of her, and her left hand is slightly raised so that it rests on the top of a short sword (Aune, *Revelation,* 920). In Revelation 17, this dignified lady becomes a debased courtesan. The seven stately hills on which she reclines are transformed into the snarling seven heads of the beast. The woman's hand no longer holds a sword but a goblet filled with a vile yet intoxicating brew, and her sober expression is transformed into a drunken stare. This mother figure, whose temples were built in the cities of Asia, is pictured as the "mother of whores and of earth's abominations" (17:5). This, John declares, is what the great city really is.

John's lampoon of the great harlot was designed to move first-century readers to resist being seduced by the power and wealth of Rome into compromising their loyalties to God, Christ, and the Christian community. The implications of the satire, however, are not confined to the first century. The harlot's traits are not simply those of Rome, but include those of Babylon, Tyre, and Nineveh. By encompassing characteristics from all of these cities, the harlot represents a power that is not limited to one place or to one time. When the harlot's arrogance, violence, and obsession with luxury are described more fully in Revelation 18, modern readers will find themselves confronting forces that belong not to a forgotten age, but to the world that they know.

Significance of the Harlot (17:7-18)

Before speaking of the harlot's downfall, John's angelic guide explains more about the harlot and the beast that she rides. Readers have already learned that the seven-headed beast is the earthly ally of Satan, the seven-headed dragon (12:3; 13:3). Previously, the beast has imitated Christ, for like Jesus the Lamb, the beast was slaughtered and yet lives (13:3, 12, 14). Now the beast is the great mimicker of God, for if God is the one who "was and is and is to come" from heaven (4:8), the beast "was and is not and is to ascend from the bottomless pit" (17:8). The similarities between God and the beast heighten the sense of conflict between them, for they represent two forms of power and two contending claims. The direction set by the beast leads to destruction (17:8), while that set by God leads to the new creation (21:1).

The angel's comments about the beast underscore that John did not write Revelation in a code, but used evocative symbols to convey multiple dimensions of meaning. First, by explaining that the seven heads of the beast symbolize seven mountains (17:9), John shows that he was not using symbols to conceal his message from his Roman captors so that it could be smuggled off the island of Patmos. The "city set on seven hills" was such a common description for Rome that not even the most obtuse Roman censor would have missed the point. Second, when people use a code, each symbol has a single meaning. On a map, for example, one symbol stands for a school and another for a church. John, however, says that the beast's heads must be understood in two ways, as seven mountains and as seven kings (17:9). Earlier, John did something similar when he said that the seven spirits of God are represented by two different symbols: the seven torches before God's throne and the seven eyes of the Lamb (4:5; 5:6).

Keeping the supple quality of Revelation's imagery in mind can help keep readers from rushing down the path of decoding only to find themselves standing knee-deep in a discouraging bog, surrounded by an impenetrable thicket of ideas with no clear way out. Some decoders assume that Revelation offers predictions of the future events that can be deciphered on the basis of today's headlines. For years, many speculated that the European Common Market might have been the ten-nation coalition represented by the beast's ten horns, which would ally itself with an apostate form of Christianity that would be based in Rome prior to the second coming of Christ (Lindsey, *Late Great Planet Earth*, 94). Since the Common Market now has more than ten member nations, others propose that the United Nations Security Council might be expanded to ten supreme nations who will rule the world (LaHaye and Jenkins, *Are We Living in the End Times?*, 169-70).

Historical interpreters reject such speculations, rightly pointing out that the book of Revelation, like the letters of Paul, was written to address the needs of its first-century readers, not to issue predictions that would be unintelligible until the end of time. Nevertheless, some historical interpreters have tried unsuccessfully to decode Revelation 17 in their own way, by relating each point of the vision to something in the first century. The challenge is that the beast's seven heads are said to represent seven kings, five who have fallen, one who is still living, and another who will come to reign for a short time. Afterward, one of the seven kings will come back as an eighth ruler, who will share his reign with the ten lesser kings that are represented by the beast's ten horns, and make war on the saints (17:9-14).

Many have tried to identify the seven kings with seven Roman emperors. But which seven? Would the sequence start at the beginning of the imperial period with Julius Caesar or Caesar Augustus, or would it begin with Nero, who conducted the first major persecution of Christians in Rome? Would the sequence include all the emperors of a given period? Those who reigned for a significant length of time? Those who were deified before John wrote? Or perhaps only those who had "fallen" by violent deaths? No enumeration of Roman emperors fully suits Revelation 17, despite many creative attempts in this direction.

A more helpful way to read the text is to recognize that John uses evocative imagery that resists decoding. Elsewhere in Revelation, the number seven indicates completeness, so that when John writes to seven churches in Asia, he presents a message to the whole church. When he says that the seventh seal is broken (8:1), the seventh trumpet is sounded (11:15), or the seventh bowl is emptied (16:17), he indicates that a vision cycle is complete. Accordingly, identifying the seven heads with seven kings seems to point to the totality of the beast's power. Picturing an eighth king as a return of one of the seven seems to play on legends that Nero would return, so that one could say of a future persecution of the people of God: "It is Nero all over again" (see p. 134 above).

Despite the ambiguity in its details, the end of the story is clear. Evil self-destructs. The beast and its allies begin by waging war against the Lamb (17:13-14), but they end up by destroying the harlot (17:16). After carrying the great harlot for a time, the beast overthrows her. The purple and scarlet gown, and the gold and jewels that gave her pride are stripped away in disgrace. She who consumed the blood of the saints is now consumed by the jaws of the beast, and her remains are burned with fire (17:16). In an ironic twist, destruction by fire means that for the harlot herself it is "Nero all over again," because under Nero the city set on seven hills was devastated by fire once before (Tacitus, *Annals* 15.38). In an earlier vision, Babylon was shattered by one of God's angels (Rev. 16:19), but here God's will is carried out when God directs the forces of evil to pursue their own destructive course. The beast comes from the bottomless pit, where destruction reigns (17:8; cf. 9:11), and destruction is what it brings, even to its allies. The sobering message of this vision is that God's judgment is carried out when he allows those who wreak destruction to become victims of their own practices.

Babylon's Funeral (18:1-24)

The vision of the demise of "Babylon" is followed by a lengthy dirge over the fallen city, a foretaste of Babylon's funeral. John does not recount this vision in a strict chronological sequence. One scene declares that Babylon has already "fallen" (18:2), but the next urges people to "come out of her," which assumes that the city is still standing (18:4). John describes the grief of the kings in the future tense (18:9), the grief of the merchants in the present tense (18:11), and the grief of the shipmasters in the past tense (18:18). Yet the angel with the millstone speaks of Babylon's fall as something in the future (18:21). The ever-shifting time frame may be due to the fact that John recounts a past vision of a future occurrence, but it also shows that his primary concern is not to detail a sequence of coming events. Rather, he writes in order to influence the way his readers live in the present, startling them into considering their current commitments in relationship to the ways of God (A. Y. Collins, *Apocalypse*, 126).

Modern readers can sense how a vision of a funeral might affect people by considering the well-known story *A Christmas Carol* by Charles Dickens. In this story a rich miser named Ebenezer Scrooge is visited by three spirits. The first shows him visions of Christmas celebrations from his past, the second shows him people celebrating in the present, and the third shows him the dark specter of the future. At the direction of this third spirit, Scrooge overhears leading businessmen talking about someone who has died. They express little genuine sympathy for the deceased, focusing instead on what will become of his money. Next he sees the dregs of society — "obscene demons" — preying like vultures on the dead man's property, and he hears poor people quietly rejoicing that their pitiless creditor is gone. Finally, the spirit shows Scrooge a desolate and overgrown graveyard, where a stone bearing Scrooge's name protrudes from the grass and weeds. Scrooge cries out, "Why show me this, if I am past all hope!" Instead, "Assure me that I may yet change these shadows you have shown me, by an altered life!"[1]

Revelation's depiction of Babylon's fall is designed to have a similar effect. Babylon the harlot is not a miser, of course, but like Scrooge she

---

1. Quotations are from Charles Dickens, *A Christmas Carol* (New York: Macmillan, 1950), 125-26.

is wealthy, grasping, and callous. Readers are first taken to the desolate graveyard, where Babylon's name is inscribed on the rubble, and obscene demons and vultures hover over the remnants of her wealth (18:2). Next, readers are allowed to overhear what the leading business people say about her downfall. Although expressing grief, their thoughts have mainly to do with the lamentable loss of her wealth (18:11-19). The oppressed do have reason to be glad, however, at the demise of their pitiless master (18:20). The point of this specter, like the point of the visions of the future in Dickens' story, is to move readers to renounce the arrogant and inhumane ways of injustice. The key verse is 18:4:

> "Come out of her, my people,
> so that you do not take part in her sins,
> and so that you do not share in her plagues."

The proper response to the vision is not fatalism, but "an altered life," to use Scrooge's words. When readers become aware of their own complicity in the practices of the harlot city and distance themselves from her ways, the vision has the effect for which it was written. We should consider the passage in more detail.

Babylon's Fall (18:1-8)

Radiant with light, the brightness of the angel who descends from heaven pierces the pall of gloom that lies over the rubble of Babylon. Echoing the words of the prophets, the angel proclaims, "Fallen, fallen is Babylon the great" (18:2); and he describes the eerie desolation that has replaced the formerly vibrant life of the city (18:2). The city once attracted the most prestigious inhabitants of the earth (17:2; 18:3), but now her smoldering ruins make a suitable dwelling only for the demons and foul spirits that drift down the deserted streets. The harlot had once preyed on the saints and the witnesses to Jesus (17:6), but here one finds "foul birds," like vultures and buzzards, circling silently above her in search of carrion (18:2b; Lev. 11:13-19).

The reasons given for Babylon's fall in Rev. 18:3 would have helped to awaken a sense of uneasiness in John's earliest readers. The angel may speak in general terms of "all the nations" and "the kings of the earth" taking part in fornication with the harlot, but John has made clear that some of the Christians addressed by the book had tendencies in this direction. "Fornication" was a metaphor for practices that violated relationships with God and the Lamb. The messages to the seven churches identified eating meat offered to idols as a form of such fornication (2:14, 20), warning that those who made themselves socially more comfortable by accommodating pagan practices would fall under divine judgment. The angel also refers to "the merchants of the earth" who have "grown rich from the power of her luxury" (18:3), but the Christians of Laodicea also fell into this category, for their primary source of security was wealth, not Christ (3:17).

When the heavenly voice cries, "Come out of her, my people" (18:4), it speaks especially to readers who are being lulled into complacency by their prosperity, or who find compromising the integrity of their faith to be a reasonable price to pay for the favors offered by the harlot. The call to "Come out of her" echoes a similar plea by Jeremiah (Jer. 51:45), but it is not meant as physical departure from an actual city. John's readers lived in Asia Minor, not in Babylon or Rome, the city set on seven hills (Rev. 17:5, 9). The angelic voice beckons them to dissociate themselves from the infidelity and materialism that were the hallmarks of the great city's trade, following instead in the ways of the Lamb.

Babylon's world is self-centered. Previous visions have shown that true glory belongs to the God who created all things and to the Lamb who redeems people by his blood. They are worthy to reign over all things (4:11; 5:12-13; 7:12; 11:15; 14:7). Babylon, however, glorifies herself and deludes herself into thinking that she is sovereign (18:7; cf. Isa. 47:8). John assumes that readers know that Babylon's splendor did not come without cost to others, and the heavenly voice declares that God will deal with Babylon in the same way that she has dealt with others (Rev. 18:6). Babylon became angry when she did not get what she wanted. Since she enjoyed giving others a taste of her wrath (14:8; 18:3), God will mix her a double in the same cup, so that she can taste wrath to the full (18:6). As she wallowed in luxury in her quarters, others faced torment and grief on the street. Therefore, judgment means that she will finally be handed the bill of suffering so that she can pay the cost herself (18:7).

The Mourners (18:9-24)

At this point, three groups of mourners appear, each standing some distance away from the fallen city, watching the smoke curling up from its ruins. The mourners include the associates of the harlot: the kings of the earth, mercantile magnates, and those who work in the shipping industry. Unlike the harsh voices of judgment that have been heard thus far, these groups display grief at Babylon's downfall (18:9, 11, 15, 19), offering eulogies that list the many splendors of the late great city. By exhibiting a more sympathetic attitude toward the harlot, the mourners give readers a way to examine their own viewpoints. Those who have been disturbed by the prospect of judgment falling on the harlot may find themselves nodding in agreement with what the kings, merchants, and sailors say. Yet if they do identify with the mourners, they have reason to be doubly disturbed, for it means that their primary loyalties lie with the self-indulgent city, and not with those who have suffered at her hands or with the God they worship.

The first group of mourners consists of the kings of the earth (18:9-10). They voice their grief by saying "Alas, alas, the great city" for "your judgment has come," yet they stand at a safe distance out of fear of having to suffer in the same way themselves. By emphasizing that the kings "committed fornication and lived in luxury" with the harlot, John also points to the sordid quality of the relationship. When the kings mourn the loss of Babylon, they actually mourn the loss of an illicit and self-indulgent relationship.

The second group of mourners consists of merchants, and here the reason for their grief seems clearly to be self-interest: "no one buys their cargo anymore" (18:11). Losing the harlot means losing income. The list of items that follows shows that the most important trade consisted in luxury items, not staples. Much of the gold and silver came from Spain, while jewels and pearls were brought from India. Textiles that were dyed purple and scarlet often came from Asia Minor, while silk was brought from China at great expense. Lavish use of ivory had led to reduced numbers of elephants in Syria and North Africa, so that Indian ivory was imported. Moroccan wood, Corinthian bronze items, Spanish ironwork, and African marble all were coveted. Expensive spices, incense, and myrrh came from Arabia and India. High demand for olive oil, wheat, and wine necessitated shipping quantities to Rome from Spain and North Africa. Cattle, sheep, horses, and chariots fill out the picture (Bauckham, *Climax of Prophecy,* 350-71).

Human beings are mentioned last on the list, and John's reference to their sale offers a climactic comment on the entire picture of commerce. The Greek expression can be translated in different ways, so that 18:13 refers to buying and selling human "bodies and souls" (NIV) or to the sale of "slaves — and human lives" (NRSV). Either way, the text recognizes that slaves are human beings, not objects. By concluding the list in this way, John underscores the brutality of a commercial system that reduces people to trade items like wood or livestock in order to supply the luxury needs of the harlot and her associates.

The dehumanizing quality of the commercial system is also reflected in the merchants' relationship with the harlot herself. She is known by her endless cravings for "dainties" (18:14), so that the merchants' relationship with her is defined by her demands for luxury items and their ability to supply them. Her demise brings an end to a profitable trade that was carried out for the sake of conspicuous consumption. As the merchants lament the fall of the harlot, their words also show that they think that her death was a pitiable waste of fine clothing. Her fine linen, her purple and scarlet gown, her gold, jewels, and pearls were such a feast for the eye that they feel genuinely pained by such a loss of wealth (18:15-17a). Babylon's materialistic obsessions are mirrored in the grief of her associates.

The third group of mourners, consisting of shipmasters and sailors, continues the pattern. Their lament over the fall of Babylon is essentially an exercise in self-pity. Throwing dust on their heads they cry out, "Alas, alas the great city, where all who had ships at sea grew rich by her wealth! For in one hour she has been laid waste" (18:19). Losing the city means losing a lucrative business partner. In weeping for her, they weep for their bank accounts.

Another angel strides abruptly onto the stage, brusquely ending the laments of the shipmasters and sailors by hurling a millstone into the sea as a portent of the violence with which Babylon will be destroyed (18:21). The angel directs the orchestra to quit playing. The harpists cease plucking the strings, and the flute and trumpet players put down their instruments (18:22). After announcing that all city businesses will be terminated and that marriage celebrations will be canceled, the angel calls for "lights out" (18:22-23). Then, in order to give the audience some explanation as to why this severe sentence is being imposed, the angel discloses Babylon's secret. Her splendor was purchased through deception, sorcery, and "the blood of prophets and of saints, and of all who have been slaughtered on earth" (18:24).

Readers have already been reminded about the deaths of Antipas and other Christian saints (2:13; 6:9; 12:11), but the judgment against the city is not linked solely to its suppression of the followers of Jesus. The angel speaks of "all" who have been slaughtered on earth. In the time of the prophets, Babylon expanded her empire at great cost of human life (Jer. 51:49) and Rome did the same as her armies overran neighboring peoples. She purchased "peace stained with blood" (Tacitus, *Annals* 1.10.4). The critique of Babylon in Revelation 18 stresses the interconnection between economic affluence, self-deceptive arrogance, and political brutality. Violence toward Christians is but one manifestation of evils that permeate a social order.

John's portrayal of Babylon's fall is a tapestry woven from threads taken from many periods of time. Much of the language echoes the threats against Tyre in Ezekiel 26–28, together with those against Babylon in Jeremiah 50–51. Allusions to many other texts also appear. The announcement of the city's fall and desolation recalls Isa. 21:9 and 13:19-22, while the fact that Babylon's sins, which are "heaped as high as heaven," should be doubly repaid links Jer. 51:9 and 16:18. The Harlot's boast that she would never be a widow paraphrases Isa. 47:8 and the list of trade goods has a counterpart in Ezek. 27:12-22. Symbolizing Babylon's destruction by hurling a stone into the sea generally follows Jer. 51:63-64, while silencing the sounds of the bride and groom recalls Jer. 25:10. Other allusions could be added to the list.

Readers in the seven churches would have identified "Babylon" with Rome, the city set on seven hills (Rev. 17:9). Yet when we consider how the description of the city and its fall combines elements pertaining to Tyre, Babylon, and Rome, we can better see that the great city in Revelation 17–18 represents something that is not confined to one time and/or place. The Christians in Asia Minor were called to resist social currents and institutions that were driven by the seduction of luxury, license, and power. Readers of later generations are called to do the same, wherever these appear.

Some may wonder whether Revelation opposes all that human culture has produced, since one could read the text as a thoroughgoing rejection of political institutions, trade, craftsmanship, musical achievements, and wedding celebrations. Yet this interpretation would miss the point. Other New Testament writers are more positive about human government (Rom. 13:1-7; 1 Pet. 2:13-17), but John confronts readers with the seamy side of a social, political, and economic life that is ultimately self-serving. He sees how the wealth of the few is paid for by the misery of the many, and how the security of some is obtained by the deaths of others. At the same time, John offers a contrasting picture of community life that is God-serving. The harpists fall silent in Babylon (Rev. 18:22), but they continue to play for God and the Lamb (15:2). Bride and groom may not celebrate in the face of God's judgment (18:23), but they will find reason to celebrate at the marriage supper of the Lamb (19:7, 9).

Hallelujah, the Lord Reigns (19:1-10)

Heavenly voices bring this cycle of visions to its climactic conclusion with a cascade of praises to God. One group within the chorus begins the sound of praise, and others continue it or respond with the "Amen." The word "Hallelujah," which means "Praise the Lord," serves as the refrain (19:1, 3, 4, 6). Those who have heard how Georg Friedrich Handel set a part of this passage to music in his "Hallelujah Chorus" can sense the play of joy, as the "Hallelujahs" are taken up by one set of voices and then another in a swelling wave of sound. In Revelation 19, a great multitude sings out "Hallelujah," and the twenty-four elders and four living creatures, who regularly appear in scenes of heavenly worship, respond by falling down before the throne to worship God (19:1, 3, 4; cf. 4:8-11; 5:14; 7:11-12; 11:16). When a voice from the throne invites everyone to praise God, the great multitude responds by singing out again, "Hallelujah!" (19:5, 6).

The multitudes praise God for the "salvation" that he has brought (19:1). In this context salvation refers to deliverance from the oppressive power of the harlot, whose smoke goes up forever and ever as a sign that her demise is permanent (19:3). Some readers may be troubled by the idea of celebrating such a victory, preferring a gentler version of the gospel; but the context suggests that joy is appropriate. The harlot was responsible for corrupting the earth and shedding the blood of the saints (19:2). Those who have been subjected to this corruption and whose lives have been threatened by her power will find blessed relief when oppression is lifted. Moreover, the justice of God, as celebrated here (19:2), consists in directing the beast to turn its rage away from the saints and toward its own ally, the harlot. Justice is done when evil self-destructs. The harlot's fiery end comes when the demonic power that she uses against others ends up destroying her (17:16).

Along with the praises, the festival choir announces that the marriage feast of the Lamb has come, and that the bride has made herself ready (19:7). Mentioning the bride recalls Old Testament passages in which God is the husband and his people are his bride (Isa. 62:5; Jer. 2:2; Hos. 2:19-20). The same idea appears in the New Testament where the church is the bride and Christ is the groom (2 Cor. 11:2; Eph. 5:25-32; John 3:29). Readers will learn in Rev. 21:2 and 9 that the bride is the New Jerusalem, which contrasts with Babylon the harlot, just as the Lamb contrasts with the beast.

Revelation assumes that readers will belong to some community and that living as a detached individual is not an option. The only question is the nature of the community to which people belong. John has depicted the harlot in strongly negative colors so that readers will be repulsed by what she represents. Here he introduces the bride in a positive way in order that readers might identify with her instead. Both the bride and the harlot are relational images. The harlot is characterized by license and the bride by marital commitment. In relation to the harlot city, which stands under God's judgment, a bride and groom have no reason to celebrate (Rev. 18:23); but those who belong to the bride have reason to celebrate the marriage feast of the Lamb (19:9). Moreover, the harlot sought to buy fine linen to satisfy her cravings (18:12), but the fine linen that adorns the bride is a gift that God has "granted" to her, and it consists of the righteous deeds of the saints (19:8). Although the harlot represents a way of life that seems glamorous, John unmasks its underlying corruption and warns of its coming demise. The bride calls people to the way of righteousness instead.

The conclusion of this cycle focuses the message of the book when John bows down before his angelic guide and is told, "Worship God" (19:10). Earlier, readers were warned against falling into the worship of the beast or other adversaries of God (13:4). Here they are warned against worshiping the angelic emissaries of God. The heavenly scenes that conclude each major section of Revelation reiterate that God and the Lamb alone are worthy of worship. This same passage clarifies the nature of true prophecy, and by implication, the nature of the prophecy that John is writing (1:3; 22:18). The spirit of prophecy is "the testimony of Jesus" (19:10). This expression can refer to the testimony that the community of faith has received from Jesus and to the testimony that they bear to Jesus in their own preaching. As we saw in chapter 2, the criterion for true prophecy is whether it moves people to worship the true God and to be faithful to Jesus (see pp. 45-47).

Chapter 7

THE END

Revelation 19–22

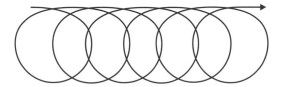

The sixth and final cycle of visions begins after the announcement that "the marriage feast of the Lamb has come" (19:7). One would think that if "the bride has made herself ready" in her gown of pure white linen, readers should soon see her process down the aisle to the sound of heavenly music. But in Revelation's predictably unpredictable vision of things, events take a different turn. The bride may be ready, but readers will not see her until a thousand years have passed; and while they wait, they see the Lamb — the groom at this wedding (19:7, 9) — thundering onto the page to slay the adversaries of God. Those hoping for a glimpse of "the marriage supper of the Lamb," with its tables laden with fine food (19:9), are instead given a revolting specter of "the great supper of God" (19:17), in which the birds of heaven are invited to feast on the slaughtered who lie on the battlefield.

Is this the End of all things? Does this carnage mark the culmination of God's purposes? John indicates that "No, there is more." And he tells of Satan being bound with a chain and hurled into the great abyss, whereas those who have resisted the beast and those who have been killed for their faith are raised to life so that they serve as priests and reign with Christ (20:1-6). Is this millennial kingdom of the redeemed the End of all things? Again, the answer is "no," for Satan is released to mount yet another attack on the saints, only to have his plot foiled by heavenly fire. All the dead are raised to stand before the throne of God, and the last judgment takes place. Then the bride of the Lamb, whose coming was announced before, descends in splendor as the new heaven and earth appear (21:1-2). The bride is the New Jerusalem, and it is here that Revelation's dizzying spiral of visions comes to its End. John takes readers on a tour of the city, showing them its pearly gates and streets of gold, its tree of life and river of living water. Yet even here John points his readers to something more.

The mystery of the End is revealed through the voice of God, who declares that "I am the Alpha and the Omega, the beginning and the end" (21:6), and through the voice of Christ, who says, "I am the Alpha and the Omega, the first and the last, the beginning and the end" (22:13). To use the words of Revelation itself, the End of all things is God and the Lamb. What is startling about this disclosure is that it brings us back to where we began. Readers are like travelers, who climb mountains and cross valleys, who swelter in the day and grope through the darkness at night, contending with plagues, tyrants, and wild beasts only to find themselves back on their front doorstep, looking at the view with new eyes. Already in chapter 1, God and Christ declared that they were the beginning and the end (1:8, 17), and the visions that followed show readers the implications of what it means to know that "the end is not an event, but a person" (Caird, *A Commentary*, 266).

Authentic prophecy is known by what it does: true prophecy moves people to worship the true God and false prophecy draws people away from God. The false prophets in John's visions show no lack of ability to perform miracles (13:13-15; 19:20), and John never faults them for issuing inaccurate predictions concerning future events. What makes them false is that they lure people into a false faith that binds them to powers that masquerade as God while serving the cause of destruction and oppression (2:20; 13:13-17; 16:13-14; 19:20). The true prophets in John's visions are not said to offer predictions of future events, but to call the peoples of the world to repentance (11:3). True prophecy is identified by its witness to Jesus and its call to "worship God" (19:10; 22:9). When Revelation moves people to faith in God and the Lamb, it brings them to the End for which the book was written.

The peculiar cyclical structure of Revelation, which we have followed throughout this book, directs attention to God and the Lamb as the End of all things. By taking readers through a dizzying spiral of visions, Revelation helps to undercut the readers' confidence that they can know the steps by which future events will unfold. Those who find a kind of security in knowing where they are on God's timeline subtly fall prey to a false faith, because God keeps the secrets of his coming hidden from human eyes (Matt. 24:36). Therefore, the kaleidoscopic changes in images that overlap with each other and convey similar messages in multiple guises actually help to show readers the limits of their own abilities to determine where they are in time. As Revelation's spirals unsettle readers, however, they repeatedly bring readers back to the presence of God and the Lamb, who are worthy of the readers' trust (Rev. 1:12-20; 4:1–5:14; 7:9-17; 11:15-19; 15:2-4; 19:1-10; 21:1–22:5).

The Great Battle (19:11-21)

Modern readers often turn to Revelation's final chapters with a mixture of dread and fascination that is fueled by the popular use of Revelation's imagery for the future annihilation of civilization. "Armageddon," the name mentioned in 16:16, is usually extended to various battle scenes that culminate in the great battle depicted in 19:11-21. Popular writers on biblical prophecy often use "Armageddon" as a synonym for "World War III," creating a composite picture of the battle by linking Scripture verses together like pieces of a jigsaw puzzle. A puzzle piece from Isa. 63:1-6, which depicts conflict in Edom or modern-day Jordan, is connected to other pieces from Joel 3:1-2 and 3:9-17, which speak of a battle in the Valley of Jehoshaphat. These in turn are linked to Zech. 12:1-9, which focuses on Jerusalem, and to additional pieces from Rev. 14:14-20; 16:12-16; and 19:11-21.

This composite picture is frequently overlaid with references to current developments in military technology and global politics. Some modern writers assume that when John writes about winged creatures, armies mounted on horses, and smoke rising from the bottomless pit, he really refers to squadrons of supersonic jet aircraft, missiles bearing nuclear warheads, battalions of tanks, laser weapons, and rising clouds of chemical gasses. The practice is so common that images from Revelation are readily used in this way by many who have never read the book itself, so that in the popular imagination, the road to Armageddon leads to the mushroom cloud that signals nuclear annihilation.

Revelation does depict warfare, but of a different sort. An important discipline in reading these texts is to ask what they say and what they do not say. In previous chapters we have discussed many of the images that John uses in his visions of battles. Here the most important point is that his account of the great battle in 19:11-21 explicitly mentions only one weapon: the word of God. No mention is made of missiles, aircraft, or tanks. All attention concentrates on the sword that comes from the mouth of Christ the warrior, the sword of his word (19:15, 21). By describing a battle that is waged and won by a word that is visualized as a sword, John shows that he is not describing an ordinary conflict, but using picture language to speak of the ultimate triumph of God over evil.

John's vision of the battle and its aftermath does not stay within ordinary limits of time and space. Recall that the conflict that climaxes in Revelation 19–20 actually began in Revelation 12, where Michael and his angels sent Satan the dragon tumbling down from heaven to earth. One would be hard-pressed to identify the date of Satan's expulsion from heaven or the place where he landed when he fell. The same is true here. The beast and false prophet, who are Satan's allies, are thrown alive into the lake of fire (19:20), while Satan himself is bound with a great chain and cast into the bottomless abyss (20:1-3). As John's vision moves effortlessly across the expanses of space, we can clearly sense that he is speaking about the defeat of God's adversaries, but not in a way that invites us to try locating the lake of fire or the door to the abyss on a map, or to ask how many feet of chain are needed to bind Satan.

It may be helpful to recall that events in Act II of Revelation unfold in the following sequence:

> Satan thrown from heaven to earth (Rev. 12)
> beast and false prophet conquer (Rev. 13)
> harlot rides on the beast (Rev. 17)
> harlot destroyed by the beast (Rev. 17)
> beast and false prophet conquered (Rev. 19)
> Satan thrown from earth into the abyss (Rev. 20)

At the beginning of Act II, John systematically introduces Satan, the beast and false prophet, and finally the harlot into the drama. Then, in reverse order, he describes the defeats of the harlot, the beast and false prophet, and finally Satan himself. Thus, the beast and false prophet conquer Christ's followers in Revelation 13, but in Revelation 19 they themselves are conquered. Similarly, Satan was banished to earth in Revelation 12, and he is finally banished from the earth in Revelation 20.

Christ the Warrior (19:11-16)

John's depiction of the overthrow of the beast and its allies focuses as much on the person of Christ (19:11-16) as on the events that take place (19:17-21). When Christ appears as a rider on a white horse, readers quickly realize that this figure is no stranger, but one whom they already know and who already walks among them. Revelation began with a vision of Christ with eyes aflame and the sword of the word coming out of his mouth (1:14, 17). The vision showed that Christ was already present with his followers, for he walked among the golden lampstands that represented the congregations. The one with the flaming eyes and the sword of the word (2:12, 18) was also called "faithful and true" (3:14), and he confronted his own followers with words of reproof and warning. Now the one who is "faithful and true" appears again with flaming eyes and the sword of the word (19:11, 15), not to reprove his followers this time, but to judge the adversaries of God, who have persistently refused to repent (9:20-21; 16:9, 11).

Christ returns as a warrior king on a white horse. Revelation is structured so that when the visions of plagues begin, a rider on a white horse appears (6:1-2), and after the plagues end, a similar rider appears (19:11). At first glance, the two figures might seem to be the same, and indeed both are conquerors; but there are important differences. The first horseman was unleashed by Christ, but the second rider is Christ himself, who comes to defeat the foes of God. The first rider received the kind of "crown" or wreath that signified victory, while the second rider wears the "diadems" that show royal power. By wearing many diadems (19:12) Christ challenges the pretensions of the dragon and the

175

beast, who display diadems on their heads and horns in a mockery of divine power (12:3; 13:1).

Christ's identity is partially, but not fully, revealed, for he "has a name inscribed that no one knows but himself" (19:12). Names are associated with power, so that invoking a name means calling upon the power of the one who bears it. Jesus' followers, for example, called on Jesus' power by praying and healing in his name (John 14:13; Acts 4:7, 10). To conceal one's true name, however, prevents others from invoking its power (Gen. 32:29; Judg. 13:17-18). Therefore, as Christ comes to the great battle in Revelation, he keeps a name secret, so that he alone has access to the power and authority that it represents. One name that is revealed, however, identifies Christ as the "Word of God" (Rev. 19:13). As the Word, he communicates the will of God to people, as well as putting God's will into effect (Isa. 55:11).

Christ's other name is "King of kings and Lord of lords" (Rev. 19:16), which is inscribed on his robe and on his thigh, where a warrior's sword normally hung (Ps. 45:3). Although God himself was known as "Lord of lords" (Deut. 10:17), Christ is not a usurper of God's power, but the agent by which God's rule is carried out. Earlier visions made clear that Christ received kingly power because he was uniquely worthy of it, for in faithfulness to God he ransomed people of every nation by his death (Rev. 5:9-14). Christ is the "King" above all the "kings" of the earth, who in previous visions allied themselves with the great harlot in order to raise a kingdom of callous luxury on the backs of its victims (17:1-18; 18:3, 9-10). As the "King of kings," Christ wields a power that is not only superior to that of other rulers, but different in kind.

Christ enters the fray wearing a robe dipped in his own blood (19:13). The red stains on his garments are visible before he has engaged his foes in combat, reminding readers about the peculiar nature of his victory. Earlier, John heard that "the Lion of the tribe of Judah, the Root of David, has conquered" (5:5), recalling Old Testament promises concerning the triumphant king who would come from David's line (Gen. 49:9-10; Isa. 11:1). What John saw, however, was that God kept the promise by sending the Lamb, who "conquered" by faithful suffering and death (Rev. 5:6-10). A similarly surprising fulfillment takes place in the great battle. The Old Testament promise comes from Isaiah 63, which pictures a divine warrior, wearing garments that are stained red, who says, "I have trodden the wine press alone," I trod the peoples "in my anger and trampled them in my wrath; their juice spattered on my garments" (Isa. 63:2-4). What John now sees, however, is that the divine warrior is Christ, who wears garments soaked in his own blood, which was shed for people of every nation (Rev. 5:9-10; 19:13). Christ can confront the nations because he has suffered for the nations.

Christ is accompanied by the armies of heaven, riding on white horses (19:14). Strangely, these armies do not wear standard military dress, but are dressed in white linen robes, which are more suitable for a festival gathering. Readers have already learned that those who accompany Christ at the great battle are "called and chosen and faithful" (17:14). This means that they are "called and chosen" by Christ, and they respond by being "faithful" to Christ. The fact that they wear white robes fits the pattern. Christ brings people into right relationship with God by sacrificing himself for them, so that they have "washed their robes and made them white in the blood of the Lamb" (7:14). Those whom Christ purifies are, in turn, summoned into a battle of faithfulness, which means resistance to sin and evil. Those who resist sin and evil by the way they live and the way they die "conquer" the powers of evil through faithfulness (3:4-5, 18; 6:11; 12:11). The white robes they receive from Christ are displayed in the righteous deeds that are the fine linen that adorns the people of God, the bride of the Lamb (19:8).

Readers are sometimes disturbed by Revelation's portrayal of the saints as the army of Christ, sensing that such a vision could sanction outbursts of violence in the name of Christ. Revelation does call Christians to take an uncompromising stand against sin and evil, but this militancy takes the form of faithful resistance against idolatry and greed. Moreover, in the cataclysmic battle of Revelation 19, what do the heavenly armies do? Nothing, according to John's account. All the action belongs to Christ: "in righteousness *he* judges and makes war" (19:11); "from *his* mouth comes a sharp sword with which to strike down the nations, and *he* will rule them with a rod of iron; *he* will tread the wine press of the fury of the wrath of God the Almighty" (19:15). John's vision of the great battle does not show the Christian community taking up arms against the nations of the world, but identifies Christ himself as the agent of God's victory. The one weapon that is mentioned is the sword of the word that comes from Christ's mouth. The rod that signifies royal rule is held in Christ's own hand, and when the wrath of God is unleashed, it is Christ, not his followers, who carries it out.

Victory Over the Beast and Its Allies (19:17-21)

Recognizing that Christ is the warrior may only heighten the readers' sense of discomfort, of course, because the battle he wages is depicted in the starkest of terms. An angel summons great flocks of birds to what is called "the great supper of God" (19:18; cf. Ezek. 39:17-20). The invitation evokes images of the skies growing dark with winged shapes, until vultures, hawks, and eagles circle overhead, as the angel reads out the ghastly menu for this feast: "eat the flesh of kings, the flesh of captains, the flesh of the mighty, the flesh of horses and their riders — flesh of all, both free and slave, both small and great" (Rev. 19:18). The adversaries of Christ gather, but what ensues can hardly be called a battle. The beast and false prophet are simply captured and cast into the lake of fire that burns with sulfur, and Christ slays the kings of the earth and their armies with the sword of his word. When Christ's word has done its work, the field is strewn with the bodies of the slaughtered, and the birds descend to gorge themselves on the remains of the dead (19:19-21).

At this point in the drama, some might wish to call a halt to the action and demand that John rewrite the script. Since John has depicted Christ as a Lamb in earlier scenes, one might argue that he should scrap this vision of battlefield carnage and replace it with something gentler and more lamb-like. Instead of conflict and victory, John could write about the Lamb and the beast reconciling their differences. Rather than wielding the sword, the Lamb would bury the sword and embrace the beast, agreeing to let bygones be bygones. While their respective armies shake hands with each other, the orchestra plays a final moving chorus as the credits roll across the screen, and the audience stands, stretches, and prepares to leave the theater.

John's vision of the warrior Christ, however, carries out a campaign not only against the beast, but against tendencies to look at the world and its evil through rose-colored glasses. The imagery is designed to be disturbing, in part because many of John's earliest readers had been lulled into complacency (pp. 66-69). John does not want readers to think that Christ's death as a sacrificial Lamb was intended to placate the forces of sin and evil. The forces that are defeated in this battle are "the destroyers of the earth" (11:18). The allies of these destructive powers were repeatedly given opportunity to repent, but at every turn they refused to do so (9:20-21; 16:9, 11). Revelation's vision cycles show that Christ did not shed his blood to assure the allies of the beast that God would not interfere with their designs. Instead, Christ died to wrest people from the kingdom of sin so they might serve in the kingdom of God (1:5-6). Obedience to the Lamb means defiance of the beast — Revelation does not envision a neutral position — and as long as the beast rages, the innocent suffer. The love of God and the justice of God converge by bringing the beast's reign to an end (cf. Ps. 9:8; 72:2; Isa. 11:4).

The horrible specter of "the great supper of God" that occurs after the battle is the counterpart to the appealing announcement of "the marriage supper of the Lamb" (Rev. 19:9, 17). The two visions are presented to readers as warning and promise. A warning vision is designed to repel people from sin and its consequences. When considering an earlier vision of the wicked being tormented with fire (14:9-10), we noted that some readers might relish such texts because they assume that the judgment inevitably falls on their opponents, not on themselves, while other readers might quickly reject the text as harsh and unchristian. We have seen, however, that the text can best be taken for what it is: a warning that is designed to bring change, not despair (pp. 139-40). The revolting description of the birds feasting on carrion is a similar warning that deserves a similar response. Readers best respond to the vision in a manner that is consistent with the rest of Revelation, not by dismissing it or by assuming that they themselves are immune from judgment, but by heeding the warning and turning from the ways of the beast to the ways of God.

The promise of "the marriage supper of the Lamb," which brings blessings to all who share in it, contrasts with the warning about the gruesome feast of the birds. The promise will be elaborated more fully in the description of the bride in Revelation 21, but here we must note how these texts relate to each other and to the readers. Warnings and promises work differently — a warning disturbs people and a promise assures them — but both serve the same end, which is that readers persevere in faith. John writes for a world in which it is easier to accommodate the beast than to resist it, a world in which faithfulness to the Lamb sets people uncomfortably apart from others in society. The warnings startle people out of an easy acceptance of the ways of the beast, while promises attract them to the ways of the Lamb.

Revelation's warnings and its promises are extended to all people. On the one hand, the book envisions people of all nations giving glory to God and the Lamb (5:9-14; 7:9-10). The saints sing, "Lord, who will not fear and glorify your name? For you alone are holy. All nations will come and worship before you" (15:4). A voice from the heavenly throne invites both "small and great" to worship God (19:5), and in the final scene, people of all nations stream into the New Jerusalem (21:24) where they find healing (22:2). On the other hand, both "small and great" are subject to judgment if they ally themselves with the beast, so that the opponents of God of every kind must know that their end will be destruction (19:17-21).

Both visions of the future stand before the readers, warning that there is judgment for all and promising that there is hope for all. Readers can best respond to the contrasting visions by heeding the warnings and by trusting the promises. Those who fall into despair because the warnings are so severe need to hear again the promises of life through the power of the Lamb, while those who fall into complacency because the promises seem so assuring are rightly startled by the warnings concerning God's judgments on sin and evil. Faith, which is the alternative to despair and to complacency, is the shape that life takes in anticipation of the End.

The Millennial Kingdom (20:1-6)

Binding of Satan (20:1-3)

The defeat of the beast and false prophet quickly leads to a mop-up operation in which an angel binds Satan, who was the power behind the beast's throne. Recall that Satan has already suffered a massive defeat, for he was cast out of heaven by Michael and the angels in Revelation 12. This meant that his sphere of operations was limited, for he could no longer come before the throne of God to denounce the righteous.

180

Satan extended his influence on earth through the beast, but now that the beast has been eliminated, Satan is exposed and vulnerable again. The angel binds Satan with a chain and throws "that ancient serpent" into the bottomless abyss, which the angel locks with a key. This action further restricts Satan's operations by barring him from earth itself for a period of a thousand years. In a previous chapter, an angel opened the door to the abyss, releasing clouds of foul smoke along with the Destroyer and his hordes of ghoulish locusts (9:1-11). The beast itself rose from the abyss to torment the followers of the Lamb (11:7; 17:8), but now with the beast out of the way, the angel pushes the dragon through the abyss's door and slams the lid shut.

The vivid images in this scene alert readers to the fact that John is using word pictures to describe things that do not neatly fit within the confines of space and time. Think first of all about the use of space in this vision. John understands Satan to be a real force that exerts its evil influence in the world, but he is not trying to persuade readers that Satan has the physical body of a dragon or that the dragon can be bound with a metal chain. John does not invite readers to speculate about exactly where on the globe the angel might capture Satan, or to wonder whether the door to the bottomless abyss is located in the northern or the southern hemisphere. John uses physical and spatial images for spiritual realities. This will also be true in his description of the kingdom of the saints in 20:4-6, which we will consider shortly.

Second, if the physical spaces in John's vision point to spiritual realities, the same is true of the references to time. John says that Satan is bound "for a thousand years" (20:2). Just as the door to the great abyss cannot be located on a map, the duration of the thousand years cannot be located on a calendar. One does not draw nearer to heaven by means of a space shuttle or nearer to the abyss by digging a shaft into the ground, and one does not enter the thousand-year period by turning a calendar page. John refers to time in order to point readers to a reality that lies beyond time.

This non-literal sense fits with other references in Revelation. When John says that the allies of the beast receive kingly power "for one hour" (17:12), he means that their reign is brief, not that it lasts for exactly sixty minutes. When he refers to persecution lasting for a three-and-a-half-year period, he repeats and varies the time reference, so that it does not fall into a neat chronological pattern (see pp. 106-7). When

Angel Casting Satan into the Abyss (Rev. 20:1-3)
by Albrecht Dürer

he uses multiples of a "thousand" to identify the number of the redeemed in 7:4-8 (twelve thousand from each tribe, for a total of
144,000), he quickly alters the imagery in 7:9 to show that this same
group actually consists of a multitude "that no one could count" (see
pp. 89-90). Similarly, John will use multiples of a "thousand" when
stating the dimensions of the New Jerusalem (21:16) — not to tell readers how much square footage to expect in eternity, but to speak about

its fullness and perfection. Fullness is what the "thousand years" signifies in 20:1-6.

Reign of the Saints (20:4-6)

After the angel has sealed the door over the abyss, John tells of a kingdom in which the saints reign with Christ for a thousand years. Tradition has long pictured the millennial kingdom as an earthly kingdom in which Old Testament promises come to fulfillment.[1] The usual practice is to draw on promises from the book of Isaiah, which envisions a time when people will live long and peaceful lives, building homes to live in and eating the fruit of their vineyards (Isa. 65:20-21). Through a transformation of the natural order, creation will become a paradise in which the "wolf and the lamb shall feed together" and "the lion shall eat straw like the ox" (Isa. 65:25). The city of Jerusalem is central to such hopes, for the prophets said that in "days to come the mountain of the Lord's house shall be established as the highest of the mountains, and shall be raised above the hills; all the nations shall stream to it." This will be the time when people "beat their swords into plowshares and their spears into pruning hooks; nation shall not lift up sword against nation, neither shall they learn war any more" (Isa. 2:2, 4; Mic. 4:1, 3).

In contrast to this tradition, however, Revelation itself does not associate any of these Old Testament passages with the millennial king-

---

1. The major ways in which theologians have dealt with Revelation's reference to the thousand-year kingdom were discussed in chapter 1. The usual labels identify ways in which this passage is incorporated into a theological system. Premillennialism affirms that Christ will return before ("pre") the millennium begins. A common form of this view is considered in chapter 1 under "Rapture, Tribulation, and Armageddon." Postmillennialism holds that Christ will return after ("post") the millennium. This approach was considered at the end of the section on "History, Politics, and Reform." Amillennialism describes theological systems that do not include an explicit thousand-year period in their understanding of time. Augustine is a representative of this approach (see pp. 7-8). Some, who take a rather quizzical view of the whole discussion, have humorously suggested other options. One is "pro-millennialism," meaning "if there is a millennium, I'm all for it." The other is "pan-millennialism," meaning "I'm sure it will all pan out in the end."

dom. John will make lavish use of Old Testament passages when describing the New Jerusalem in Rev. 21:1–22:5, and we will see that his vision of the city weaves lines from Isaiah, Ezekiel, Zechariah, and other Old Testament writings into a resounding symphony of promise. Clearly, John could have paraphrased or alluded to Old Testament passages in his description of the millennial kingdom if he had seen fit to do so; but this is not the case. He describes the thousand-year reign of the saints in remarkably spare prose, without the allusions to Old Testament texts that he includes so freely in other visions. The passage is so short that it can be quoted in full:

> ⁴And I saw thrones and they sat upon them, and judgment was given unto them: and I saw the souls of them that were beheaded for the witness of Jesus, and for the word of God, and which had not worshipped the beast, neither its image, neither had received his mark upon their foreheads, or in their hands; and they lived and reigned with Christ a thousand years. ⁵But the rest of the dead lived not again until the thousand years were finished. This is the first resurrection. ⁶Blessed and holy is he that hath part in the first resurrection; on such the second death hath no power, but they shall be priests of God and of Christ, and shall reign with him a thousand years. (20:4-6 KJV)

Some interpreters use this passage as a container that they fill with promises from the Old Testament, but this was not John's practice. Instead, he follows the lead of the book of Isaiah itself, which indicates that its promises will be fulfilled when God creates "new heavens and a new earth" (Isa. 65:17). The new heaven and earth that John announces in Rev. 21:1 will be the world of the New Jerusalem, the city to which the nations go up to worship the Lord, as the prophets said (21:24-26).

John does not actually say whether his vision of the thousand-year reign of the saints takes place on earth or in heaven, which is surprising given the usual assumptions that are made about this passage. On the one hand, he may well be speaking of a kingdom on earth, since the scenes that follow refer to the opponents of God coming from the four corners of the earth to attack the saints, and warn that fire will come down from heaven to destroy these enemies (20:7-10). On the other hand, the vision could refer to a heavenly kingdom, since John introduces it simply by saying that he "saw thrones," and in previous visions the throne of God and the thrones of the twenty-four elders were said to be located in heaven (4:2, 4; 11:16). Therefore, the thrones in 20:4 might be heavenly as well. In either case, noting John's vagueness about the location is a helpful way to check speculation about the nature of the millennial kingdom.

John speaks of the saints' whereabouts in relational rather than in geographical terms. Each time we might expect him to say that they "reigned on earth," he says that they "reigned with Christ" (20:4, 6). The point bears repeating. If we ask, "Where are the saints?" we receive the answer, "They are with Christ." The relational answer "with Christ" points us to the heart of life in the millennial kingdom. John is more concerned with "who" than with "where." Having assured readers that the saints will be "with Christ," John leaves most other questions unanswered, as if to say, "What more do you need to know?"

Readers may venture further by asking, "Who, specifically, will reign 'with Christ' in this kingdom?" John's prose is, again, remarkably vague on the point and most modern translations paraphrase the text to make it read more smoothly. The King James Version was quoted above because it conveniently preserves the ambiguity of the Greek. Those who share in the millennial kingdom are described in three ways in 20:4. John refers to: (1) those who sit on thrones, (2) those who were beheaded for their witness, and (3) those who had not worshipped the beast. The question is whether these descriptions apply to one, two, or three different groups. If John envisioned three groups, he might have thought of (1) the twenty-four elders sitting on thrones, giving a just verdict on behalf of (2) the martyrs and (3) all the faithful. If John referred to two groups, they would be two of those listed above. If he spoke of only one group, however, it would be the martyrs sitting on thrones as vindication for their faithfulness.

John may have been content with such imprecise language because for him, the martyrs epitomize and represent the faithful. When John spoke of "those who had been beheaded for their testimony" (20:4), he presumably referred to all martyrs, not only those who met their deaths in this particular way. Similarly, his earlier visions spoke as if all the faithful would die at the hands of the beast and its henchmen (13:15), so that in effect being faithful meant being a martyr. Jesus "conquered" by suffering death faithfully (5:6), and his followers also "conquer" by remaining faithful to the point of death (12:11); but faithfulness, rather than the manner of death, is the key point. John was not making strict predictions about a future time when every faithful Christian would be "beheaded," but he was calling all of his readers to show the kind of endurance and faithfulness that would accept martyrdom if necessary (13:10; 14:12; Bauckham, *Theology*, 107). The martyrs represent the faithful.

Those who have been faithful to the point of death are raised to life at the beginning of the millennial kingdom — something that constitutes the "first resurrection" — while the rest of the dead are raised to life only after the thousand years are complete (20:4-6). In other words, the martyrs and those like them are raised first, and this "first resurrection" gives them everlasting life and vindication from society's negative judgment against them. Having been raised, they will not die again or be subject to further judgment by God, but will reign with Christ. The second phase of the resurrection will occur in 20:11-15, when the rest of humanity is brought back to life. Those who are raised in this second phase are subject to God's judgment, with the result that some receive eternal blessing and others experience the eternal punishment that is called "the second death" (20:14).

Revelation is unique among New Testament writings in referring to resurrection in two phases. Its emphasis on the "first resurrection" that brings both life and vindication offers incentive to readers to persevere in faith at all costs. In the opening messages to the churches, the risen Christ assures his readers that even if society condemns those who prove faithful, God will not condemn them. They can "be faithful until death" in the confidence that Christ will give them "the crown of life." God may subject his opponents to the punishment that is "the second death," but he will vindicate the faithful, who will reign with Christ (2:10-11). This message is designed to promote faithful endurance (13:10; 14:12), not to make readers despair of grace. Eternal life belongs to all whose names are included in the Lamb's book of life, not only to a select spiritual elite. The resurrection may occur in two phases, but the result is finally the same: all the redeemed are brought to everlasting life, and all reign with Christ forever (22:5).

Final Conflict and Final Judgment (20:7-15)

Victory Over Satan and His Allies (20:7-10)

John's final cycle of visions turns like a great wheel, moving readers from scene to scene. The millennial kingdom was not the climax of the cycle, but merely one point along the way to the New Jerusalem. The scene shifts when Satan, released from his prison, gathers the nations known as Gog and Magog to mount yet another attack upon the saints (20:7-10). The names of the adversaries come from Ezekiel 38–39, which says that in the latter years a figure named Gog from the land of Magog will muster his hosts to attack those who are living securely on the mountains of Israel. God warns that he will destroy these armies by fire, and the carnage will be so great that the birds will be called to feast upon the slain.[2]

Revelation's last chapters point to the fulfillment of Ezekiel's visions, but they do not follow Ezekiel's sequencing. John spoke of the birds feasting on the slain (Ezek. 39:17-20) before the millennium, in Rev. 19:17-21; but he envisions Gog and Magog's attack on the saints and their destruction by fire (Ezek. 38:1-16; 39:5) after the millennium, in Rev. 20:7-10. John certainly affirms that God will protect his people and destroy their adversaries, as promised in Ezekiel; but he seems remarkably unconcerned about the chronological sequencing of the fulfillment. Ezekiel describes the order of events one way, John describes it in another; but the outcome is the same — deliverance — and deliverance is what is important. Recognizing this does not make the vision of Satan's release and the abortive attack against the saints by Gog and Magog any less peculiar, but some insights into its significance can be gained by considering each of the principal players in this short dramatic episode.

First, Satan has served a thousand-year prison sentence in the great

---

2. Premillennial dispensationalists identify Gog as Russia, and argue that the invasion depicted in Ezekiel 38-39 will take place in connection with the great tribulation that culminates in the battle of Armageddon. See, for example, Hal Lindsey, *Late Great Planet Earth,* chapter 5, "Russia is a Gog," and chapter 12, "World War II." Tim LaHaye and Jerry Jenkins opened a bestselling series of novels with the Russian invasion of Israel that fulfills Ezekiel 38-39 (*Left Behind,* 6-15).

abyss with no time off for good behavior. But upon his release, he promptly resumes his former way of life by practicing deception and enticing the nations into opposing the people of God. In Revelation 12, Satan mounted a campaign in heaven against Michael and his angels, but Satan lost and was thrown down to earth. Defeat brought no change in Satan, however, for scarcely had he landed, when he mounted another campaign against the people of God (12:13-17). With the aid of the beast and its false prophet (13:1-18), he sent out foul spirits to gather the kings of the earth for war against the forces of God (16:13-14); but Christ threw the beast and false prophet into the lake of fire, and Satan himself was confined to the abyss (19:19–20:3). Still, there is no change in Satan, for upon his release, he takes up where he left off by summoning the nations for war against the people of God (20:7-11). The pattern shows that Satan does not change or compromise. Therefore, those who encounter his power must resist it without compromise (2:10, 13, 24), confident that God himself will not compromise, but will finally bring Satan's rampage to an end.

Second, we can consider the role of the nations. John's description of the battle in 19:17-21 implied that all the forces hostile to God were annihilated; his account of the binding of Satan in 20:1-3 stated that during the millennium, Satan would not deceive the nations; and the vision of the thousand-year kingdom in 20:4-6 focused on the faithful reigning with Christ. When Satan is released, it seems incredible to think that there will be any nations left to deceive! One wonders how anyone on earth would heed the Devil's call after such a lengthy Satan-free period. John does not explain this, but lets readers live with the question. And perhaps a part of the vision's function is precisely to evoke such astonishment. The passage offers a pointed commentary on the human condition by indicating that whenever Satan is active, some will indeed be responsive to him. Any kingdom short of the new creation, with its new heaven and new earth, will include those who have a propensity to evil. Finally, restraining evil is not enough. Its seductive power must be brought to an end. Those who are drawn by its siren song are warned that disaster waits for those who yield to it.

Third, we can consider the role of the saints. The vision of the millennial kingdom depicted the saints coming to life in order to reign with Christ. They served as priests of God and were no longer threatened by divine condemnation (Rev. 20:4-6). When Satan is released, the saints are said to be residing in a "camp," perhaps recalling how the people of Israel lived in a camp during their sojourn in the wilderness. The saints also have a "beloved city," which evokes images of Jerusalem, the city that is loved and blessed by God (Ps. 78:68; 87:2). Ezekiel's oracles concerning Gog and Magog fill out the picture by speaking of the people dwelling in quiet and safety (Ezek. 38:8, 11, 14). The intrusion of Gog and Magog is a disturbing reminder that security is not something that the people of God ever possess in themselves. Despite all that has occurred, they are not immune from attack and finally have no security except in God. Peace and salvation are his gifts (Caird, *A Commentary*, 257).

Resurrection and Last Judgment (20:11-15)

John's vision of the last judgment begins when he sees a great white throne (20:11). In the millennial kingdom, only the faithful were brought back to life, but now all the dead are raised to stand before the throne of God. The power of God is palpable in this scene. Heaven and earth flee from God's presence. Death, Hades, and the sea, which hold the dead prior to this time, "give up the dead" that are in them (20:13), as if surrendering them to God. The result is that all people, great and small, render an account to the Sovereign.

The judgment is based on not one but two sets of books: the book of life and the books in which people's deeds are recorded (20:12). Each set of books has its own function. The book of life has to do with divine grace while the books of deeds have to do with human account-ability. The book of life is like a civic record, in which the citizens of the city of God have their names inscribed (21:27). John has already said that people are inscribed in this book "from the foundation of the world" (13:8; 17:8), which means that they cannot obtain access to the book of life by their own efforts, but are included in the book as an act of divine grace. Some cities expunged from the citizenship rolls the names of those who were condemned and executed, but the risen Christ said that he would not blot the names of the faithful out of this book, even though they were condemned by human beings (3:5; see pp. 68, 129-30).

The other set of books includes the records of what people have done during their lives. The book of Esther tells of an earthly book in which the king would keep a record of the good deeds that people performed, so that they could be rewarded (Esther 6:1-2). The book of Daniel, in turn, speaks of more comprehensive books that are kept in the archives of heaven. On the day of judgment, these books will be opened and people will be held accountable for their actions (Dan. 7:10). The idea that people's deeds are subject to final divine judgment appears in various New Testament writings (e.g., Matt. 25:31-46; John 5:28-29; 1 Cor. 3:10-15; 2 Cor. 5:10).

John speaks of some being thrown into the lake of fire, along with Satan, the beast, the false prophet, Death, and Hades. This is where the adversaries of God receive the fiery eternal condemnation that is the "second death" (Rev. 20:13-15). Warnings about punishment by fire are not unique to Revelation, but occur in Jesus' parables and other passages (e.g., Matt. 13:36-43, 47-50; Luke 16:19-31). The question is how one should take such threats. Warnings are not given to make people despair of grace, but to bring change and to avert disaster. John includes warnings in his book because he understands that the threat of divine judgment is real *and* because the hope of avoiding judgment is real. Earlier, we saw that the stark warning about fiery judgment in Rev. 14:9-11 was accompanied not by a call to despair, but by a call to faithfulness and a promise of blessing (14:12-13; see pp. 138-40). Similarly, the vision of Babylon's flaming collapse was not intended to make readers resign themselves to a hopeless future, but to call them away from sin (18:4; see pp. 162-63). Warnings of judgment are designed to unsettle the readers while the promises of salvation and blessing are designed to encourage them. Together, they serve the same purpose, which is the readers' perseverance in faith.

Note that in the judgment, both divine grace and human accountability are important, but God's decision finally is based on the grace that is represented by the book of life. John does say that people are "judged according to their works, as recorded in the books," and that they are "judged according to what they had done" (20:12, 13). Clearly, he understands that God holds people accountable for their way of life. At the same time, John does not suggest that salvation is ultimately based on human achievement, so that only those who achieve a certain score in their books of deeds merit a place in the kingdom. God's favorable judgment is an expression of grace. People can hope for a place in

190

the heavenly city because God wants them there and writes their names in the book of life (20:15; 21:27).

Many readers find it unnerving to find John speaking about God writing people's names in the book of life from the foundation of the world. Those who take John seriously naturally want to know, "Is my name included in God's book?" Revelation does not list the names that are in the book of life, but it does give readers enough information to know that the comments about the book of life are designed to encourage faithfulness, not despair. John's counsel can be summarized this way: Trust that the Lamb, who died to liberate people from "every tribe and language and people and nation" for life with God (5:9-10), also died for you. Trust that God wants you to put this faith into practice — then leave matters concerning the final judgment in God's hands.

The New Jerusalem (21:1–22:5)

The final chapters bring Revelation's cycles to a climax with a vision that unfolds in brilliant color and cascades of harmonious sound. The dissonant echoes of conflict and judgment give way to a majestic chorus of concord and hope. Visually, the vision begins with a panoramic view of the new heavens and new earth, and a glimpse of the New Jerusalem coming down out of heaven in the distance. Next, an angelic guide brings John closer to the city, so that attention focuses on the city itself. Readers are told of its walls and gates, which are made of gemstones, pearls, and gold. Then they are taken into the city, where the river of the water of life flows from the throne of God and the Lamb, and the tree of life bears fruit and produces leaves for the healing of the nations. When the vision comes to its End, it comes to God and the Lamb, where the redeemed gather around the throne in worship. At last they see the face of God, and reign in his light forever.

Creator and New Creation (21:1-8)

Revelation envisions the salvation of the whole of creation, not only the redemption of individual souls. Like Paul, who speaks of the day when

191

"the creation itself will be set free from its bondage to decay" to "obtain the freedom of the glory of the children of God" (Rom. 8:21), John points to a new creation as the goal of God's purposes. The resurrection of the faithful is part of the resurrection of the world. Recall that when John first came before the throne of God, the four living creatures that had the faces of a lion, an ox, an eagle, and a human being, led the hosts of heaven in a chorus of praise to the Creator of all things (Rev. 4:6-11). When the Lamb received a scroll from God, waves of praise spread through the entire created order, until every creature "in heaven and on earth and under the earth" joined in singing praises to God and the Lamb (5:13). This vision of a creation tuned to the praise of its Creator anticipates the outcome of the saving work of God and Christ. In subsequent visions, the creation is the scene of conflict, as powers opposed to God seek to exert their influence over the world and its people. God responds by "destroying the destroyers of the earth" (11:18), so that in the end, "the kingdom of the world" can truly be "the kingdom of our Lord and of his Christ" (11:15).

The new creation is marked, in part, by an *absence* of powers that oppose God and diminish life. The demise of the harlot brought an end to a power that reduced the creation and its people to mere commodities that could be bought and sold to satisfy the self-indulgent tastes of the powerful (18:11-19). The defeat of Satan, the beast, and their allies eliminated powers that dominated the nations and oppressed the faithful (19:19-21; 20:7-10). The resurrection of all the dead brought an end to death itself (20:14). Therefore, in the new creation there is an absence of death, mourning, crying, and pain, for all those marks of the former, fallen world have passed away, together with the sea from which the beast arose (21:1, 4; cf. 13:1). At the same time, the new creation is characterized by the *presence* of the God who gives life. The anguished cry, "Where is your God?" will no longer be heard (Ps. 42:3), for in quick succession, a voice from the throne declares that God's dwelling will be "with humankind"; he will dwell "with them," and "God himself will be with them" (Rev. 21:3). Instead of the toxic waters of judgment (8:11; 16:3-4), God will invite them to drink freely from "the spring of the water of life" that flows from his throne (21:6; 22:1).

The voice from the throne declares that the God who promises all these things is "faithful and true" (21:5). To underscore this, each verse in this section recalls passages from the writings of the prophets, weaving older melodies into a new symphony of promise. Seeing a new heaven and a new earth echoes Isa. 65:17. The descent of the holy city, New Jerusalem, which appears in splendor like a bride adorned for her husband, recalls Isa. 52:1; 61:10; 65:18. Announcing that the dwelling of God is among people marks the fulfillment of Ezek. 37:27, while saying that God will dwell with them and they will be his peoples affirms Zech. 2:10-11; 8:8. To say that God will wipe away every tear from their eyes and that death will be no more corresponds to Isa. 25:8. For mourning, crying, and pain to end, and for the former things to pass away fulfills Isa. 65:17, 19. God makes all things new (Isa. 43:19), for he is the beginning and the end (Isa. 44:6). To the thirsty, he gives water as a gift from the spring of the water of life (Isa. 55:1). The chorus of echoes of Old Testament passages sounds a resounding "yes" to the promises of God.

The heavenly voice breaks out of this assuring vision of the future in order to address the time in which the readers live. God is assuredly "faithful and true," but what about the readers? At the beginning of Revelation, Christians are called to "conquer" through their faithfulness to God and the Lamb. The Lamb "conquered" by offering himself as a sacrifice for others before being raised to everlasting glory (Rev. 5:5-6). Those who are freed by the Lamb become part of a resistance movement against pressures to abandon faith, whether these pressures come from overt hostility, from the temptation to compromise one's faith in order to assimilate more comfortably into pagan society, or from the complacency that wealth induces (see chapter 2 above). From an earthly perspective, yielding to pressure often seems easier than paying the price that faithfulness entails. Therefore, each message to the churches ends with a promise to "the one who conquers," expanding the readers' perspective beyond the challenges of the moment, so in the vision of the New Jerusalem they can see what God has prepared for the faithful (2:7, 11, 17, 28; 3:5, 12, 21). These promises are summarized and reaffirmed here in the promise that the outcome of faith is inheritance of all the blessings of life in the presence of God (21:7).

The promise is coupled with the warning that the cowardly, the faithless, polluted, murderers, fornicators, sorcerers, idolaters, and liars have no place in God's city (21:8). Most readers who take a candid look at themselves will find that their records are marred by at least one item from this list of sins, and the result is a realization that no one is immune from judgment. Nevertheless, the warning does not mean that anyone who has ever committed one of these sins will be excluded from the New Jerusalem. God's city is not reserved for those who have never sinned, but for those who are cleansed by the blood of Christ (7:14; 22:14). The heavenly voice names sins in order to move people to reject sins and to trust in the grace Christ provides, while remaining part of the resistance movement that "conquers" by resisting evil through faith.

Holy City — Holy People (21:9-21)

Revelation addresses readers who are pulled in two directions, toward faithfulness and unfaithfulness. Accordingly, John wrote what might be called a "Tale of Two Cities," because he identifies faithfulness with the holy city and unfaithfulness with the harlot city. Recall that in an earlier vision, "the holy city" and its temple represented the people of God, who were oppressed by the nations, and yet preserved so that God's witnesses could testify before the peoples of the world (11:1-3). Also recall that the people of God were pictured as a woman, who was pursued by the dragon and yet was preserved by God in the wilderness (12:1-6, 13-17). The vision of the holy city and the vision of the woman both depict the same thing: the situation of the people of God on earth, as they live among powers that seek to overwhelm them and to end their existence as a community of faith.

Not all of John's earliest readers would have seen their situation in such stark terms. In the cities where they lived — Ephesus, Smyrna, Pergamum, Thyatira, Sardis, Philadelphia, and Laodicea — conditions varied. In some cities, Christians were threatened with violence, but in other cities the danger was a more subtle pressure to enhance their position by assimilating to the wider culture, or to find security in prosperity. John sought to startle his readers into a greater awareness of the situation by depicting the counterpart to the community of faith as the harlot, who uses both the seduction of wealth and the threat of violence to extend her control over the peoples of the world (17:1–18:24). John is aware that wealth and power are alluring, and that many are willing to compromise their integrity for the sake of comfort and prestige. Therefore, he seeks to bolster his readers' will to resist by portraying the seamy side of the worldly powers that find violence intoxicating and reduce human relationships to a commercial transaction. He also presses upon readers that the harlot may seem alluring now, but her future is bleak, for the way of harlotry leads to destruction.

Up to this point, the visions of the cities give readers little reason to celebrate. If readers identify with the "holy city," they can expect to be threatened by worldly powers (11:1-3); and if they identify with the harlot city, they can anticipate destruction (17:16). Neither option is particularly appealing. The vision of the New Jerusalem alters this by showing readers that "the holy city" of the future will bring a blessedness that is worth living for. Readers have incentive to identify with the community of faith in the present, despite the challenges involved, because faith has a future.

The harlot allures readers in the present, but the bride calls them to the future. The bride is the community of the redeemed in glory, a city that encompasses the whole people of God. The persecuted woman in Revelation 12 bore the traits of the people of God from many periods, and the bride in Revelation 21 does as well: the city's twelve gates bear the names of the twelve tribes of Israel, and its twelve foundations are named for the twelve apostles of the Lamb (21:12-14). The dimensions of the city are 12,000 stadia on each side, a number that corresponds to the numbers of people brought into the redeemed community (7:4-8; 21:16). The city is described as a walled structure made of stones, but in its essence the city is a community of people, whose "pillars" are the human beings who belong to God and the Lamb (3:12; Eph. 2:19-22).

When John announced that the bride of the Lamb had made herself ready for the marriage feast, he said that she was clothed with fine white linen, which was woven from the righteous deeds of the saints (Rev. 19:7-8). When readers actually meet the bride in the vision of the New Jerusalem, they find that her appearance is even more splendid than anticipated. Along with fine linen, a bride might hope to wear gold and jewels to her wedding (*Joseph and Asenath* 18:5-6). The Lamb provides ample splendor for the community that is his bride, for the city of the redeemed is ornamented with gold and precious stones. Jasper, sapphire, agate, emerald — twelve types of gems in all — adorn the foundations of the city, each of its twelve gates is formed from a single pearl, and its streets are paved with gold (Rev. 21:18-21).

This dazzling conclusion to John's "Tale of Two Cities" is designed to give readers a reason to pursue the way of faith in the present. The contrasts between Babylon and New Jerusalem, between the harlot and the bride, seek to alienate readers from powers that oppose God, while drawing them more firmly to a vision of life with God. Readers are called away from Babylon (18:4) and toward the New Jerusalem. There will be no reason for a bride and groom to rejoice in Babylon (18:23), but there will be celebration at the marriage feast of the Lamb in God's city (19:7, 9). Babylon will be a dwelling for demons (18:2), but the New Jerusalem will be the dwelling of God (21:3). The harlot may exhibit a splendor that comes from the exploitation of people (18:12-13), but the bride manifests the glory that comes from God (21:11-21). Nations are corrupted when they seek to amass wealth for themselves by trafficking with the harlot, yet God calls the nations to a vision of the bridal city, where they will bring their glory into the presence of God and the Lamb (21:24-26). Babylon is filled with impurity and deception (17:4-5; 18:23), but there is nothing impure or false in the New Jerusalem (21:27). The harlot makes the nations drunk on idolatry and sin (17:2; 18:3), but the bride invites the nations to drink of the water of life and to be healed by the leaves from the tree of life (22:1-5; Bauckham, *Theology*, 131-32).

The New Jerusalem's holiness and perfection is expressed in its shape, which is a perfect cube, measuring 12,000 stadia on each side (21:16). These dimensions, if taken literally, would mean that the base of the city would be about 1500 miles square — an urban center that would cover most of the western half of the United States — and that it would stretch 1500 miles into space. Nevertheless, the point of description does not seem to be a precise indication of the *quantity* of city space in eternity, but an indication of the *quality* of life there. Note that Ezekiel, too, saw a vision of a restored Jerusalem in which God's glory would be manifest and rivers of water would flow from the sanctuary (Ezek. 40:1-4; 43:1-5; 47:1-12); but in his vision the city with its twelve gates measured only a little more than 1.5 miles on a side (Ezek. 48:8-9, 30-35). John speaks of a New Jerusalem that will be a thousand times greater than this, affirming that God will both keep and surpass the promises that were made through the prophets.

The cubic shape also suggests that the holy city is a holy sanctuary. According to the Old Testament, the inner chambers of the tabernacle

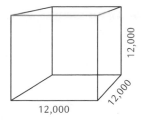

and the temple were cubic in shape (1 Kings 6:20). Ordinary worshipers could not enter such a sacred space. Only the high priest, whose turban was inscribed with the name of God and who wore a breastplate adorned with twelve gems, was to come before the Lord in the cubic chamber (Exod. 28:17-20, 36-38). When the tabernacle and the temple were dedicated, however, the glory of the Lord was manifested in the sanctuary in such a way that no one could draw near (Exod. 40:34; 1 Kings 8:11). According to Revelation, the entire city and the entire community is God's sanctuary (cf. 1 Cor. 3:16; Eph. 2:21-22), but here God's glory is manifested in such a way that people are drawn to it (Rev. 21:23-24), and all worshipers come before the Lord bearing God's name upon their foreheads (22:4). The limitations of the old order give way to new life for all the redeemed in the presence of God.

Glory to God and the Lamb (21:22–22:5)

Before looking further at the New Jerusalem, it may be helpful to consider how Revelation's imagery has been taken up and transformed in popular culture. Modern readers encounter details from Revelation in humorous portrayals of heaven that appear in publications ranging from congregational newsletters to national magazines. Among the stock features are the pearly gates (21:21), which are usually pictured as a single ornate gate with two doors, which are situated on fluffy clouds. Typically, one door in the gate stands slightly ajar so that Saint Peter can peer out at a new arrival in heaven. Peter is regularly pictured as a white-bearded fellow, dressed in a long white robe (7:9) with a halo hovering over his head. Angels playing harps are optional (15:2). In the caption below the picture, readers commonly find that Saint Peter is interrogating the newcomers about their qualifications for admission into heaven, or explaining that visiting hours are over, or perhaps cautioning that the streets of gold are torn up due to repairs.

Modern readers who are familiar with such scenes find surprises in Revelation's own vision of the New Jerusalem. First, there is not one set of gates but twelve gates, three on each side of the city. From every direction — north, south, east, and west — the gates provide access to the presence of God. Second, the gates stand open day and night. They are never shut (21:25), and the radiance of the city attracts the nations of the world, who bring their glory to God and the Lamb, the source of all glory (21:24, 26). The pearly gates are not designed to keep the nations away from God, but to provide them with a way to approach God. Third, Saint Peter's name is presumably inscribed on the city's foundations, along with the names of the other apostles (21:14), but John does not suggest that Saint Peter serves as a gatekeeper. We might better assume that his attention, like that of the other servants of God, is absorbed by worship around the throne of God and the Lamb (22:3-4).

John declares that he saw "no temple in the city," yet he immediately explains that in fact the city does have a temple: God and the Lamb (21:22). We have already noted that in Revelation "the End" is not an event, but God and the Lamb, and now we find that the "temple" is not a building, but God and the Lamb. The whole of the New Jerusalem, with its cubic shape, is a sanctuary that is filled with the glory of God. It contains no other structure that serves as a focus for worship. Since attention focuses directly on God and the Lamb, whose radiant power and presence are manifested throughout the city, the term "temple" is applied to them rather than to a building.

The "nations" are among the worshipers that draw near to this temple. John declares that "the nations" will walk by the light of God and the Lamb, that "the kings of the earth" will bring their glory into the New Jerusalem, and that people bring to the city of God "the glory and honor of the nations" (21:24, 26). At first glance, we might wonder where these kings and nations come from, since the kings of the earth and the nations were said to have been destroyed by the word of Christ and by heavenly fire (19:17-21; 20:7-10). John, however, is not outlining a simple sequence of events, but presenting readers with contrasting visions that include both warnings of judgment and promises of salvation.

In some visions, the nations are awed by the power of the beast and deceived into opposing God (13:7; 17:1, 15; 19:15; 20:8) and the kings of the earth are beguiled by the opulence that they can obtain for themselves through the harlot, so that they make war on the Lamb (16:14; 17:2; 18:3, 9-10; 19:19). In each case, this path leads to destruction. Other visions declare that the Lamb offered himself to liberate people of every nation to serve God (5:9-10; 7:9). People of every tribe are called to repent and to give God the glory, rather than to follow the path of self-glorification that leads to disaster (14:6; 18:7-8). At the end of Act I of Revelation, God lessened his judgments and many on earth gave him glory (11:13). In the middle of Act II, those who conquer the beast declare that God is "King of the nations" and that "all nations will come and worship" before him (15:3-4).

The vision of the New Jerusalem ends the spiral of warning and promise by underscoring that God's will is finally for the redemption of the nations. A voice from the throne recalls the traditional covenant promise that begins, "I will be their God." But instead of concluding, "they will be my people," using the singular, Revelation says "they will be his peoples," using the plural (21:3; Zech. 2:11; cf. Lev. 26:12; Ezek. 37:27). God claims not only one people but many peoples. Revelation is part of a long story in which people are repeatedly drawn away from the one true God, so that they worship the gods of the nations (Deut. 6:14; Judg. 2:11-12; 1 Kings 14:23-24). The vision of the New Jerusalem is the rightful culmination of this story, for in it the situation is reversed, and the nations come to worship the one true God. Such a future, in which the peoples of the world come to worship the Lord and to walk in his light, is the future for which the prophets hoped (Isa. 60:1-3, 5, 11).

This climactic vision brings together God's particular promises to his chosen people and his intentions for the world as a whole. The city in the vision is named for God's chosen city, Jerusalem, the place out of all the earth that he chose for his sanctuary. At the same time, this city encompasses a garden like the one that he prepared for all humankind, for within the city flows the river of the water of life, together with the tree of life that grew in Eden (Gen. 2:9-10). Genesis tells how the ancestors of all humankind disobeyed God, so that the earth was cursed because of their sin, and they were driven away from the tree of life to toil and die (Gen. 3:1-24). Revelation, however, holds out the hope that in the city of God nothing will be "accursed" any longer and that people will taste of the tree of life. They will no longer need to toil to eke a living from the earth, for the tree of life will give them fruit continually (Rev. 22:2-3). The prophets had spoken of living water and fruitbearing trees in the city of God (Ezek. 47:1-12; Zech. 14:6-8), but where Ezekiel simply said that their leaves would be "for healing" (Ezek. 47:12), John adds that the leaves will be "for the healing of *the nations*" (Rev. 22:2).

In the end, those who gather around the throne see the face of God and reign with him forever, in the glory of God's everlasting light (22:4-5). This marks the final reversal of the story that began when Adam and Eve sinned, and hid themselves from the face of God in shame, seeking refuge in the shadows (Gen. 3:8). God's light, purity, and power threaten the darkness of human sin, uncleanness, and mortal weakness. The Lord told Moses that no human being could see his face and live (Exod. 33:20), and when Isaiah had a vision of God's heavenly throne he cried out in terror, "I am lost, for I am a man of unclean lips and I live among a people of unclean lips; yet my eyes have seen the King the Lord of hosts!" (Isa. 6:5). Just as the sun's blazing rays can destroy the eyesight of those who gaze at it, God's burning holiness can destroy those who come directly into his presence. Therefore, the Law of Israel stipulated that the high priest, with the Lord's name inscribed on the turban that crossed his forehead, was to come into the presence of God under a protective cloud of incense to make atonement for the people (Exod. 28:36-38; Lev. 16:11-19).

In the New Jerusalem, the barriers of sin and mortality are removed by the grace of God, and the redeemed find themselves again in the garden. Instead of hiding from God's face, they turn towards God's face, for just as the privilege of being God's people is extended to the nations, the privilege of serving as high priest is extended to all worshipers, who bear God's name on their foreheads (Rev. 22:4). The promise that the righteous might one day see the Lord comes to its fulfillment (Ps. 11:7; Matt. 5:8; 1 John 3:2). The night of sin and death is gone; the light of God's salvation and light has come. Faith gives way to sight, uncertainty issues into understanding (1 Cor. 13:12). The story of God's people reaches its culmination when they "rest and see, see and love, love and praise. This is what shall be in the end without end" (Augustine, *The City of God* 22.30).

The End Is Near (22:6-21)

The resplendent colors of the New Jerusalem fade from view after Rev. 22:5. The radiant hues of its jewels and gold, its streams of water and lush foliage are engulfed by the brilliant light of God that washes over the city. As the city's contours vanish in the light, the majestic harmonies of worship that rose from the assembly of the redeemed may linger in the reader's mind, but they too fade along with the vision. What remains of the book of Revelation takes readers from the incomparable grandeur of the eternal city back to the world of ordinary life. In 22:6 John stands alone with his angelic guide, who repeats that "these words are trustworthy and true," and who reminds readers of the way their journey through Revelation began, by paraphrasing its opening verse: "the Lord, the God of the spirits of the prophets, has sent his angel to show his servants what must soon take place" (22:6; cf. 1:1).

Yet John and the angel are not alone, for a voice calls out, "See, I am coming soon!" (22:7). The speaker stands offstage and his identity is not given, but the voice is persistent in calling out the message. Each time the voice is heard, readers do "see" the speaker's identity more clearly. When the voice declares a second time, "See, I am coming soon!" the readers learn that the speaker is "the Alpha and the Omega, the first and the last, the beginning and the end" (22:12-13). Finally, the speaker's face comes into focus when the voice says, "It is I, Jesus" (22:16). By identifying himself in this way, Jesus again takes readers back to the beginning of the book, where Jesus first appeared to John and announced that he, "the first and the last," walked among the golden lampstands that represented his churches (1:17-20).

The Christ, who declares that he is "the first and the last, the beginning and the end," is the one who appears in both the first and the last chapters of Revelation. He constitutes the book's beginning and its end. The Christ who is present with his churches in Revelation's first chapter also says, "See, I am coming soon!" in its final chapter. When Revelation invites the saints to pray, "Come, Lord Jesus" (22:20), it can ask that the "grace of the Lord Jesus be with all the saints" even now (22:21). The grace of the Lord Jesus can be present among his followers because Jesus himself is present among his followers. By calling himself the Root of David (22:16), Jesus recalls promises that were made through the prophets and fulfilled by the Lamb, whose death already ransoms people of every nation for God (5:5-10; cf. Isa. 11:1; Jer. 23:5; Zech. 3:8). As "the bright morning star" (Rev. 22:16; cf. 2:28; Num. 24:17), the risen Jesus is now the harbinger of a new day of salvation that approaches when he himself approaches.

Revelation's emphasis on God and Christ as the End of all things (Rev. 1:8, 17; 21:6; 22:13) helps readers understand what it means when it says, "Blessed is the one who keeps the words of the prophecy of this book" (22:7; cf. 22:10, 18, 19). In comments at the beginning of this chapter, we noted that throughout Revelation, prophecy is known by what it does: true prophecy moves people to serve the true God and false prophecy draws people away from God. Prophecy can have to do with the future, but it is not primarily prediction. This final section of Revelation reinforces the point. After hearing that those who keep the words of the prophecy will be blessed, John mistakenly worships his angelic guide, but is quickly told that those who keep the words of the book "worship God" (22:7-9; cf. 19:10). Revelation does not suggest that people receive blessing or "keep" the words of its prophecy by speculating about the date of the battle of Armageddon. Rather, the "blessed" are those who "wash their robes" through faith in Christ and faithfulness to Christ (22:14), pursuing righteousness and holiness, and resisting evil, impurity, falsehood, and other forms of sin (22:11, 15).

Further help in understanding what John has written comes from the angel's directive, "Do not seal up the words of the prophecy of this book, for the time is near" (22:10). In contrast to the book of Daniel, which was to have been sealed up and kept secret until the end times (Dan. 12:4, 9), Revelation was an open book from the time it was written onward. To call Revelation "prophecy" means that it is a form of communication that called its first readers to repentance, perseverance, and hope in God and the Lamb. It is not a coded prediction whose true message is concealed from readers until the final years of world history. Asking what Revelation communicated to the Christians in the seven churches helps to discipline our thinking, as we consider how it continues to communicate with readers living centuries after John of Patmos penned the book's final "Amen" (22:21).

Two reasons why Revelation can and should speak to people today can be summed up around the poles of Christ and culture. First, readers often find that their cultural situations are analogous to those of the seven churches. Although Christians in the West may not be preoccupied with questions about eating meat offered to idols, many are aware of contemporary pressures to relinquish one's faith commitments because of the appeal of assimilating into the wider culture, the complacency that arises from prosperity, or the threat of violence. As modern readers confront such issues, Revelation continues to challenge and encourage them. Second, Revelation speaks not only of relationships to culture, but of relationships to the God "who was and is and is to come" (4:8). Because God and the Lamb are not confined to one period of time, Revelation's call to fear and hope in God and the Lamb are not confined to one period either. Whether readers live in the first century or the twenty-first century, God and the risen Christ are there.

Reading Revelation nearly two millennia after it was composed does leave us with questions about what it means to say that Jesus is coming "soon" (22:6, 7, 12, 20). This question is not unique to Revelation, since Paul, for example, could write as if he expected Christ to return within his lifetime (1 Thess. 4:17). The New Testament leaves its readers to live with tension. Some passages announce that Christ will soon return, and that Christians must remain awake and watch for him (Matt. 24:34; Mark 13:30, 37). Other passages declare that God alone knows when Christ will return, and that it is not for others to know "the times or periods that the Father has set" (Acts 1:7; Matt. 24:36; Mark 13:32). In the same way, Revelation declares that "the time is near" (Rev. 22:10), only to confound the readers' sense of timing with a kaleidoscopic spiral of visions that periodically repeats similar messages through different images and interrupts its forward movement with suspended judgments and heavenly interludes. Revelation can tell readers that the marriage feast of the Lamb "has come" and that the bride is "ready," yet it does not allow readers to see the bride until more than a thousand years have passed in its visionary world (19:7-8; 21:2, 9). Readers are left with the assurance *that* the End will come, but without knowing *when* it will come.

Before John put down his pen, he wrote a warning to any who would tamper with the message of his book: those who add to what he has written will have plagues added to them, and those who take away anything will have their share in the tree of life and holy city taken away (22:18-19). Similar exhortations appear in Israel's Law (Deut. 4:2;

12:32) and in other sacred and official writings from antiquity. Although we might be tempted to speculate as to whether any of the alterations that have occurred in Revelation's wording as it has been copied and recopied over the years would warrant such harsh condemnation,[3] a more helpful question would be to ask why John — like Paul (Gal. 1:6-9) — shows such urgency about maintaining the integrity of the message, and to reflect on what maintaining its integrity means.

Revelation confronts readers with an astonishing range of visions that both threaten and encourage them. Those who recognize the integrity of the book must come to terms with both. Christians in the so-called mainline churches have often had difficulty with the threatening side of the book. Repulsed by those who intimidate people with Revelation's warnings of fiery judgment or who turn its visions of conflict into a script for World War III, many Christians relegate Revelation to the margins of their lives. They might occasionally read a passage about heavenly glory during one of their worship services, but otherwise find it best to keep Revelation out of public view (see pp. 31-32 above). For such readers, the challenge is to hear Revelation's summons to see and resist the forces of sin and evil that are afoot in the world, especially as these manifest themselves in preoccupations with wealth, callousness toward violence, and the notion that it does not really matter what one calls "god." Revelation's visions are designed to disturb readers in order to bring them to renewed lives of faith and faithfulness.

Other readers have difficulty coming to terms with the expansive hope that Revelation offers. Preoccupied with the secrets of the seven seals, the ghoulish armies massing for battle, and the prospect of cosmic destruction, they pass quickly by the scenes of heavenly glory and cosmic praise that culminate in the eternal city of God. By reading Revelation as a script for a future drama that will be played out in lockstep fashion, they follow a course in which faith becomes fatalism. For them, the challenge is to take the ominous visions not as simple predictions, but as warnings that are designed to move readers to repentance and endurance. Moreover, the book's repeated spirals may move down-

---

3. As an example of fluctuation in wording, note that in 22:14, some ancient manuscripts read "do his commandments," a reading that appears in the King James Version. Other manuscripts read "wash their robes," a reading that appears in the NRSV, NIV, and other modern translations.

ward into visions of threat, but they return each time to scenes of glory in the presence of God. To hear the book in its integrity means hearing the promises that God and the Lamb extend to those of every tribe and language and people and nation. Therefore,

> "The Spirit and the bride say, 'Come.'
> And let everyone who hears say, 'Come.'
> And let everyone who is thirsty, come.
> Let anyone who wishes take the water of life as a gift."
>
> (22:17)

In light of such invitations and promises, the book calls each of its readers to respond "Amen. Come, Lord Jesus!" (22:20), and to embrace the benediction that occurs in its final verse: "The grace of the Lord Jesus be with all the saints. Amen" (22:21).

INDEX